Photographing Iceland

An Insider's Guide to the Most Iconic Locations

Martin Schulz

PHOTOGRAPHING ICELAND

An Insider's Guide to the Most Iconic Locations

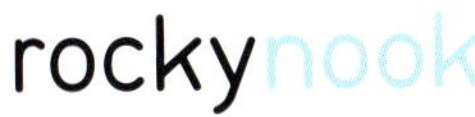

Photographing Iceland
Martin Schulz
www.martin-schulz.photography/en

Editor: Joan Dixon
Translation: Jeremy Cloot
Interior design: Anna Diechtierow
Layout production: Petra Strauch
Cover design: Aren Straiger
Project manager: Lisa Brazieal
Marketing coordinator: Mercedes Murray

ISBN: 978-1-68198-408-7
1st Edition (1st printing, October 2018)

Original German title: Island fotografieren
German ISBN: 978-3-86490-509-4

Rocky Nook, Inc.
1010 B Street, Suite 350
San Rafael, CA 94901
USA

www.rockynook.com

Distributed in the U.S. by Ingram Publisher Services
Distributed in the UK and Europe by Publishers Group UK

Library of Congress Control Number: 2018937758

This book is printed on acid-free paper.
Printed in China

For my dear wife Alice,
without whom none of this would be possible.
And for my wonderful son Erik—welcome to life on Earth.

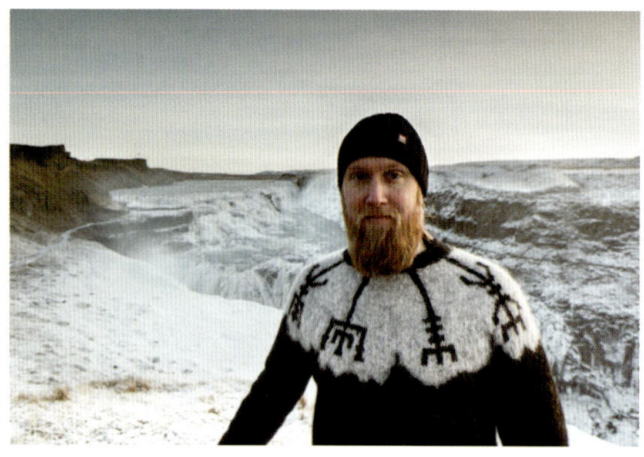

Over a period of many years, photographer **Martin Schulz** has traveled throughout Iceland at all times of the year. Even after numerous visits, he continues to be enthralled by the island's monumental grandeur and he knows all of its most fascinating locations.

Landscape photography is the cornerstone of Schulz's work. His images capture the innate beauty of our planet, and they show his respect and admiration for the natural world. For more of his enchanting, atmospheric images, visit *www.martin-schulz.photography/en*.

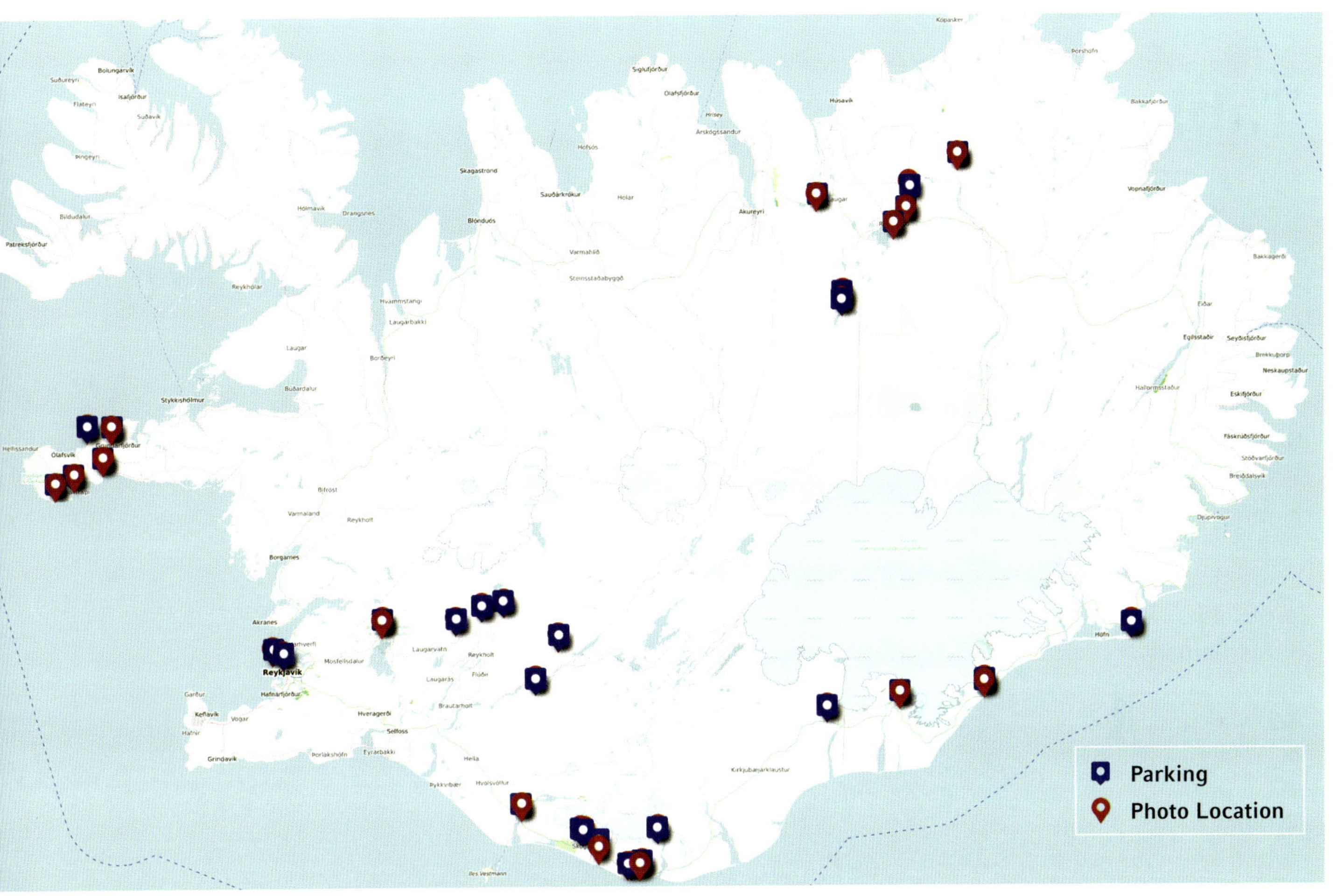

Parking
Photo Location
Bolungarvík
Suðureyri
Ísafjörður
Flateyri
Súðavík
Þingeyri
Bíldudalur
Patreksfjörður
Hólmavík
Drangsnes
Reykhólar
Skagaströnd
Blönduós
Sauðárkrókur
Hólar
Hofsós
Siglufjörður
Ólafsfjörður
Hrísey
Árskógssandur
Akureyri
Húsavík
Kópasker
Þórshöfn
Bakkafjörður
Vopnafjörður
Varmahlíð
Hvammstangi
Laugarbakki
Laugar
Borðeyri
Búðardalur
Stykkishólmur
Hellissandur
Ólafsvík
Bifröst
Varmaland
Reykholt
Borgarnes
Akranes
Reykjavík
Mosfellsdalur
Laugarvatn
Laugarás
Flúðir
Hafnarfjörður
Garður
Keflavík
Vogar
Hafnir
Grindavík
Hveragerði
Selfoss
Þorlákshöfn
Eyrarbakki
Brautarholt
Hella
Hvolsvöllur
Þykkvibær
Kirkjubæjarklaustur
Höfn
Djúpivogur
Breiðdalsvík
Stöðvarfjörður
Fáskrúðsfjörður
Eskifjörður
Neskaupstaður
Hallormsstaður
Egilsstaðir
Seyðisfjörður
Eiðar
Bakkagerði

Table of Contents

Introduction

Iceland—the land of fire and ice. A land of active volcanoes, black beaches, steep cliffs, magnificent waterfalls, and icebergs that float past huge lava fields. Iceland is a land of contrasts that covers just 40,000 square miles but offers an extreme variety of landscapes.

Not long ago, Iceland was still a secret spot for photographers, and photo tours often turned into adventures involving arduous treks and long trips along unpaved roads.

Nowadays, countless travel agencies have got the island covered, and tourism has become one of the country's leading economic factors. New tourist infrastructure is continually expanding, and many of the most striking attractions are now easily accessible by car. Nevertheless, you only have to take a few steps off the beaten path to get away from the tourist crowds and to enjoy photographing Iceland's natural environment at your own pace.

The ever-increasing numbers of tourists means the country is in a state of constant change. New parking areas and public restrooms are being built and many once rugged paths are being paved. Dangerous areas are fenced and signs are posted to protect both the environment and the visitors. All this comes with a financial cost, so some landowners have started charging parking and entry fees on their land. These fees are a topic of hot debate and it often takes months before such fees are approved by the government. I have noted all the current fee-paying attractions; however, with the rapidly changing situation, what might have been free at the time of writing might cost money by the time you get there.

Despite all the changes Iceland is going through, it hasn't lost its appeal as a photographic destination. If you are visiting Iceland for the first time, you are sure to find subjects worth stopping for at every turn. And you can capture breathtaking, people-free photos of the better-known places, if you visit them at the right time of day and the right time of year.

Since my first visit 10 years ago, I have been captivated by Iceland and its natural wonders. Now, 20 visits later, it still hasn't lost its allure for me. There are simply too many places to discover, and the quality of the light is breathtakingly different from season to season. Countless times, the grandeur of Iceland has brought me back down to earth by reminding me how relatively insignificant an individual is on this beautiful planet, and it has taught me great respect for Mother Nature. I have been fortunate to have shared all these wonderful experiences with my wife, Alice, who supports and motivates me through all my photographic adventures.

With this book, I am excited to introduce you to the beauty of Iceland and to share my enthusiasm for this wonderful place. I will help you choose the appropriate photo gear for your purposes and will give you tips on finding the best locations and the best times to capture Iceland's incomparable marvels.

PLANNING YOUR TRIP

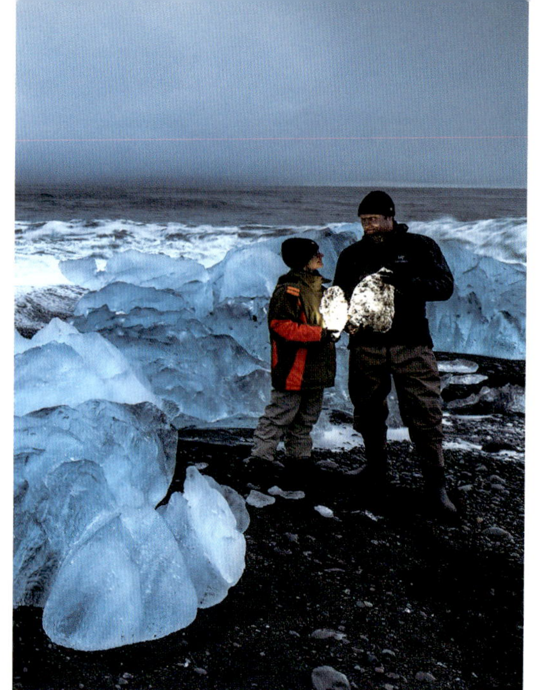

Good planning is the key to every successful trip, so this is where we will begin.

Iceland has an extremely low crime rate and is very safe to visit. In the 10 years I have traveled the island, I haven't had a single negative experience.

On the downside, Iceland isn't a cheap place to visit: lodging, food, and rental cars are considerably more expensive in Iceland as compared to other countries. The book includes some tips to help you keep your costs at a reasonable level.

Almost from the start of my Iceland travels, I found it more effective to stay several nights at a strategically located hotel rather than to move to a different location every day. This approach saves time and effort with packing and checking in and out, and it also reduces traveling time, thus allowing more time to take photos at your chosen locations. Staying put also means that a day's bad weather won't ruin your plans, as you can simply head out again the next day when the weather improves. All the tours described in this book are based on this method of travel.

HOW THIS BOOK IS ORGANIZED

The book is divided into five tours, each covering a contiguous geographical area but with locations that you can approach in any order you like. Each tour begins with a selection of starting points (usually a place of lodging). Each location covered also includes useful pointers, such as the best time of day or year to visit the site, appropriate clothing, the GPS coordinates of the site, and the best place to park. The coordinates are also provided in Quick Response (QR) codes in the margins. If you have Google Maps installed on your phone, a quick scan of a QR code will take you directly to the corresponding location on the map.

Each of the five tours follows a route that begins and ends in Reykjavík—taking you to the recommended lodging and back again—so you have the opportunity to visit each location on a return journey to Iceland.

When traveling in Iceland—especially when you are alone—always pay close attention to the weather and road conditions. The website recommendations listed at the end of this section are great for checking weather and road conditions, and they provide other useful information, too (see page 18).

FLIGHTS

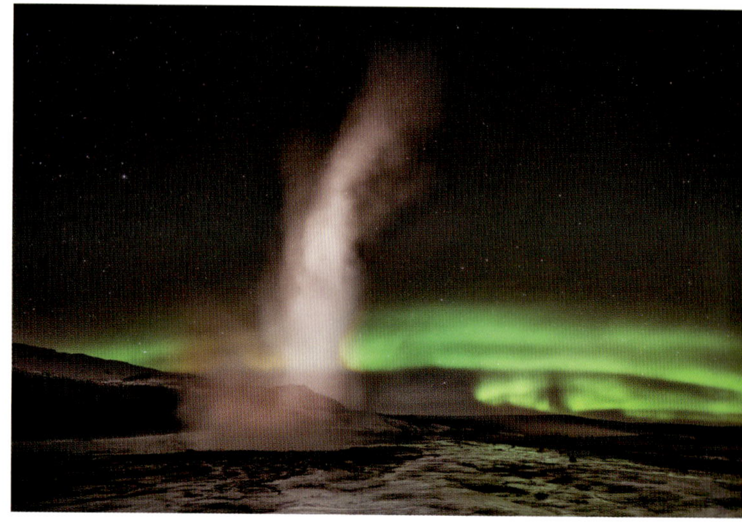

The price of a flight to Iceland varies widely depending on where you fly from and with which airline you fly. The cheapest flights currently on offer are on WOW air, which departs from 14 major North American cities, including Los Angeles, Chicago, Boston, and New York.

Icelandair flies from a wider selection of locations and lands at Keflavík airport, which is a 45-minute drive from Reykjavík. If you book early, Icelandair flights seem to have competitive fares. Check their website for special offers. Spring and fall are great times to shop for bargains.

On flights to Europe, both Icelandair and WOW air allow for free multiday stopovers in Iceland, giving you a perfect opportunity to take a break in your journey and enjoy the wonders of Iceland while you are there. For more details, search for "stopover" on both airlines' websites.

Other airlines fly to Iceland, too, but usually with multiple stopovers. The more stopovers you make, the greater the risk of luggage getting lost along the way, so I always try to book a direct flight, at least for the inbound leg of my journey.

CAR RENTALS AND TRAFFIC

A reliable car is probably the most important piece of gear needed for a safe and successful trip in Iceland. Route 1 (also known simply as the Ring Road) circumnavigates the island and is paved most of the way, with only a few stretches of gravel. When you are away from Route 1, you will usually encounter gravel roads that are often quite rutted; however, some of these roads are drivable with a regular car if you drive slowly over humps and take care to avoid potholes. Nevertheless, a four-wheel-drive (4WD) SUV is highly recommended and is mandatory in many circumstances.

The only time I didn't rent an SUV was on my very first trip to Iceland, and I ended up cursing my lack of maneuverability and the time I wasted driving around obstructions on unpaved roads. Since then, I have always rented a 4WD vehicle. Increased ground clearance ensures that I don't damage the underside of the car, and 4WD capability offers increased safety and speed on gravel roads.

A 4WD is mandatory on many of Iceland's roughest roads, which are noted with an F in the roads' names. Not only is it against the law to drive on an F-road without 4WD, but also, you immediately lose your insurance coverage and are liable for all damages if you attempt to drive on an F-road in a regular car. Furthermore, you risk heavy fines if the police catch you breaking this law.

If you are visiting Iceland in winter, a solid 4WD vehicle is a must. Make sure your rental vehicle's tires have studs, which are normal gear for Icelanders. Even Route 1 is often covered in a thick layer of ice in winter.

The speed limits in Iceland are 90 km/h (55 mph) on paved roads and 80 km/h (50 mph) on all other roads. These speed limits are strictly enforced by cameras and by the police using portable speed traps. Speeding violations are costly, so don't be tempted to break the local laws even if many Icelanders do.

Always remember that Icelandic roads are much more hazardous than the roads at home. Most roads take you on a raised bed through rough landscapes full of lava boulders and steep drops. If you accidentally veer off the road, there is no way to slow down before you hit a rock or land in a gully. The edges of the roads often have unrepaired frost damage that can easily force you off the road. Countless sheep often cross the road without warning, too.

I have seen plenty of badly damaged vehicles lying abandoned beside the road, some of which had obviously overturned several times. It is no surprise to learn that tourists are involved in the majority of traffic-related deaths in Iceland.

Natural factors also pose risks when driving in Iceland. Floods, snowdrifts, and storms often cause road closures. Always check road and weather conditions before you begin a trip. (See the websites listed on pages 18–19.)

When you rent a car in Iceland, you will be offered an array of additional insurance options. Although these may seem outrageously expensive, it is worth spending the extra money to make your trip safe and simple. You are sure to be offered "Gravel Protection" against damage caused by loose stones and "Sand and Ash Protection," which insures you against storm damage. Even if the cost of the extra insurance seems exorbitant, it is definitely cheaper than the $10,000 that a paintjob and bodywork could cost.

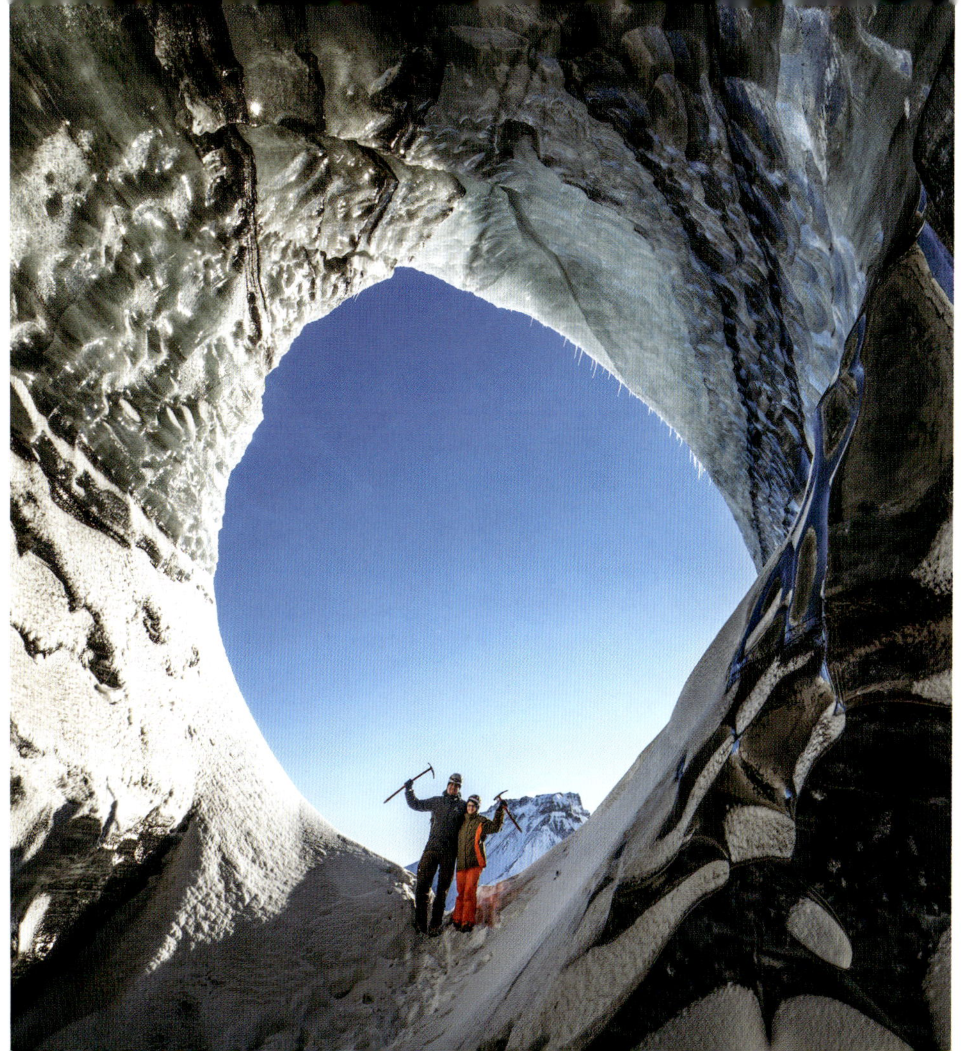

LODGING

Over the years, increasing numbers of tourists have seen parallel growth in the number of new—and often very nice—hotels and hostels on offer. Whether you decide to stay in a regular hotel, a private vacation home, or a simple mountain hut, there are plenty of choices at all the major online booking websites. Always book as early as possible to get the best rates.

To help you find a place to stay, each tour starts with a few tips about where to look in the nearest town or the surrounding area.

If you prefer to camp out, there are plenty of well-appointed campsites scattered around the island. Note that camping off the beaten track and relieving oneself out of doors are prohibited in many areas.

CLOTHING AND THE WEATHER

When Icelanders chat, the conversation quickly turns to the weather, which affects every aspect of island life and is, understandably, one of the most important everyday topics. One of Iceland's best-known adages states that if you don't like the weather, wait an hour!

The weather in Iceland is extremely changeable. Especially in the highlands, a sunny day can quickly turn rainy, and fog and mist can reduce visibility to zero in no time. I always check the Meteorological Office's website before setting out for the day, and I check it again before getting out of the car at each stop to make sure I have the right clothing with me.

When dressing for an outing, the proven "onion principle" is the best way to go as you can easily find yourself needing a T-shirt, a sweater, and a rain jacket all on a single summer's day!

Always take high-quality rain protection with you. Iceland is always windy and, without an additional rain protection layer, blue jeans or trekking pants can quickly become sopping wet. It's a good idea to bring additional clothing in the car in case you get wet and need to change in the middle of an excursion.

Although the Gulf Stream gives Iceland a relatively mild climate, you should never underestimate the effect of the constant, biting wind. Always bring extra warm clothing along, especially if you are traveling in winter.

To help you get started, here is my personal packing list.

Protecting Your Gear:

A high-quality backpack is essential to protect your expensive camera gear from the extreme Icelandic environment. I use the Tilopa backpack made by f-stop (*www.fstopgear.com*) and I highly recommend it. The quality and thoughtful construction make this backpack the perfect companion.

What to pack:

- Underwear
- Socks
- T-Shirts (short- and long-sleeved)
- Sweater
- Fast-drying trekking pants
- Rain jacket
- Rain pants
- Sturdy hiking boots
- Spare pair of shoes
- Flip-flops
- Swimming gear
- Pajamas
- Beanie
- Jeans and a casual shirt for Reykjavík

Winter extras:

- Thermal underwear
- Snow pants
- Down jacket

EQUIPMENT

As well as high-quality photo gear, you will need solid hiking gear to ensure that you reach your location safely.

In addition to your regular photo gear, I recommend that you take along the following:

- Headlamp and/or a flashlight
- Rubber boots or waders
- Spikes for your boots (in winter)

Recommended photo gear:

- DSLR
- Wide-angle lens
  (the widest and brightest you can get)
- Zoom lens
  (up to 400mm, depending on your shooting style)
- Tripod
- Ball head
- Remote shutter release
- Filter holder
- Filters
- Panorama gimbal head
- Plenty of rechargeable batteries
- Battery charger
- Plenty of memory cards
- Lens cleaning cloths
- Towel for your camera
- Weatherproof backpack

It is always a good idea to bring along a laptop and/or an external hard drive for backing up your photos.

Check out *www.martin-schulz.photography/en/equipment* for a complete list of my gear.

Don't forget to bring a plug adapter for your battery charger and laptop. Iceland uses the regular European Schuco type power outlets.

If, like me, you take your planning seriously and want to find out in advance about the lighting at your chosen location, you should take a look at The Photographer's Ephemeris. This app is available for iOS and Android and gives you all the data you need to plan sunrises, sunsets, and phases of the moon for your shoots. It even includes tips on recognizing the constellations, and has gained a reputation as a kind of Swiss Army Knife for photographers.

The captions for the images in this book include the settings used to capture each shot. Where I used a graduated neutral density filter, you will see the acronym GND, where the number indicates the strength of the filter. (For more on gray filters, see the Photo Skills section on page 178.)

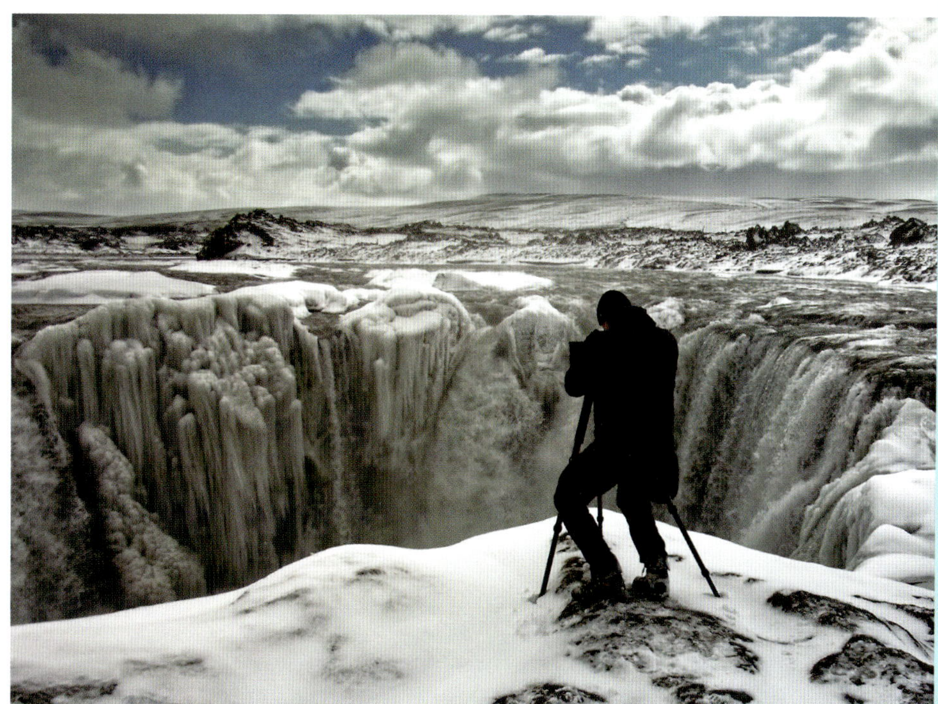

THE ICELANDIC LANGUAGE

Even though most Icelanders speak excellent English, the official language of the island is Icelandic.

Because of Iceland's isolated location, modern Icelandic is still very similar in many ways to the Norse tongue from which it developed. Today's Icelandic alphabet includes two ancient runes that are not found in any other language: Eth (Ð, ð, which is pronounced like "th" in "this"), and Thorn (Þ, þ, which is pronounced like "th" in "thing").

Other linguistic peculiarities make it difficult for beginners to pronounce the names of mountains and rivers, and sometimes even the names of the people they are talking to!

Here are a couple of examples, which I hope will make things clearer:

If an Icelandic word contains the letters "ll" they are usually pronounced "tl." This means the volcano that became famous for disrupting worldwide air traffic in 2010 is spelled "Eyjafjallajökull" but pronounced "Eyjafjatlajökütl" (or phonetically as ey-yah-fjat-la-ye-keu-tl).

The letter "á" is usually pronounced "ow," which means that the amazing waterfall "Háifoss" is actually pronounced "Howifoss."

The combination "rn" is spoken as if there is an extra "t" in the middle; so "Barnafoss" is pronounced "Bartnafoss."

GENERAL BEHAVIOR

Iceland is a small nation, and the Icelanders often appear quite reserved; however, should you ever need help, you are sure to get it. This is especially true in emergencies. If your car were to break down in the remote highlands, every Icelander passing by would stop to assist you.

On the downside, the more popular Iceland has become as a destination, the higher the number of tourists who behave recklessly and who end up requiring help from the locals. For example, people have needed to be rescued while attempting to swim across a torrential glacial river and while taking a family trip up a glacial spur in a small sedan. Never forget that the Icelandic environment rarely forgives these kinds of mistakes.

Exploring a glacier without a professional guide is extremely dangerous and can be fatal. Ignoring the strength of the waves and currents at the black beaches of Vík means risking your life. Iceland still has very few fences or locked gates and you can move freely around most of the natural wonders it has to offer. Please don't risk your life for a photo and always respect nature while on your travels. Where things are cordoned off, there are good reasons for it—usually due to the fragile nature of Iceland's vegetation, which must be left untouched if it is to survive. Even a single footprint in the wrong place could cause damage that might take years to recover from.

IMPORTANT AND HELPFUL WEBSITES

[1]

ROAD CONDITIONS AND GENERAL INFORMATION ON DRIVING:

[1] *www.road.is/travel-info/road-conditions-and-weather*
This website lists up-to-date driving conditions, road closures, and other driving hazards.

[2]

[2] *www.safetravel.is*
Find general information on traveling and driving in Iceland.

[3]

[3] *http://en.ja.is/kort/?type=map*
A useful detailed online map of the island.

[4]

WEATHER:

[4] *en.vedur.is/weather/forecasts/areas*
This is the official website of the Icelandic Meteorological Office, offering forecasts and detailed information on current conditions.

[5]

[6]

[7]

[8]

[9]

[10]

[5] *en.vedur.is/weather/forecasts/aurora*
This page lists northern lights forecasts.

GUIDED TOUR AGENCIES:

[6] *www.icelandtravel.is*
Highly recommended for guided northern lights tours and adventure tours on snowmobiles or to the ice caves.

[7] *www.katlatrack.is*
This is my favorite tour operator for highland tours in the South.

[8] *www.iceak.is*
This is my favorite tour operator for highland tours in the North.

NEWS AND CURRENT AFFAIRS:

[9] *www.icelandreview.com*
Icelandic news.

[10] *www.visitreykjavik.is*
All about Reykjavík.

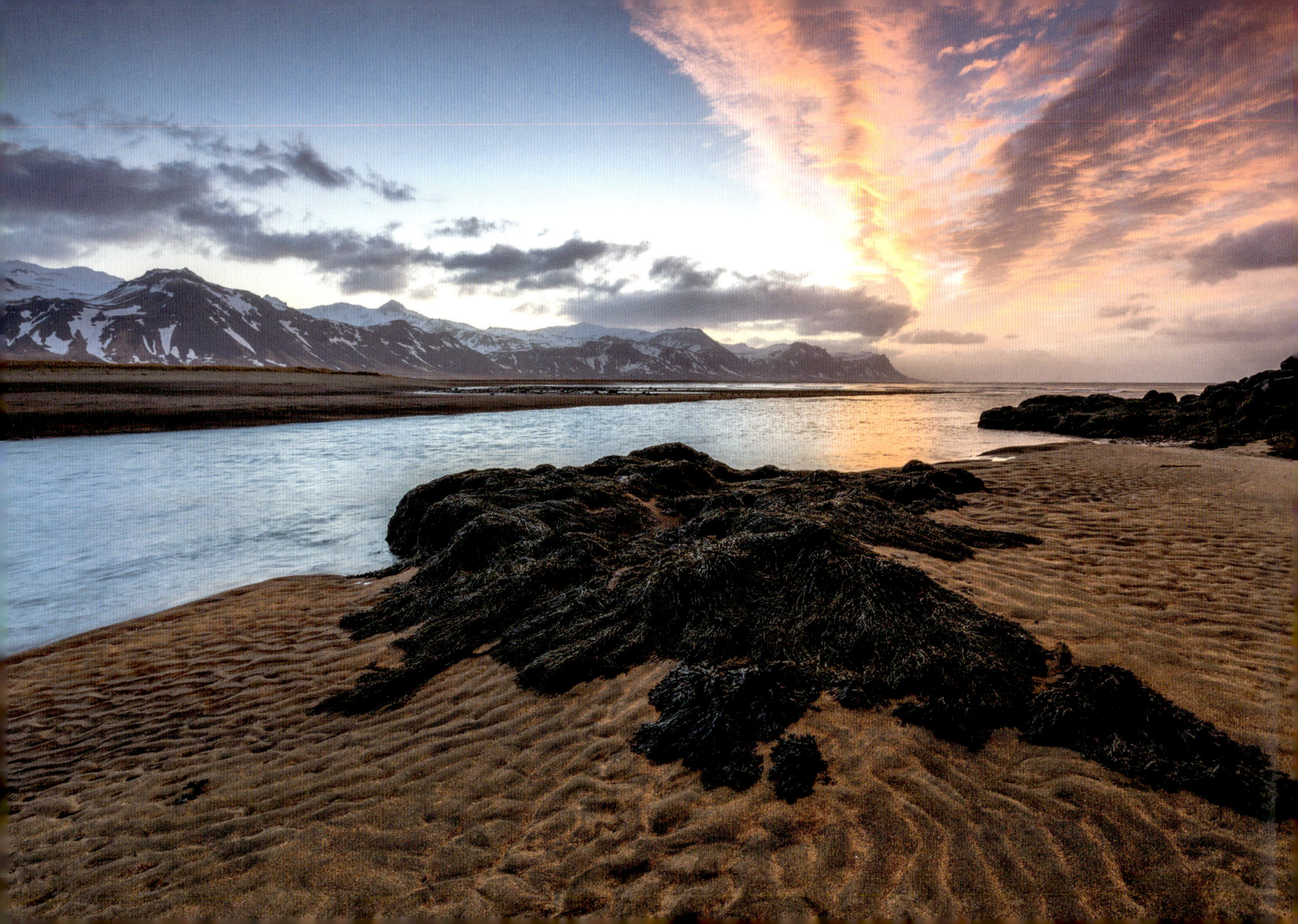

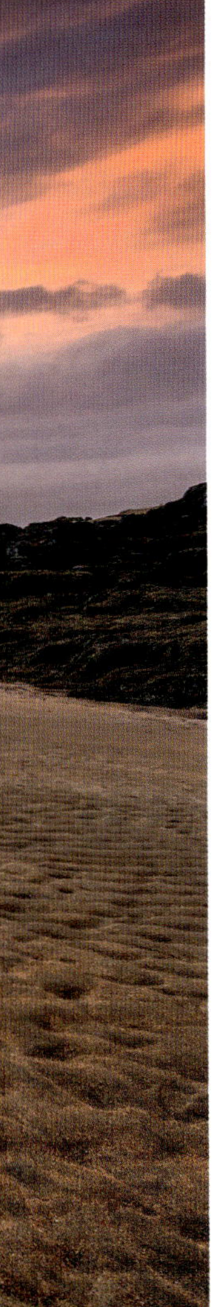

TOUR 1

THE SNÆFELLSNES PENINSULA

The Snæfellsnes Peninsula, which sticks out into the ocean like a finger, is about a two-hour drive from Reykjavík. Its name means "Snow Mountain Island" and this beautiful place exists thanks to the activity of the Snæfellsjökull volcano. On a clear day, the volcano itself can be seen from the tower of the Hallgrímskirkja church in Reykjavík, and it is a fascinating sight with its rounded flanks and glacial peak.

Snæfellsnes is a great starting place to get acquainted with Iceland, and is often described as comprising elements of the entire country in a miniature territory: it has cliffs, lava fields,

TOUR 1 BASICS
Overall time required: 2–3 days
Travel time: A little over two hours from Reykjavík
Lodging: Ólafsvík or Grundarfjörður to the north
Hótel Búðir (*www.hotelbudir.is*) is highly recommended

and glaciers, as well as many of the other features that make Iceland unique. It is also home to Kirkjufell, which is Iceland's most photographed mountain.

To get there, head north from Reykjavík on Route 1, and drive along the west coast past countless traffic circles until you reach the banks of the Hvalfjörður fjord. This long fjord has a toll tunnel beneath it that costs 1,000 Icelandic Krona (about $9.75 at the time of writing) to use. If you want to save your money, and if you have about 45 minutes to spare, you can take the old road around the fjord. About a half-hour's drive north of Hvalfjörður is the pleasant town of Borgarnes, which is a great place to take a break, to fill the car with gas, and perhaps to stock up on food.

In Borgarnes, turn off Route 1 onto Route 54, which takes you directly to the Snæfellsnes Peninsula. Ólafsvík and Grundarfjörður both offer plenty of lodging. Hótel Búðir is a favorite of mine. It is perfectly situated on the south side of the penninsula next to a small church, and is surrounded by tiny bays full of red sand and black lava outcroppings. It is an ideal base for photographers, and offers great views of the surrounding countryside from the skylights on the top floor. The hotel is great, too, for a romantic break with a candlelit three-course meal or a cozy drink in the lounge.

On this tour, the return journey takes you past some of the same places on your way back to Reykjavík.

TOP TIP

If you fancy a break with a great cup of coffee and an Icelandic waffle, then you should definitely stop at *Blómasetrið – Kaffi Kyrrð* in Borgarnes. This is a flower and gift shop with all sorts of interesting things, and an eatery that has unquestionably earned its name *Café Tranquility*. Katrín and her mother make sure everyone feels right at home in this snug atmosphere (*www.blomasetrid.is)*.

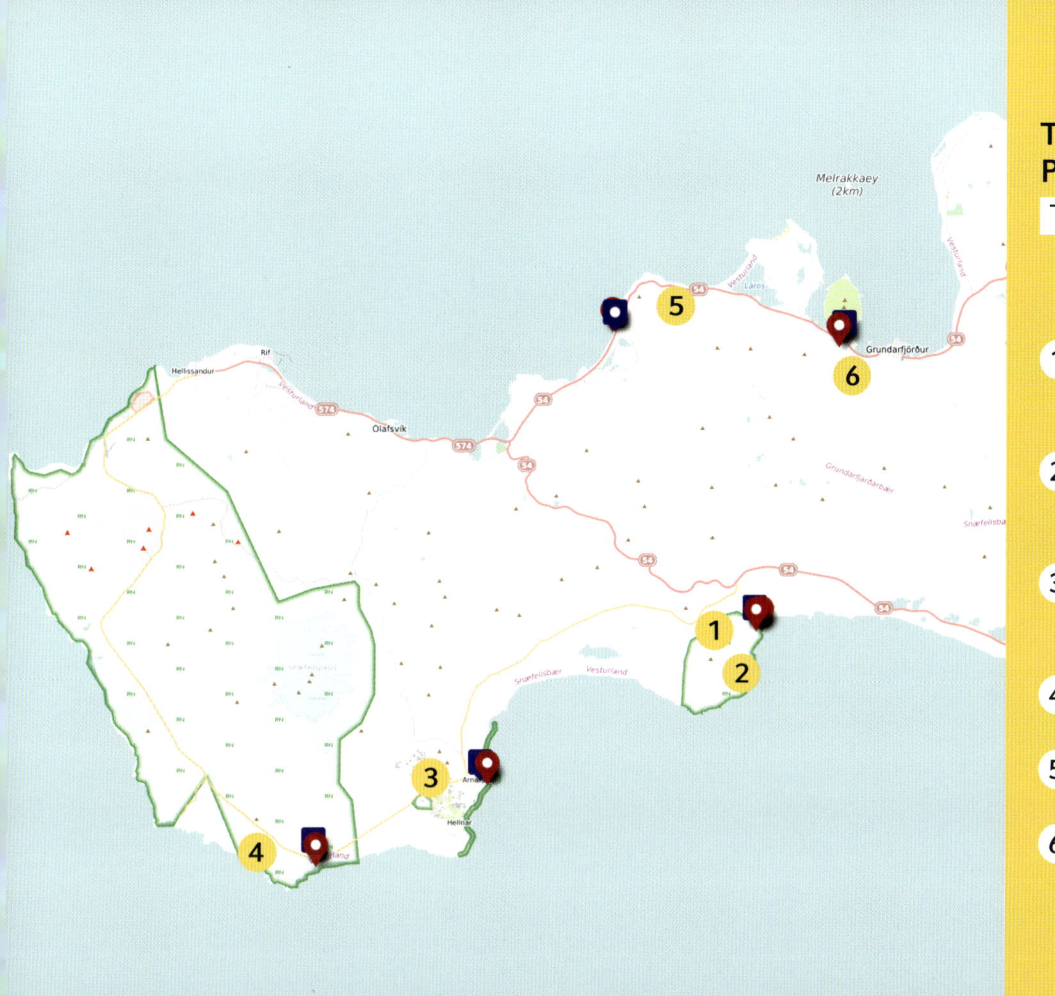

THE SNÆFELLSNES PENINSULA

TOUR 1

1. THE RED BEACHES OF BÚÐIR
2. THE BLACK CHURCH AT BÚÐIR
3. THE COAST AT ARNARSTAPI
4. LÓNDRANGAR
5. SNÆFELLSJÖKULL
6. KIRKJUFELL

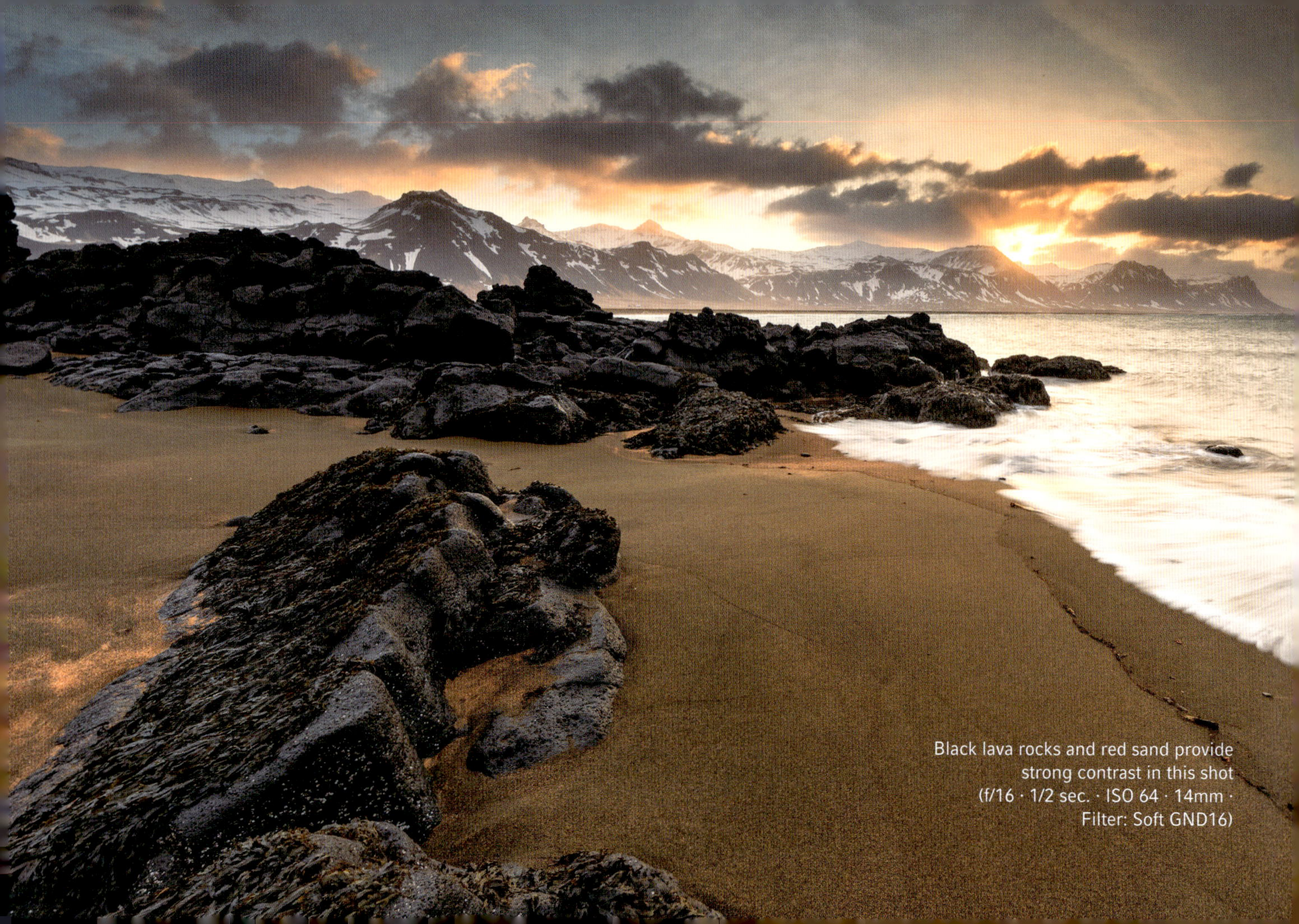

Black lava rocks and red sand provide strong contrast in this shot (f/16 · 1/2 sec. · ISO 64 · 14mm · Filter: Soft GND16)

Parking Area

Photo Location

1 THE RED BEACHES AT BÚÐIR

Location: 2-minute walk from Hótel Búðir or the hotel parking area
Best time of day: Sunrise
Best time of year: Fall or winter
Equipment: No special requirements
Tour type: Self-drive
Parking area coordinates: 64.823042, –23.385359
Location coordinates: 64.821993, –23.378591

You can walk to several beautiful little bays from Hótel Búðir or from the hotel's parking area. The best route to take is the footpath that leads directly off the hotel yard. The first beach you see offers wonderful patterns in the sand and makes a great photographic starting point. If you follow the same path all the way to the coast beyond the bay, take the small step down that you can see just before the path turns to the right, and climb down to the beach below. Although it is small, this bay offers a perfect combination of red sand and black lava rocks, spread along the entire beach. Depending on the water level when you are there, there are countless angles to capture the waves from as they rush up the beach and break on the rocks. Shooting from the rocks provides a great viewpoint and keeps your feet dry while you work. If you look out to sea and to the left, you will see a range of mountains that provides a great background for your photos.

In winter, the sun rises directly to the south (i.e., over the horizon out to sea) and the high water level means that some of the lava rocks will be surrounded by water, making winter the

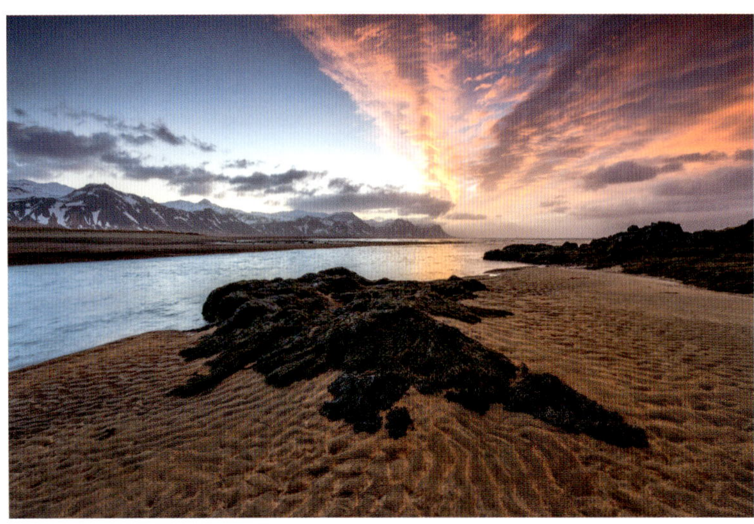

Sunrise at the red beaches of Búðir
(f/16 · 0.6 sec. · ISO 64 · 14 mm · Filter: Soft GND16)

best time of year for taking photos at this particular location.

This doesn't mean it's not a beautiful place in summer or fall; however, because the sun rises in a northeasterly direction at those times of year, you will probably have more luck with your photos if you go to the beaches that lie farther to the east.

TOP TIP
The beaches farther to the west make an ideal photo opportunity, but are great for walking, too, taking you along the lovely scenic coastline and through the Búðahraun lava field. Take your time to get to know the area and pick your favorite spot for shooting in the lovely morning or evening light.

2 THE BLACK CHURCH AT BÚÐIR (BÚÐAKIRKJA)

Distance: 1-minute walk on foot from Hótel Búðir or the hotel parking area
Best time of day: Sunrise or at night
Best time of year: Fall or winter
Equipment: No special requirements
Tour type: Self-drive
Parking area coordinates: 64.823042, –23.385359
Location coordinates: 64.821710, –23.383975

Parking Area

Photo Location

Búðir used to be an important trading post, but its small black-tarred church is now the only remaining witness to earlier times. The present church is not actually the first to be built here. It was erected in 1848 and renovated over the course of the 20th century, but it is the oldest church in Iceland and is a protected monument. You have probably seen photos of this church, perhaps showing the graveyard in the foreground.

My favorite way to photograph the church is as follows: Starting at the gate to the graveyard, walk around to the left until the church is behind you. You will now see a broad path that is almost a road. Follow this path to the next corner until you see a small downward slope. Now turn around. The path is now in the foreground and leads your eye directly to the church, while the mountains in the distance make for a grand background. On a clear day, you can even include the majestic Snæfellsjökull in your images.

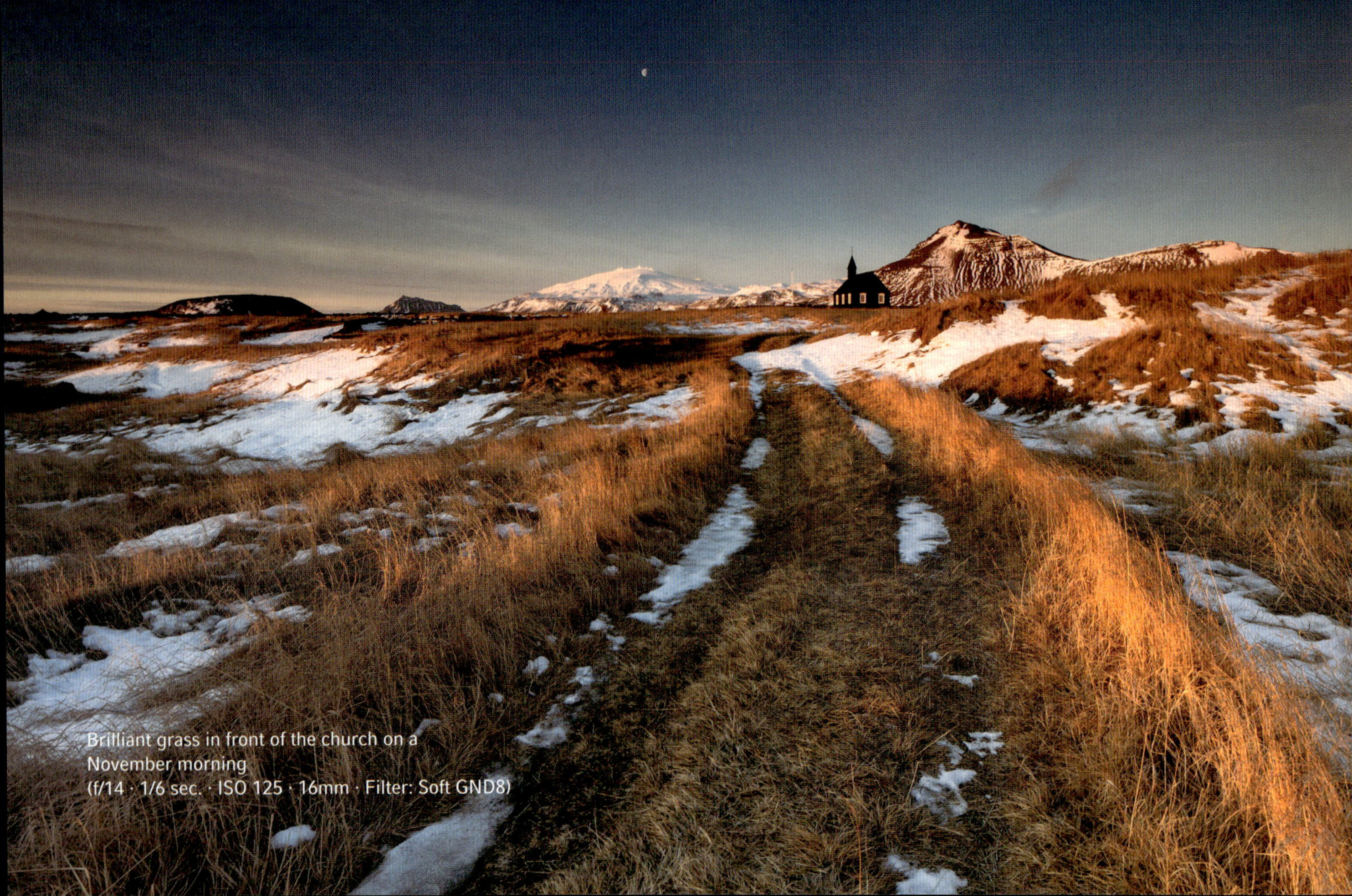

Brilliant grass in front of the church on a November morning
(f/14 · 1/6 sec. · ISO 125 · 16mm · Filter: Soft GND8)

This location is especially beautiful in late winter when the sun is a little higher in the sky and gives the grass a subtle golden shimmer.

The short distances involved make it a snap to do a combined tour of the red beaches and the black church. After you have visited the beach at sunrise and experienced the dawn, the rising sun transforms the church into your next magical subject.

TOP TIP

Búðakirkja and the surrounding beaches are a great location for photographing the northern lights. If you stay at Hótel Búðir, you can even have the hotel staff wake you if there is solar activity during the night. For more details, see the chapter on photographing the Northern Lights on page 189.

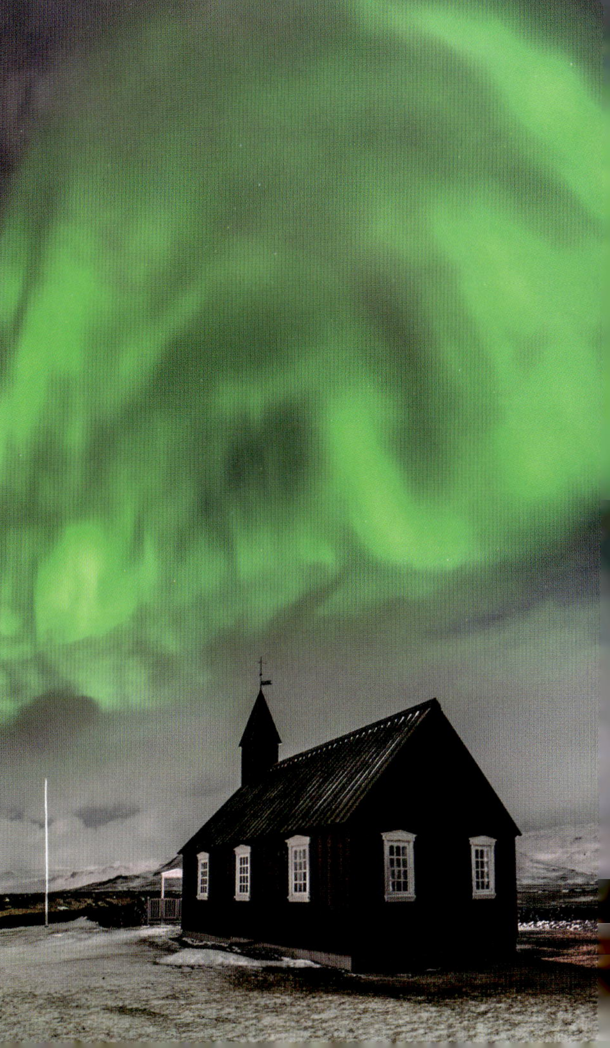

Dazzling northern lights over the Búðakirkja (f/2.8 · 10 sec. · ISO 640 · 15mm)

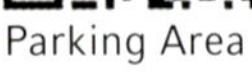

Parking Area

Photo Location

3 THE COAST AT ARNARSTAPI AND GATKLETTUR

Distance: 20 minutes from Búðir
Best time of day: Sunrise or sunset
Best time of year: Summer, fall, or winter
Equipment: No special requirements
Tour type: Self-drive
Parking area coordinates: 64.766344, –23.628184
Location coordinates: 64.765370, –23.622035

The fishing village of Arnarstapi is just a 20-minute drive from Búðir. If you take Route 574 toward the west from Búðir, you will see a fantastic view toward Snæfellsjökull. In clear weather, there are countless views of this wonderful glaciated volcano to be seen between the peaks of the mountains. The volcano's peak is where Jules Verne's *Journey to the Center of the Earth* began. To reach Arnarstapi, simply follow the road signs. Once you have passed a number of houses on the right, you will see two small red wooden houses with thatched roofs on the left. Take the next turn to the right. You will arrive at a small parking area where marked paths lead to the coast.

During the middle ages, Arnarstapi was an important fishing center, and the many sheltered bays in the area are relatively easy to reach by boat. The coast around Arnarstapi is full of caves, eroded cliffs, and freestanding rock arches. Close to the parking area is a rock sculpture depicting the mythical figure Bárður Snæfellsás. Legend has it that Bárður was the first settler in this area and, because he had troll's blood in his veins, he was bigger and stronger than anyone else. He founded the

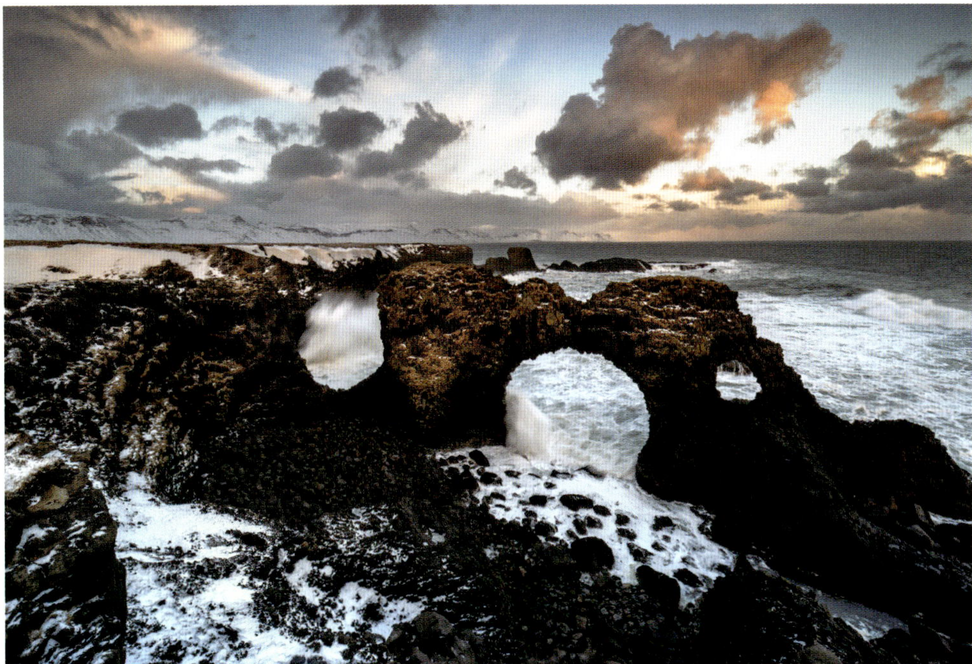

Sunset on a cold winter's day (f/14 · 1/4 sec. · ISO 64 · 14mm · Filter: Soft GND16)

community of Hellnar and lived there on a farm. The saga of Bárður also tells of evil deeds. He is said to have killed his nephews because they neglected to look after his daughter, who drifted all the way to Greenland on an ice floe, where she was credited as having discovered the largest island in the north. Although she is said to have returned home safely, it was too late to save Bárður's unfortunate nephews.

The raging sea clearly shows how the rock arch was formed (f/11 · 1/50 sec. · ISO 250 · 24mm · Filter: Soft GND16)

If you follow the marked paths to the coast on the left, you will come to Gatklettur, the most impressive rock arch on the entire coast. A wooden platform at the site gives you plenty of opportunities to photograph the arch with the mountains we saw from the beaches at Búðir in the background. At high tide and when winter storms rage, water shoots through the two holes in the formation and makes a great subject for dramatic photos. Try using an extended exposure time to capture the dynamic movement of the waves. It requires patience to capture this type of shot, and not every wave is powerful enough to shoot through both holes. Observing this phenomenon without a camera is a great way to gain an impression of how the ocean has made its mark on the coast over the centuries.

TOP TIP

In summer, this whole area is a breeding ground for Arctic terns ("krías" in Icelandic). If you get too close to their nests, you might be attacked by adult birds defending their young. Krías always attack from above, so holding your tripod up high is a good way to reach the coast safely without suffering painful pecks to your head.

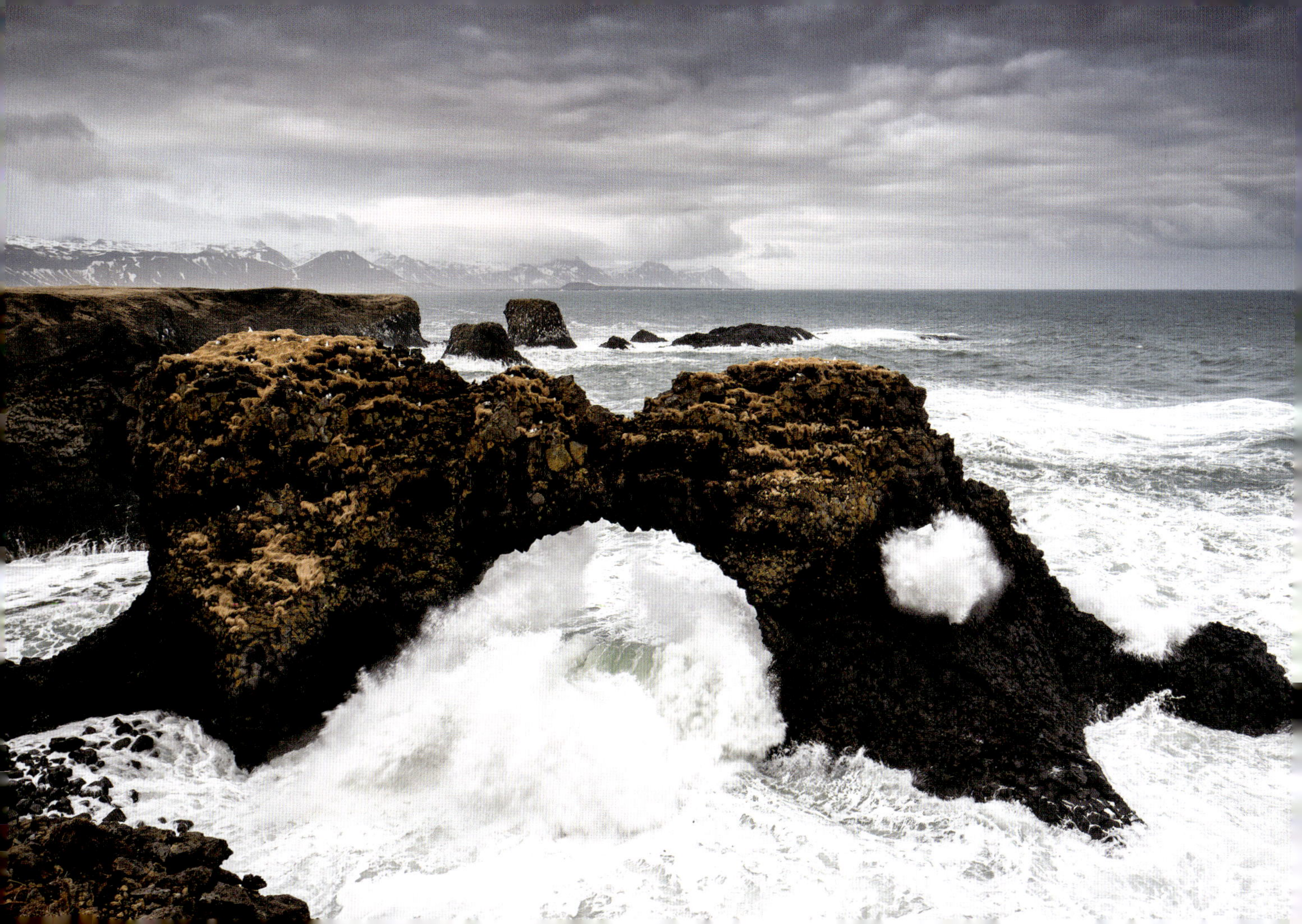

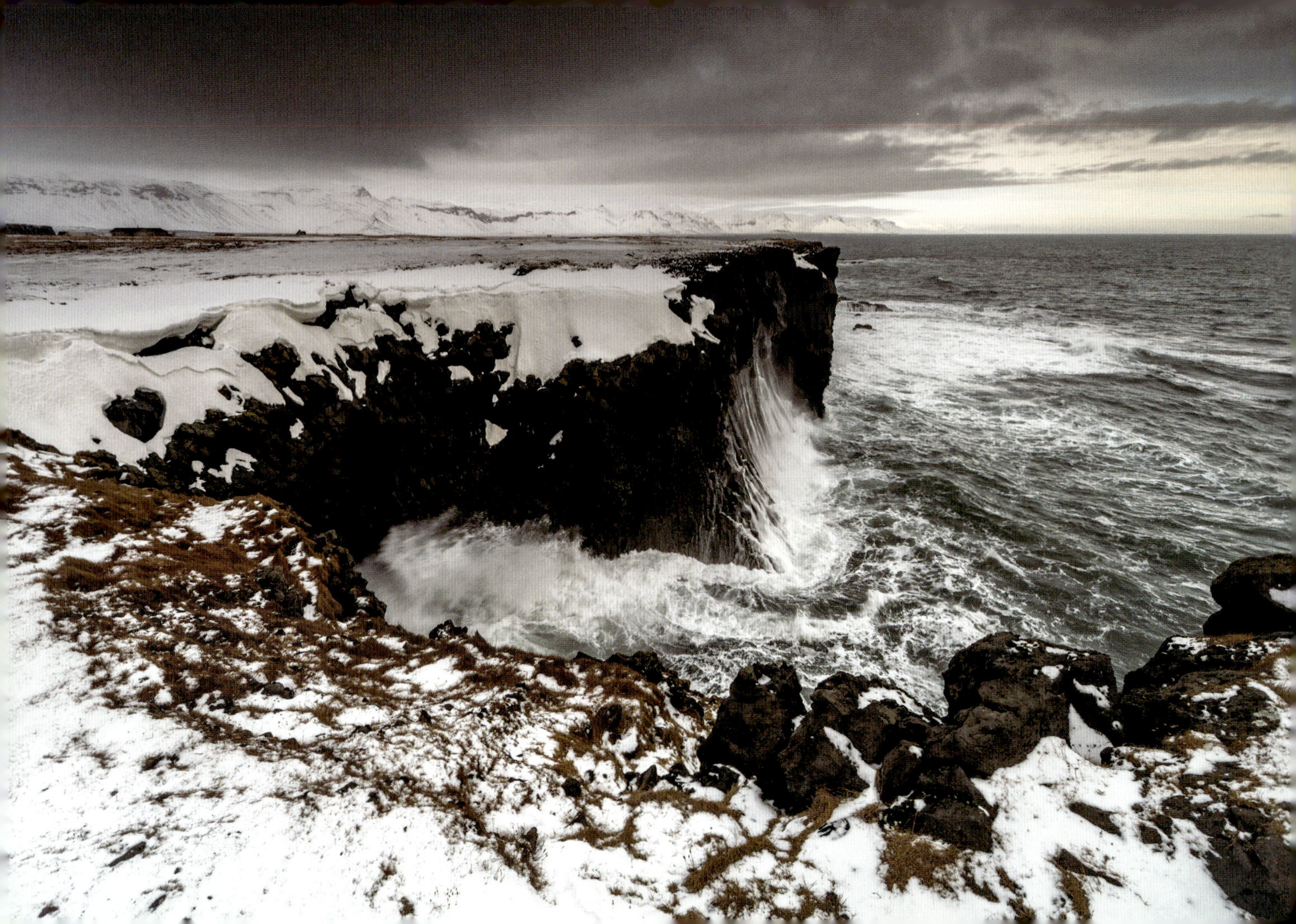

Big waves breaking on the basalt coastline (f/11 · 1/20 sec. · ISO 125 · 14mm · Filter: Soft GND8)

Before you go back to the parking area, it is worth taking a quick detour along the coast to the west. There is another wooden platform a couple of minutes' walk away, and from there you have a great view of the basalt columns that form large portions of the coastline. When the swell is strong, the crashing waves break high on the cliffs make a great photo subject. The receding waves can be beautiful, too, as they flow back down the black basalt and into the ocean. The crystalline structure of the rock makes fascinating patterns and is a great subject in its own right.

TOP TIP

There is 2-mile-long long walk leading westward along the coast from Arnarstapi to Hellnar. Alongside the natural basin called Baðstofa—which, according to legend, was used by Bárður Snæfellsás as a swimming pool—there is also a nice little café called Fjöruhúsið, where you can get a good cup of coffee and homemade dishes and freshly baked breads and pastries. For more details, see *www.facebook.com/FjoruhusidHellnum* and check the opening times before you go.

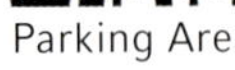

Parking Area

Photo Location

4 LÓNDRANGAR

Distance: 10 minutes from Arnarstapi
Best time of day: Sunrise or sunset
Best time of year: Summer, fall, or winter
Equipment: No special requirements
Tour type: Self-drive
Parking area coordinates: 64.737666, –23.775863
Location coordinates: 64.735287, –23.774026

If you follow Route 574 to the west from Búðir or Arnarstapi, you will soon see a spectacular rock formation on the coast to your left, called Lóndrangar. The two rock stacks (250 and 200 feet high) are the remains of a much larger volcanic crater that has been eroded by the wind and the sea. There is a large parking area right next to the road, which makes a great base for a visit to this spot. Simply follow the path toward the coast for a couple of minutes to a pair of wooden platforms, where you will find great views of the rocks. I prefer the platform to the left because it is closer to the water and makes it easier to capture impressive images with the steep drop of the stacks in the foreground. The swell is particularly strong in winter. If the wind allows, try capturing some images using longer exposure times. This produces a soft-focus effect in the breaking crowns of the waves and adds sparkle to your images.

Lóndrangar at sunset during a storm (f/8 · 1/15 sec. · ISO 400 · 14mm · Filter: Soft GND16)

TOP TIP

If you want to get even closer to the stacks, drive farther toward the west, take the first turn to the left, and follow the road to the lighthouse at Malariff. There is a parking area next to the Gestastofa Visitor Center. From there, various paths lead eastward toward the stacks at Lóndrangar.

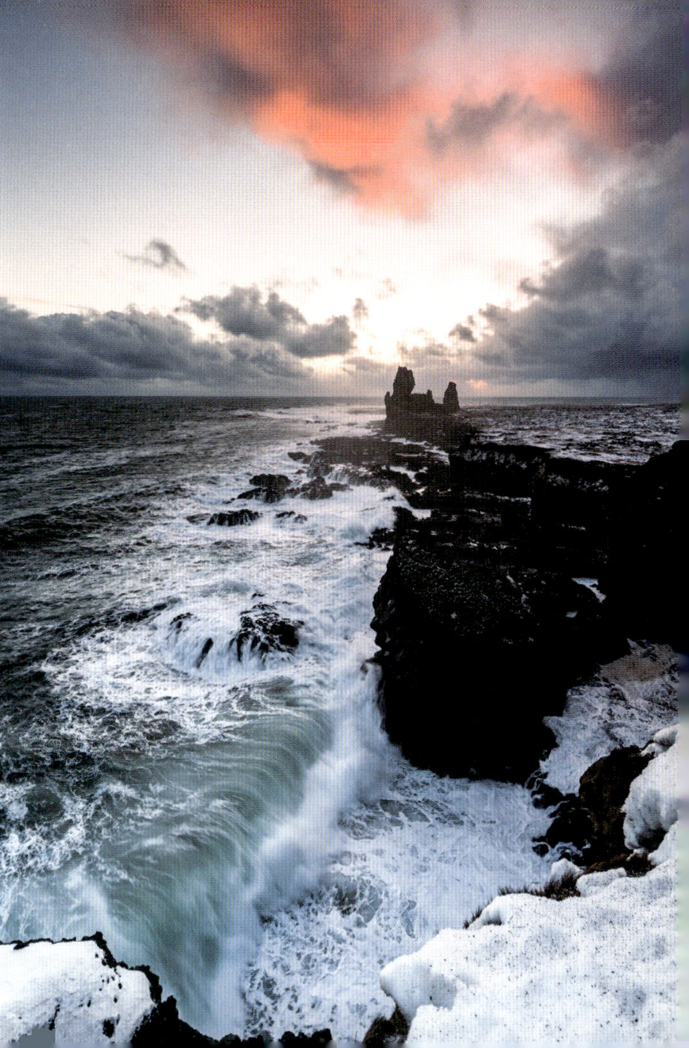

Parking Area

Photo Location

5 BLACK SAND AND GLACIERS AT SNÆFELLSJÖKULL

Distance: About an hour's drive from Arnarstapi, or 25 minutes from Búðir (via Route 54)
Best time of day: Sunrise or sunset
Best time of year: Summer, fall, or winter
Equipment: No special requirements
Tour type: Self-drive
Parking area coordinates: 64.931114, –23.508354
Location coordinates: 64.931337, –23.510500

As you drive farther west, Snæfellsjökull will accompany you to your right, and you are sure to find numerous great photo spots along the way. One particularly impressive and seldom seen view of the glacier is from the north side of the Snæfellsnes Peninsula. To get there, either continue on Route 574 to the west or, if you start from Búðir, take Route 54 to the north, which takes you over a beautiful mountain pass. Once you are over the pass, continue on Route 54 toward Grundarfjörður.

You will soon see a long beach with black sand to your left. There is a small parking area just before the end of the beach. When you head out across the beach, remember that arctic terns (krías) breed here too, so you may need to use your tripod to fend off overhead attacks.

If you look along the coast, you will see the beautiful, snow-capped Snæfellsjökull in the background. This is another great location for using long exposure times to soften the look of the waves in your photos.

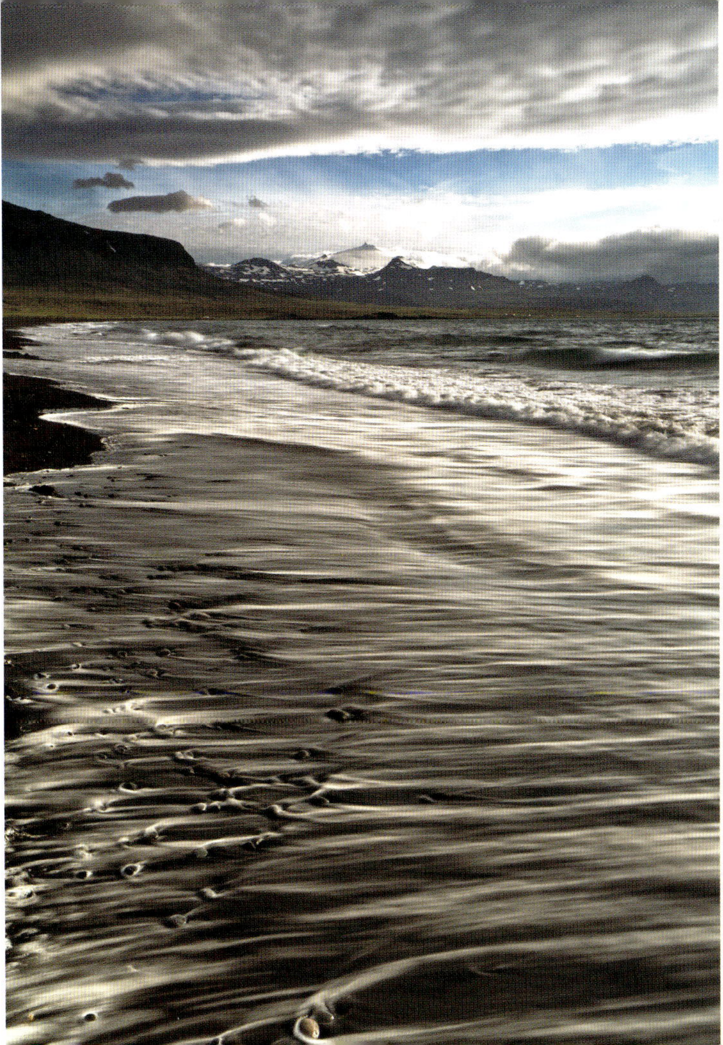

A view along the beach to the majestic Snæfellsjökull (f/18 · 1/2 sec. · ISO 50 · 32mm · Filter: Soft GND16)

WARNING!

The mountain pass on Route 54 is often difficult to negotiate in winter and is sometimes closed completely. If this is the case, you will need to adjust your journey plan to allow plenty of extra time for driving around the tip of the Snæfellsnes Peninsula.

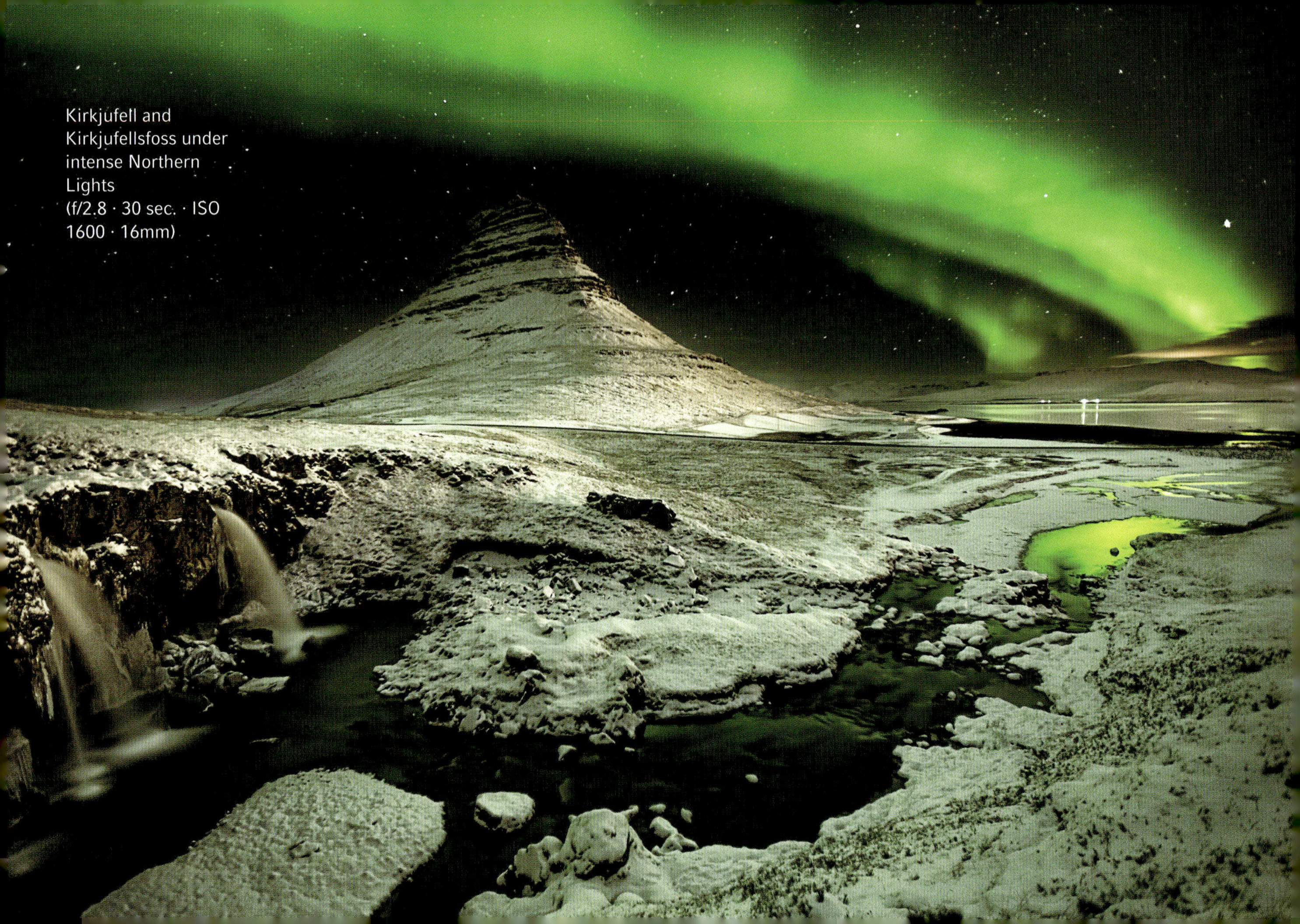

Kirkjufell and Kirkjufellsfoss under intense Northern Lights (f/2.8 · 30 sec. · ISO 1600 · 16mm)

6 KIRKJUFELL

Distance: 30 minutes from Búðir via Route 54, or 75 minutes on Route 574
Best time of day: Sunrise, sunset, or nighttime
Best time of year: Fall or winter
Equipment: No special requirements
Tour type: Self-drive
Parking area coordinates: 64.927435, –23.307114
Location coordinates: 64.925912, –23.311860

Parking Area

Photo Location

Kirkjufell is the most photographed mountain in Iceland. Before Iceland became as popular as it is today, I had discovered this unique mountain and the many ways to capture its beauty. Viewed from the south, it looks like a church tower, while from the west it looks like the nave of a church, so its name, which means Church Mountain, is no surprise. Kirkjufell is 463 meters (1,500 feet) high and is located on a peninsula near the small town of Grundarfjörður. Its distinctive shape is due to the glaciers that once surrounded it. If you are surefooted and have a head for heights, you can climb it from its southwest side.

The tiered waterfall Kirkjufellsfoss is another photographic highlight located opposite Kirkjufell on the right-hand side of the road. There is a parking area next to the lower basin, which you can't miss as you drive along Route 54 toward Grundarfjörður.

Because the number of tourists in Iceland has increased rapidly in recent years, the Icelanders have begun to think hard about how to preserve the natural environment, which is their most important tourist attraction. The

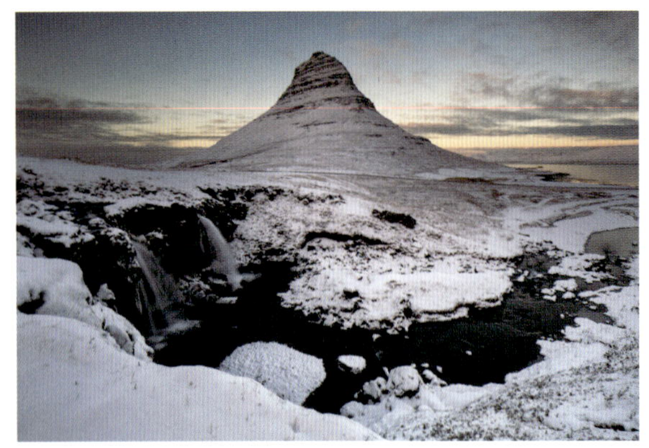

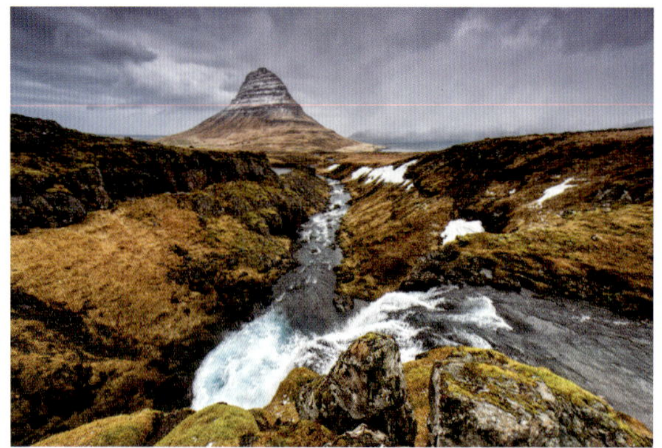

Left:
Sunset at Kirkjufell in the snow (f/16 · 1/6 sec. · ISO 50 · 16mm · Filter: Soft GND8)

Right:
Kirkjufell in fall (f/10 · 1/160 sec. · ISO 200 · 14mm · Filter: Soft GND16)

well-maintained paths on both sides of the Kirkjufell waterfall are just one part of the new infrastructure required to guide tourists around popular sites. If you want to photograph the waterfall with the mountain in the background, take the right-hand path up to the bridge, where you can switch sides and look for a spot to shoot from.

I am constantly on the lookout for new ways to combine well-known subjects in my photos, and here, too, I have found a new spot that is even better than the others. Starting from the old bridge over the waterfall with your back to Kirkjufell, walk for about 15 minutes on the right side of the river toward the mountains until you reach a smaller (but no less beautiful) waterfall. To get there, you have to find a small gap in the fence that is in your way. Last time I was there, the fence was open and I was easily

The west side of Kirkjufell at low tide (f/11 · 11 sec. · ISO 400 · 14mm · Filter: Soft GND16, ND64) ▶

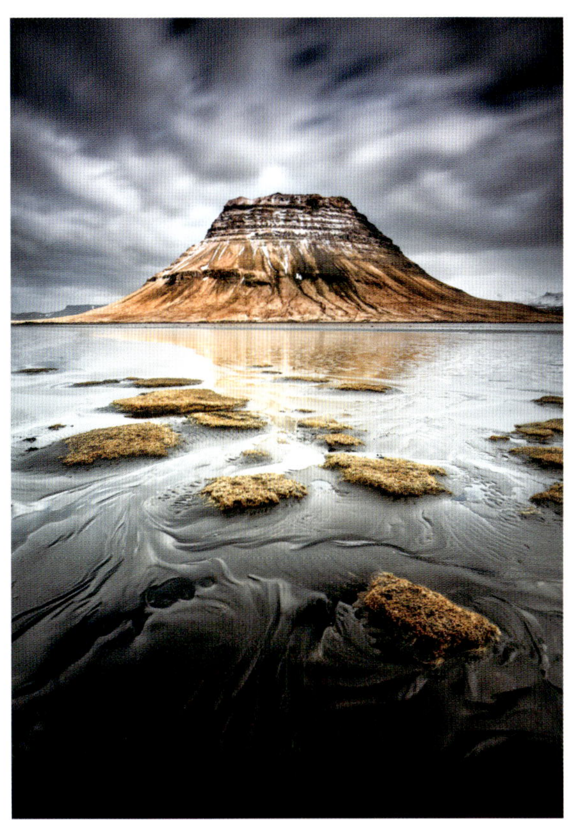

able to continue on uphill. You will probably be welcomed by a small group of horses that graze there, and, once you have passed them, you will soon see the waterfall (GPS coordinates: 64.921949, –23.319123).

If you are on the lookout for a completely different view, it is worth taking a detour to the west of Kirkjufell. To get there, turn left out of the parking area and drive toward Ólafsvík. Once you have passed Kirkjufell, you will see an ocean inlet to the right that reaches all the way to the road. Take the first turn to the right just past the inlet and drive about 100 yards along the side road (GPS coordinates: 64.944603, –23.342185). Park there and walk to the water. At low tide, and on less windy days, the black sand and the reflection of the mountain make irresistible photographic subjects.

Waterfall

Side road

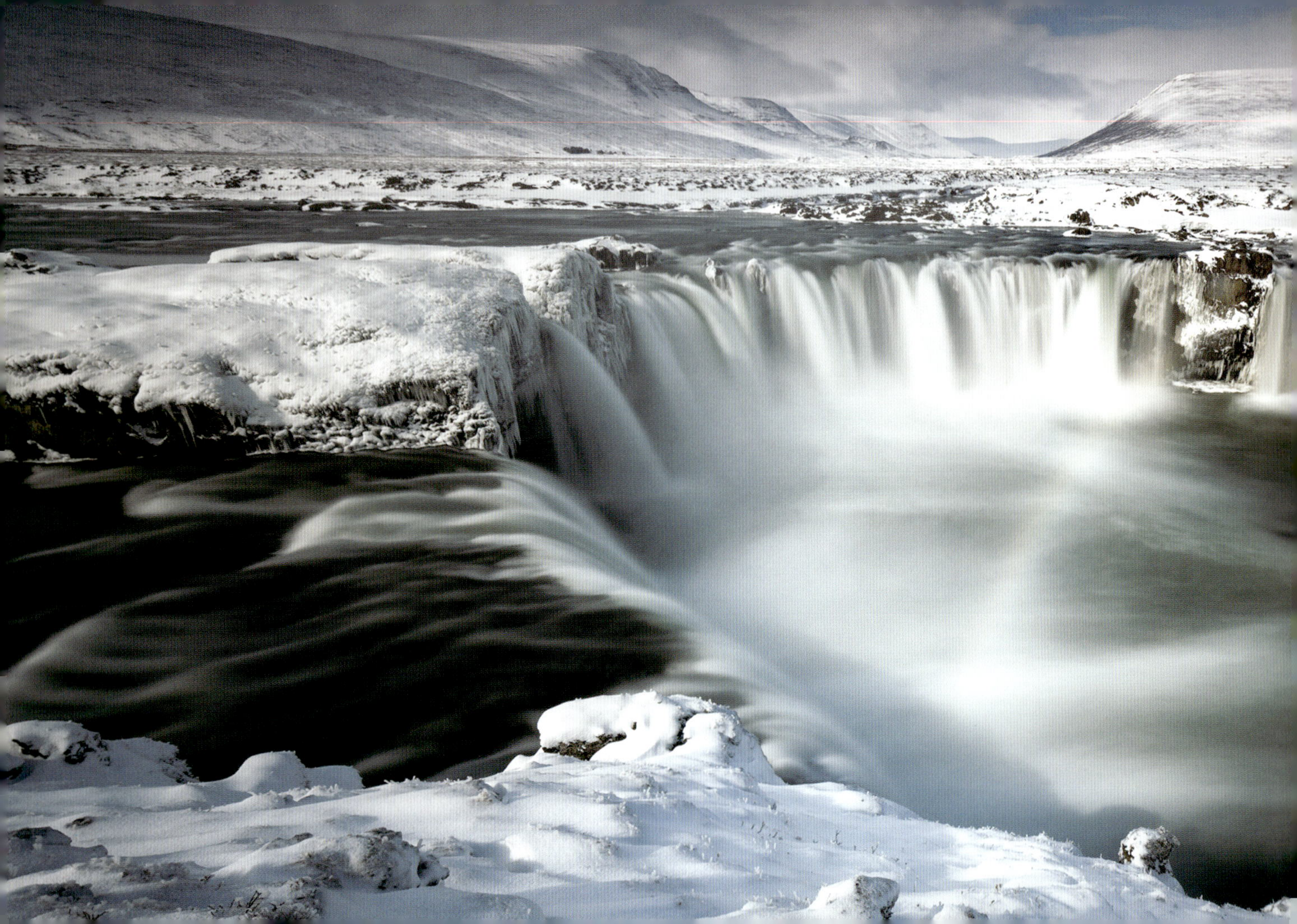

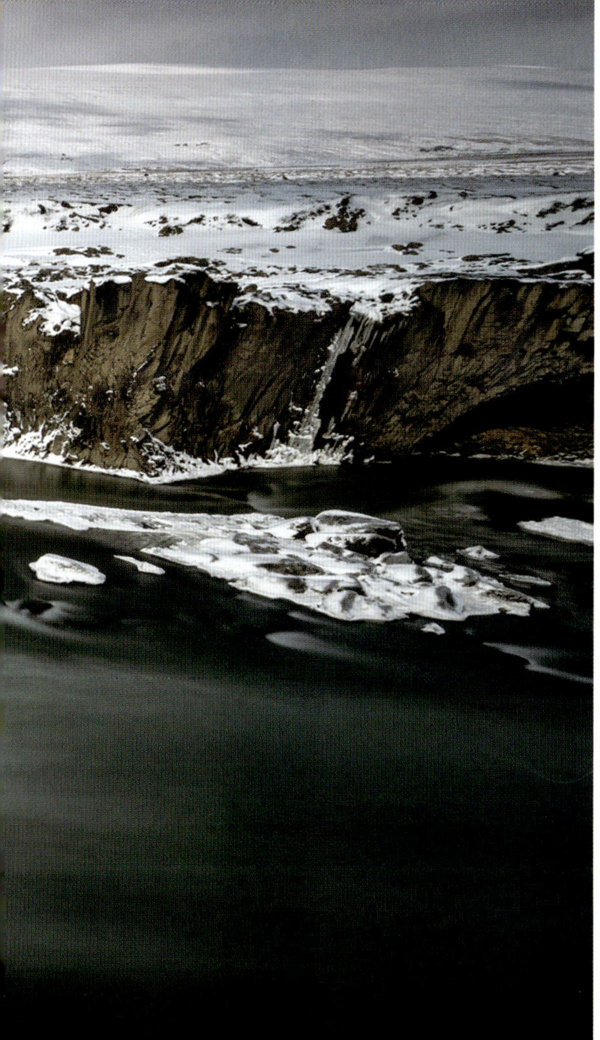

TOUR 2
THE NORTH

This tour takes you to Iceland's far north. As on the first tour, leave Reykjavík heading north on Route 1 (the Ring Road) and drive along the west coast on the banks of the Hvalfjörður. This long fjord has a tunnel under it that costs 1,000 Icelandic Krona to use. Heading north for about half an hour, you will reach the small town of Borgarnes, which is an ideal place for a coffee break and to fill your car with gas. The combined flower shop and café *Blómasetrið – Kaffi Kyrrð* (*www.blomasetrid.is*) is a great place to take a break on your journey. From Borgarnes, continue northward on Route 1 and drive through several valleys and over two mountain passes, which are often snowed over in winter and are very foggy in fall. On clear days, the views of the mountains along the way are spectacular and offer plenty of photo opportunities. Akureyri is

TOUR 2 BASICS
Overall time required: 5–6 days
Travel time: Approx. five hours from Reykjavík to Akureyri. Add an hour if you aim to stay in Laugar.
Lodging: I recommend staying in Laugar, which is perfectly located for tours in the northern area. The travel times listed in this chapter all assume you are staying in Laugar. If you are staying in Akureyri, add an hour to each tour. If you are traveling in winter, the short days make it a sensible option to plan an overnight stop on long drives.

the main town in the north of Iceland, and offers plenty of places to buy food and gas. It is also a nice place in its own right, and it is worth taking a break to explore the town.

Although Akureyri is a great place to spend some time, it is better to travel on for about an hour more to Laugar and look for lodging there. Saving time at your destination is always a good idea, especially when you are planning a photo trip that depends on capturing the mood of the moment at the right time of day. Laugar is close to the Goðafoss Waterfall and is only 20 minutes from Lake Mývatn.

If you are traveling in winter, the road and weather conditions often make an overnight stop along the way unavoidable. In Iceland, driving in bad weather, and especially at night, can be very dangerous. Depending on the exact date and location, Icelandic winters can have just a few hours of daylight. In the summer, however, it never gets completely dark because on the longest days, the sun sits just slightly below the horizon.

This tour takes you along the same route on the return trip to Reykjavík.

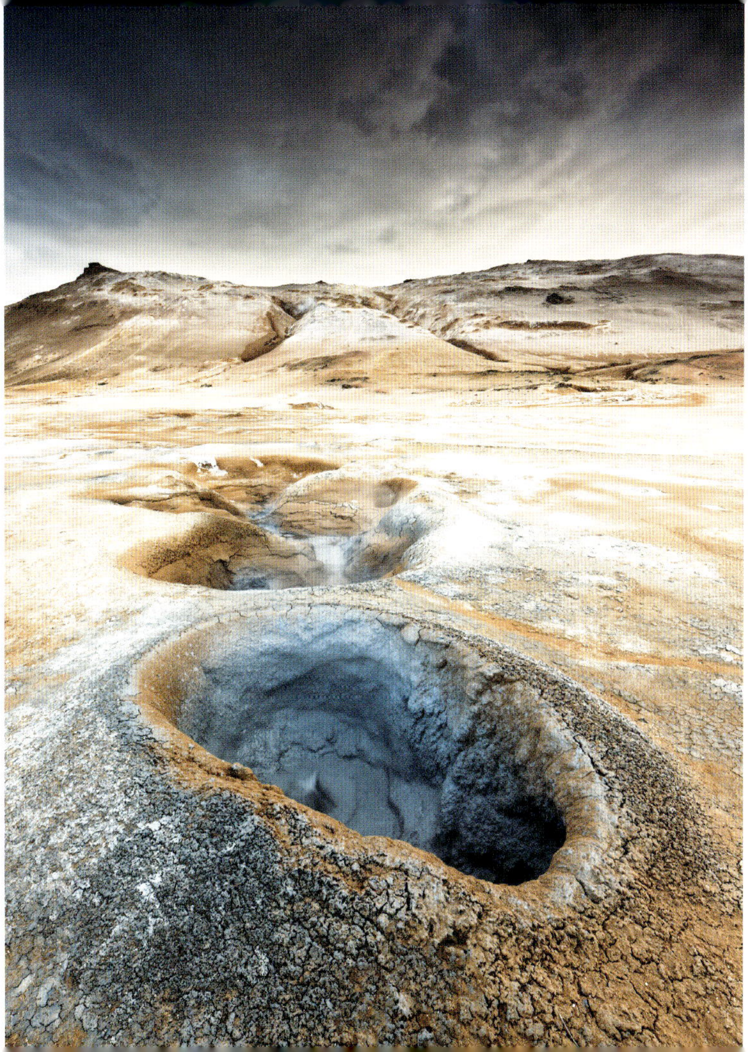

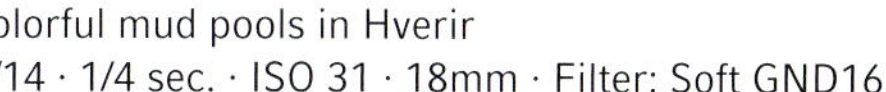

Colorful mud pools in Hverir
(f/14 · 1/4 sec. · ISO 31 · 18mm · Filter: Soft GND16)

TOP TIP

If you desire an unusual experience, plan a detour to Húsavík. This tiny town is located way up north, about a half-hour drive from Laugar, and is known for its whale-watching tours. The conditions on the coast at Húsavík are ideal for meeting these giants of the ocean. There are various tour operators working directly from the harbor. And don't forget to take your longest lens with you if you want to capture every detail of an unforgettable trip.

WARNING!

This tour has two separate destinations, both of which require a 4WD vehicle. This is not only for your safety, but also because it includes F-roads, where a 4WD vehicle is mandatory by law. If you drive on an F-road in a regular car, your insurance coverage will be void and you risk police fines, too. If you don't want to take the self-drive approach but still want to visit these destinations, there are guided tours to "The Fantastic Falls" available year round from IceAk in Akureyri (*www.iceak.is*). For more details, see the section on Aldeyarfoss on page 53.

It is important to check the weather forecast regularly all year round. Storms can occur at any time. Watching the weather is particularly important in winter, especially if you are travelling in the north of Iceland, where roads are often closed. The official Icelandic road maintenance website also provides useful information about weather-related road conditions.

Icelandic Meteorological Office: *en.vedur.is*

Road Conditions: *www.road.is*

See the *Introduction* section for more details on these websites.

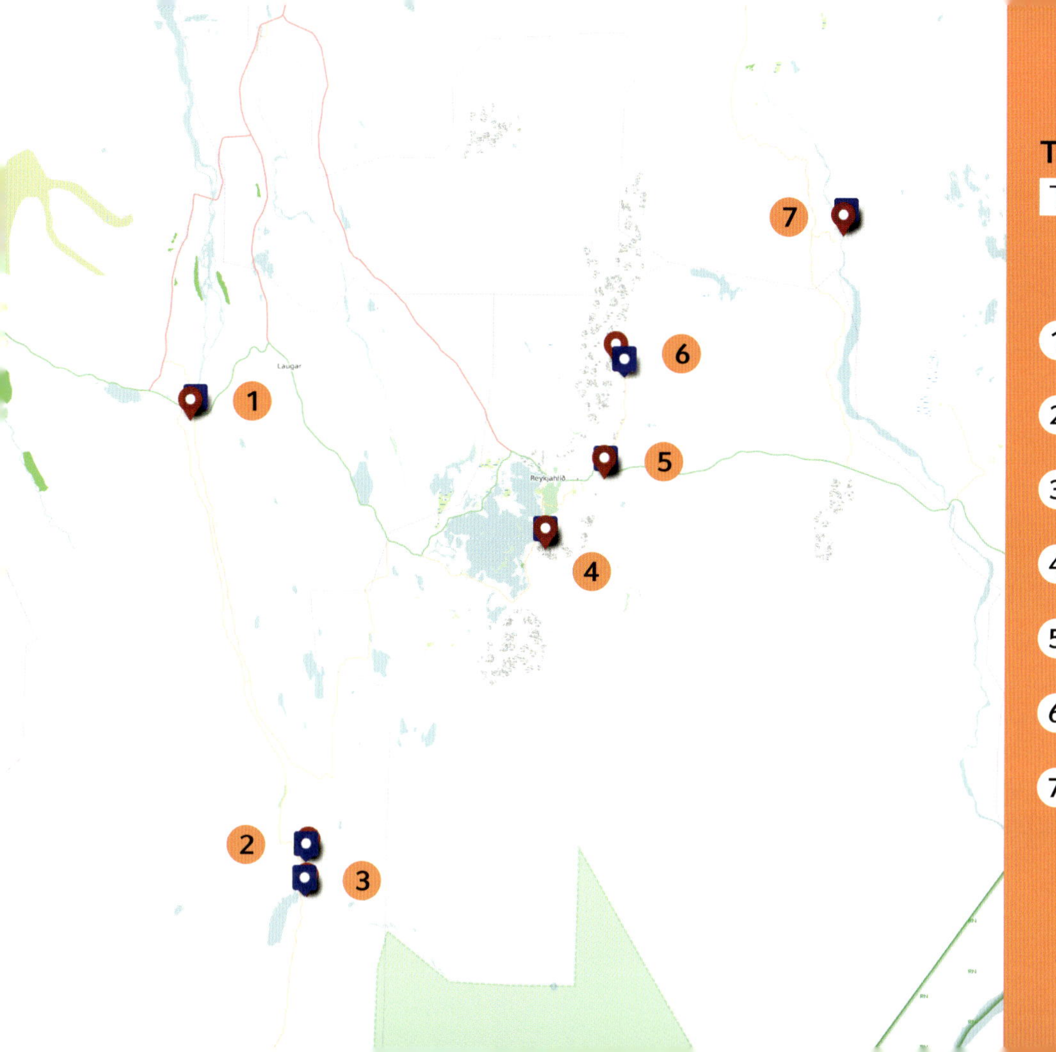

THE NORTH

TOUR 2

1. GOÐAFOSS
2. ALDEYARFOSS
3. HRAFNABJARGAFOSS
4. DIMMUBORGIR
5. HVERARÖND AND HVERIR
6. LEIRHNJÚKUR
7. DETTIFOSS

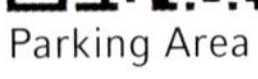
Parking Area

Photo Location

1 GOÐAFOSS

Distance: About 10 minutes from Laugar
Best time of day: Sunrise or sunset
Best time of year: Summer, fall, or winter
Equipment: No special requirements
Tour type: Self-drive
Parking area coordinates: 65.685981, –17.538408
Location coordinates: 65.683069, –17.548265

The rocks provide a perfect foreground for the view up to the mighty waterfall (f/20 · 1/4 sec. · ISO 31 · 20mm · Filter: Soft GND16)

This imposing three-tiered waterfall is located directly on Route 1 at Bárðardalur, about halfway between Akureyri and Mývatn. If you are staying in Laugar, it is only a 10-minute drive, making it easy to reach for a sunrise or sunset photo session.

According to legend, the falls got its name—which means Waterfall of the Gods—when Þorgeir Ljósvetningagoði Þorkelsson threw his last remaining pagan icons into the water here in about 1000 AD and declared Christianity to be the official religion of Iceland.

Roads on both the east and west sides of the river lead to the parking areas close to the edge of the 40-foot falls.

Both sides of the falls offer great photo opportunities, but I prefer the eastern side, where you can shoot from a wooden platform at the top or take a path down to the foot of the falls. If you take the footpath from there toward the falls, you will find a boulder covered in grass and moss close to the riverbank, which makes a wonderful foreground subject at any time of year.

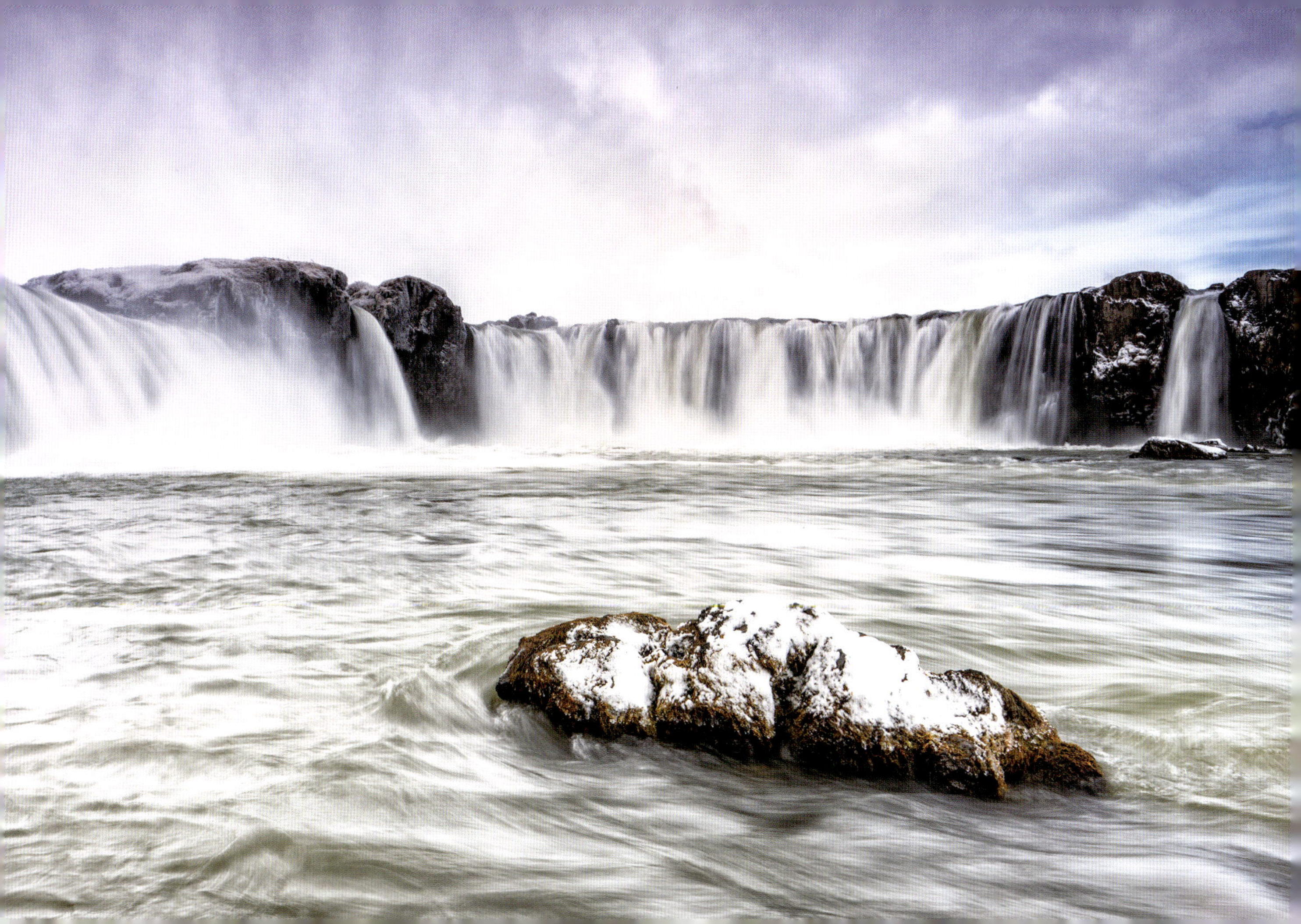

WARNING!
If you walk down the side of the waterfall in winter, take great care when approaching the water. It is not always clear where the ground ends and the thin layer of ice on the water begins.

TOP TIP
Even if the light is most appealing at sunrise or sunset, you will often find rainbows formed by the spray above the falls when the sun is higher in the sky. This type of shot is best captured from the eastern side of the river.

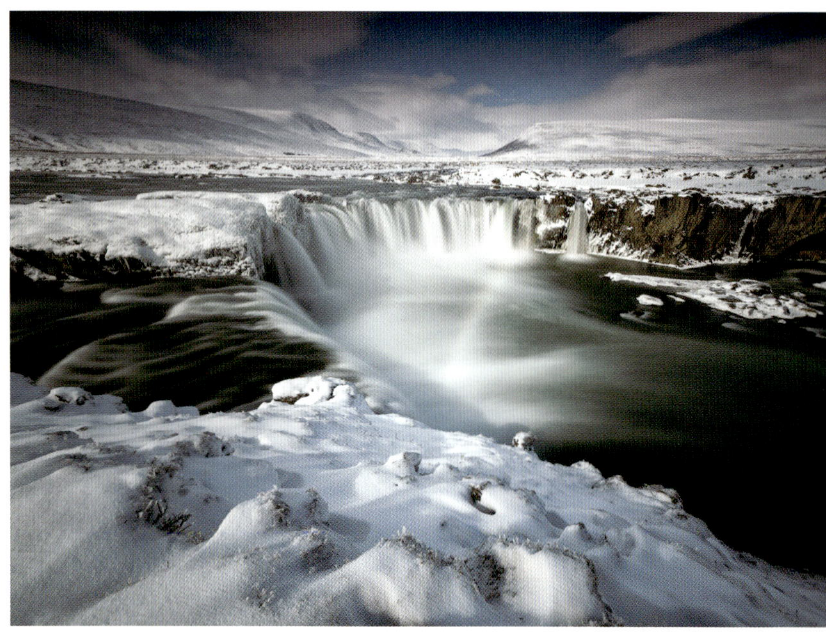

Goðafoss in the snow with a rainbow
(f/16 · 18 sec. · ISO 125 · 14mm · Filters: Soft GND8, ND64)

2 ALDEYARFOSS

Distance: One hour from Laugar, 45 minutes from Goðafoss
Best time of day: Sunrise or sunset
Best time of year: summer, fall, or winter
Equipment: No special requirements
Required vehicle: 4WD
Tour type: Self-drive in summer or fall, guided in winter
Parking area coordinates: 65.364250, –17.341240
Location coordinates: 65.366019, –17.338321

Parking Area

Photo Location

Aldeyarfoss is one of Iceland's most captivating waterfalls and is only a 45-minute drive from Goðafoss.

The trip begins on an easy gravel road (Bárðardalsvegur Vestri, Route 842) to the west of the river Skjálfandafljót, which feeds both Goðafoss and Aldeyarfoss. If you are starting from the eastern side of Goðafoss, simply turn left onto Route 1 and cross the river, drive past the western approach to the falls, and take the next road to the left. Follow this road until you almost reach Bólstaður Farm. This is where Route 842 ends and Route F26 (Sprengisandur) begins, and this is the road that takes you to Aldeyarfoss. Even if this stretch of the road isn't particularly challenging, note that this is an F-road where a 4WD vehicle is mandatory. If you ignore this law and use a regular car, you lose your insurance cover and risk a traffic fine.

There is a sign-posted parking area above the falls at Aldeyarfoss. You will find an easy footpath opposite the restrooms, which takes you to the upper bank of the pool that the waterfall flows into.

From the edge of the pool, you will immediately see an overhanging cliff opposite the falls that, for obvious reasons, is one of this location's most popular photo spots. You need to have a head for heights to shoot from there; but if you prefer, you can set up your camera to the right of the cliff instead. From this vantage point, you can capture the entire pool and the waterfall in a single shot.

To the left, toward where the river continues its flow, is a narrow path that you can see over the edge of the rocks. This path takes you to the foot of the falls. While on the path, stay close to the rock face almost all the way down and only head off to the left for the final quarter of the descent.

WARNING!
Taking this path is recommended only in summer, and then only if you are sure-footed on loose ground.

Once you reach the bottom, you'll be at eye level with the falling water, and you are sure to feel the power of its enormous spill. There is also a smaller pool at this level, which is great for capturing reflections of the waterfall on fine days. Selfies are popular here, too, but extra care is required, as you need to get really close to the water to capture yourself and the falls.

TOP TIP
Try using a range of exposure times to capture your shots. If you get it just right, the water flowing into the pool appears star-shaped with the waterfall at its center. The right exposure time to use depends on the amount of water the river is carrying and the speed of its flow at a given time.

Aldeyarfoss in snow and ice at sunrise (f/14 · 8 sec. · ISO 40 · 15mm · Filter: Soft GND16, ND64)

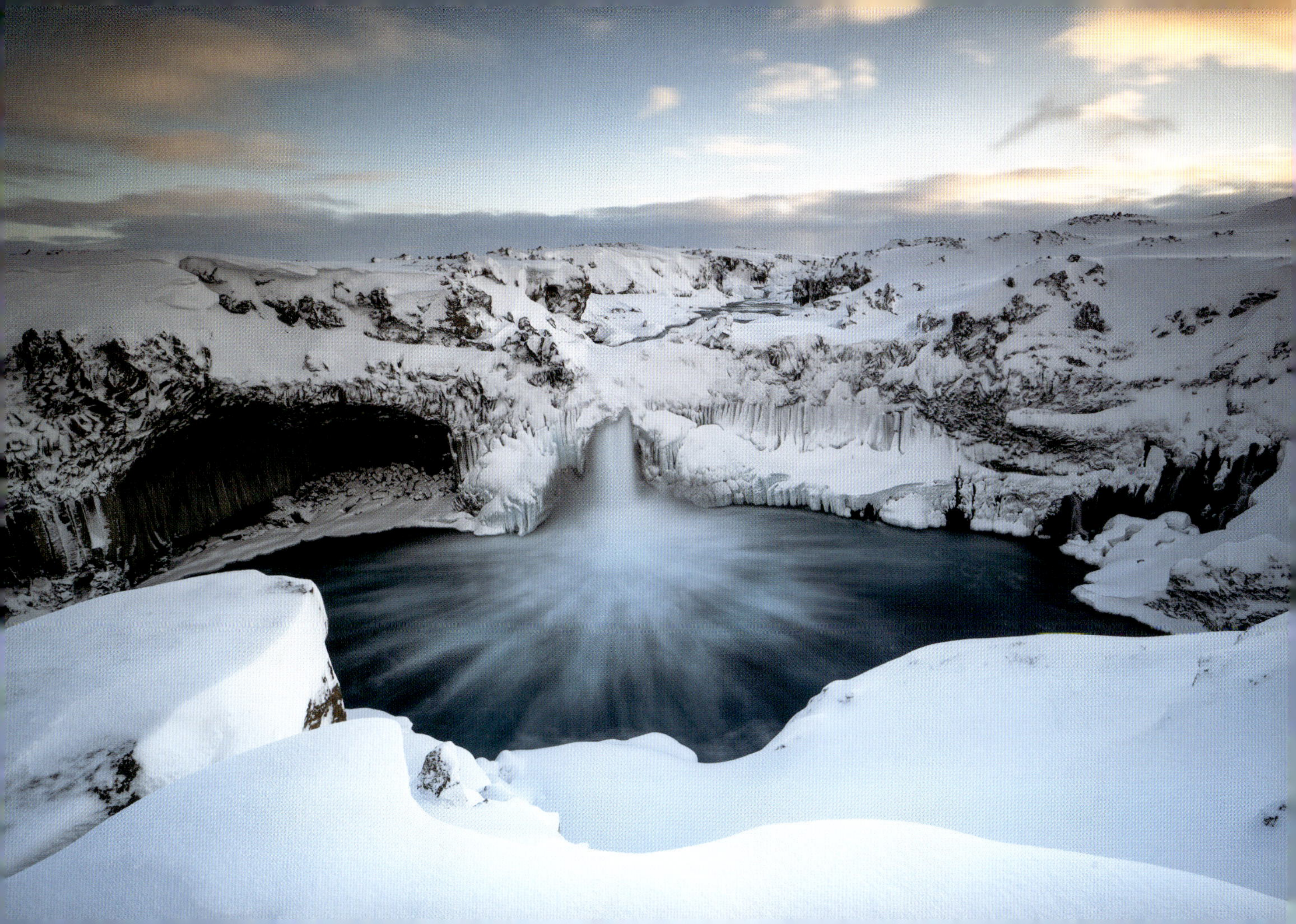

A breathtaking view of the pool at Aldeyarfoss (f/18 · 1.3 sec. · ISO 31 · 16mm · Filter: Soft GND16)

TOP TIP

Aldeyarfoss is impossible to reach using your own vehicle in late fall or winter. Masses of snow and deep drifts make the road impossible to negotiate, even in the best available SUV. However, there are plenty of guided tours here in winter. I have been on several and have been blown away every time by the amazing ride and the fantastic winter landscapes.

I can thoroughly recommend *IceAk* in Akureyri (*www.iceak.is*). Þórður and his guides offer unforgettable trips and know just where to take you to get the best-possible photos. *IceAk* offers a standard group tour to "The Fantastic Falls," which includes Goðafoss, Aldeyarfoss, and Hrafnabjargafoss. You can also book a private tour that is put together according to your personal wishes, enabling you to stay for as long as you like at each of your chosen locations.

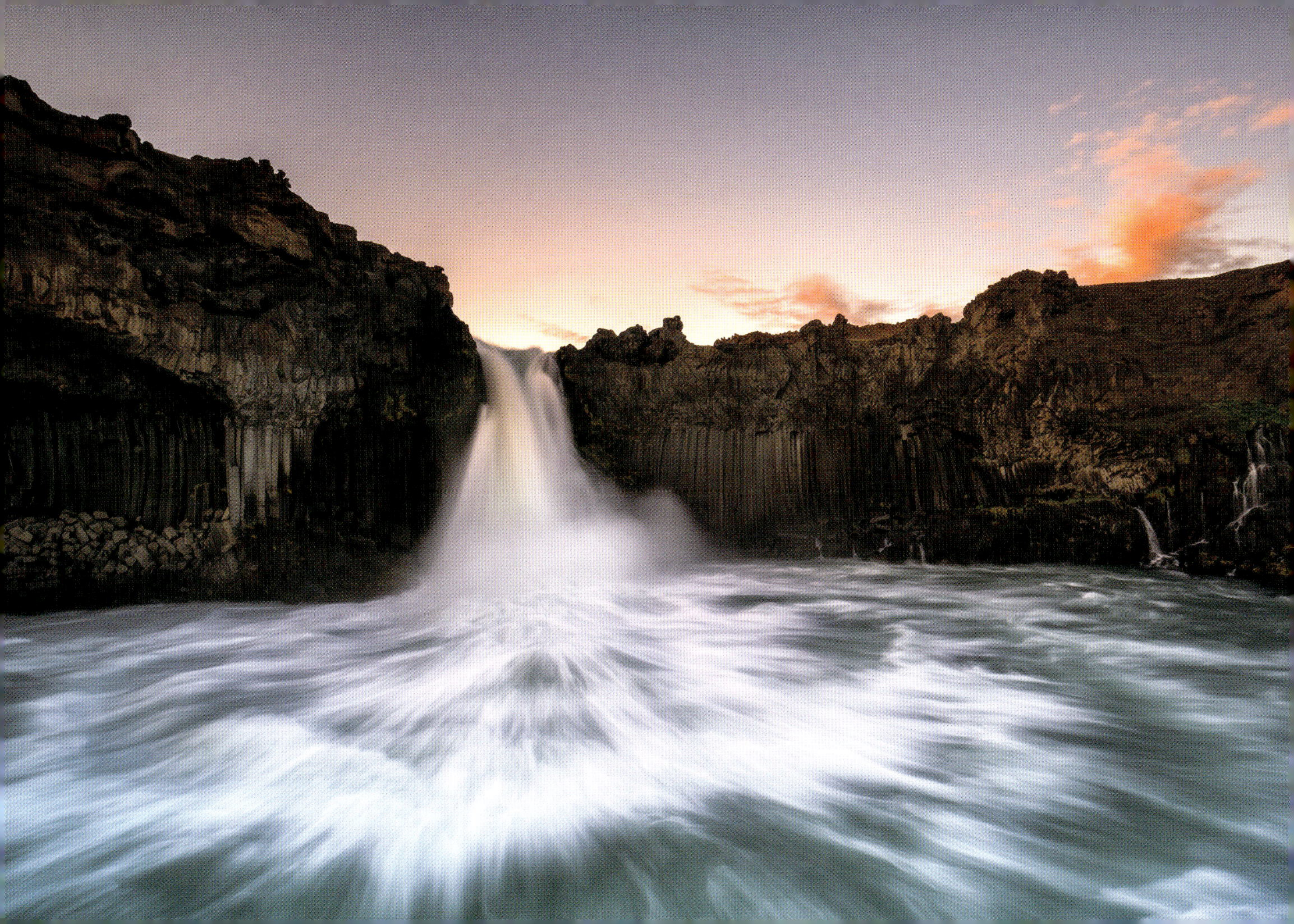

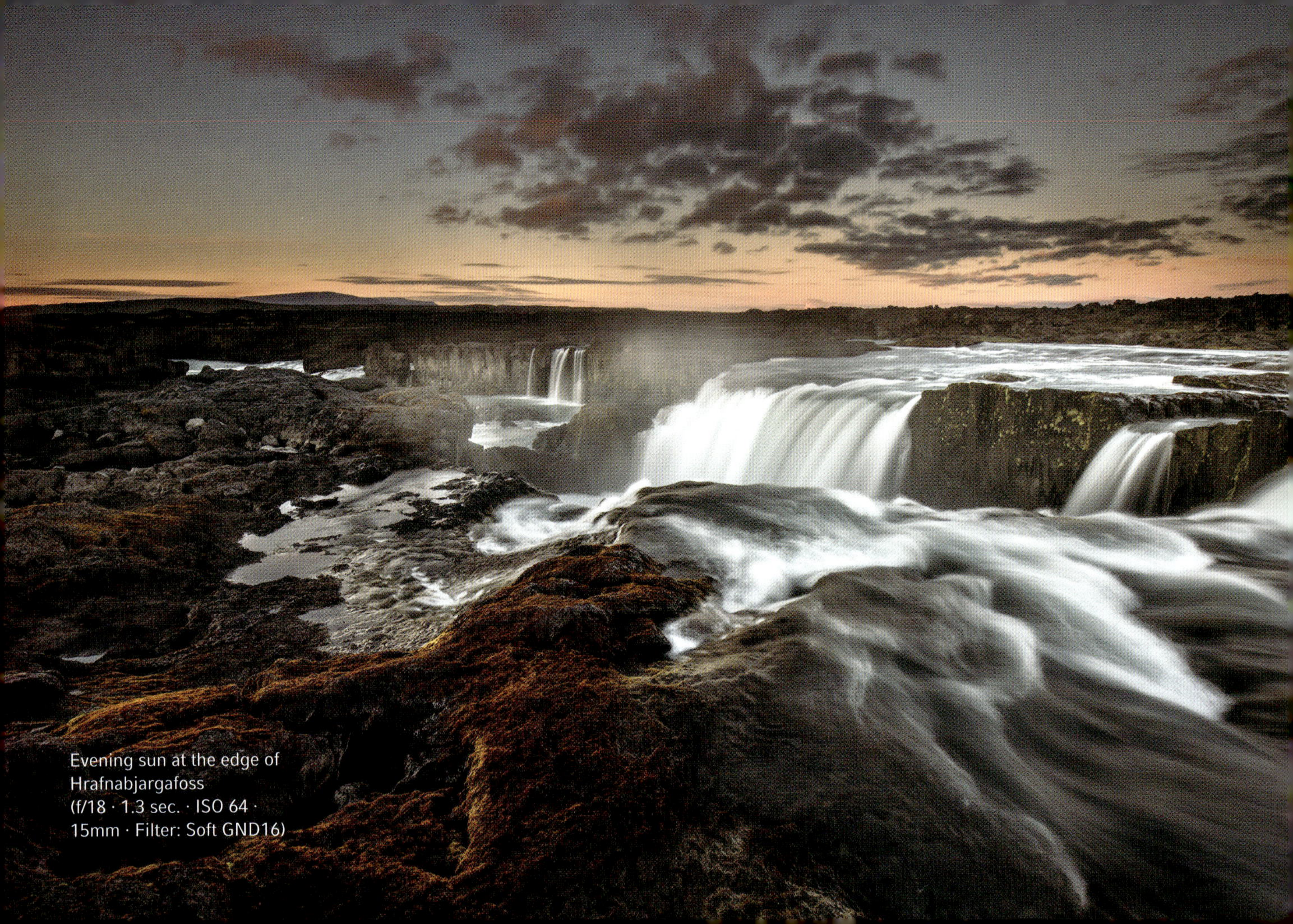

Evening sun at the edge of Hrafnabjargafoss (f/18 · 1.3 sec. · ISO 64 · 15mm · Filter: Soft GND16)

Parking Area

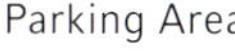

Photo Location

3 HRAFNABJARGAFOSS

Distance: One-and-a-quarter hours from Laugar, about an hour from Goðafoss
Best time of day: Sunrise or sunset
Best time of year: Summer, fall, or winter
Equipment: No special requirements
Vehicle: 4WD required
Tour type: Self-drive in summer or fall, guided in winter
Parking area coordinates: 65.339202, –17.344741
Location coordinates: 65.339870, –17.340916

Hrafnabjargafoss is another very interesting waterfall that is just a 15-minute drive from Aldeyarfoss, toward the highlands. Despite a number of guided tours that go there, this particular location is still something of an insider tip, and you will seldom find individual tourists there. Follow the F26 until you see a sign to turn toward Hrafnabjargafoss, and then follow the rough, stone-strewn road until you reach a small parking area.

WARNING!
Drive slowly on this road and take care to avoid the larger rocks you are sure to encounter. It is easy to get a flat tire, and dealing with the consequences can be a real hassle in such a remote region. This is one of the places where you will quickly appreciate having an SUV with decent ground clearance.

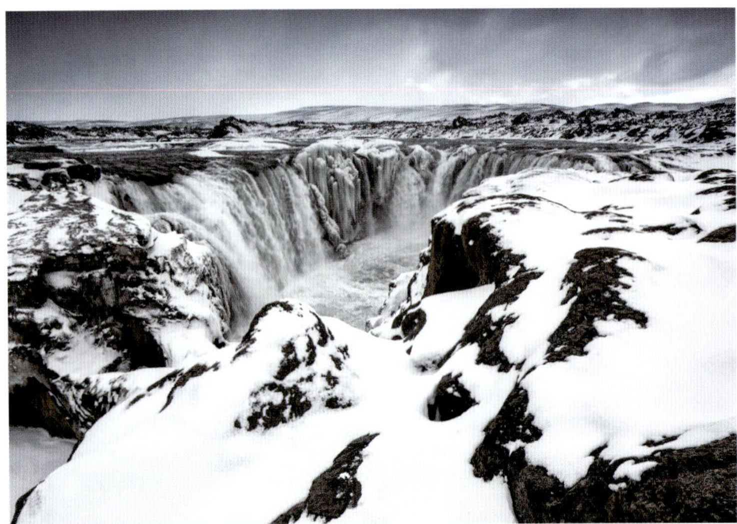

It is always worth a trip to this remote waterfall, even in winter (f/14 · 1/40 sec. · ISO 31 · 20mm · Filter: Soft GND8)

From the parking area, follow the sound of the waterfall across a small lava field. Summer and early fall offer many excellent photo opportunities. I prefer shooting at the right-hand edge of the falls, where you can capture the flowing water and the moss-covered lava while including several other waterfalls in the background. In summer, the sun often bathes the sky in wonderful colors at times when the moon is already visible above the horizon.

If you take a guided tour in winter, you will find Hrafnabjargafoss to be one of the most changeable waterfalls in Iceland. Depending on the amount of snow and ice, it can appear much smaller or much larger. Parts of the falls are often frozen over and covered in a thick layer of ice. The guides from *IceAk* and other tour operators know the area extremely well and will always take you safely to the best locations.

Taken together, Hrafnabjargafoss and Aldeyarfoss make a great combined tour in summer or fall.

4 DIMMUBORGIR

Distance: 30 Minutes from Laugar
Best time of day: Any time—the more clouds, the better
Best time of year: Summer, fall, or winter
Equipment: No special requirements
Tour type: Self-drive
Parking area coordinates: 65.591552, –16.913016
Location coordinates: 65.591031, –16.913451

Parking Area

Photo Location

Dimmuborgir is another interesting location close to Lake Mývatn. Its name means "dark castles" and it is, in fact, a spectacular labyrinth of lava rock formations. To get there, follow Route 1 toward Mývatn and as soon as you reach the lake, turn onto Route 848. Shortly thereafter, you will see a sign to turn toward Dimmuborgir.

Dimmuborgir itself consists of countless intertwined paths snaking through a huge lava field with formations that are often several meters high. It doesn't take long to lose sight of where you started, but the paths are clearly marked, so you can concentrate fully on your remarkable surroundings without worrying about getting lost. The lava formations are reminiscent of towers and high castle walls, often with circular "windows," and it is easy to see how this area got its name.

Around 2,300 years ago, as the lava from the Þrengslaborgir and Lúdentsborgir volcanoes flowed toward Mývatn, some of it backed up in a hollow to form a lava lake. The surface began to petrify and, deeper down, contact with the water below formed steam vents around which the lava cooled. The natural

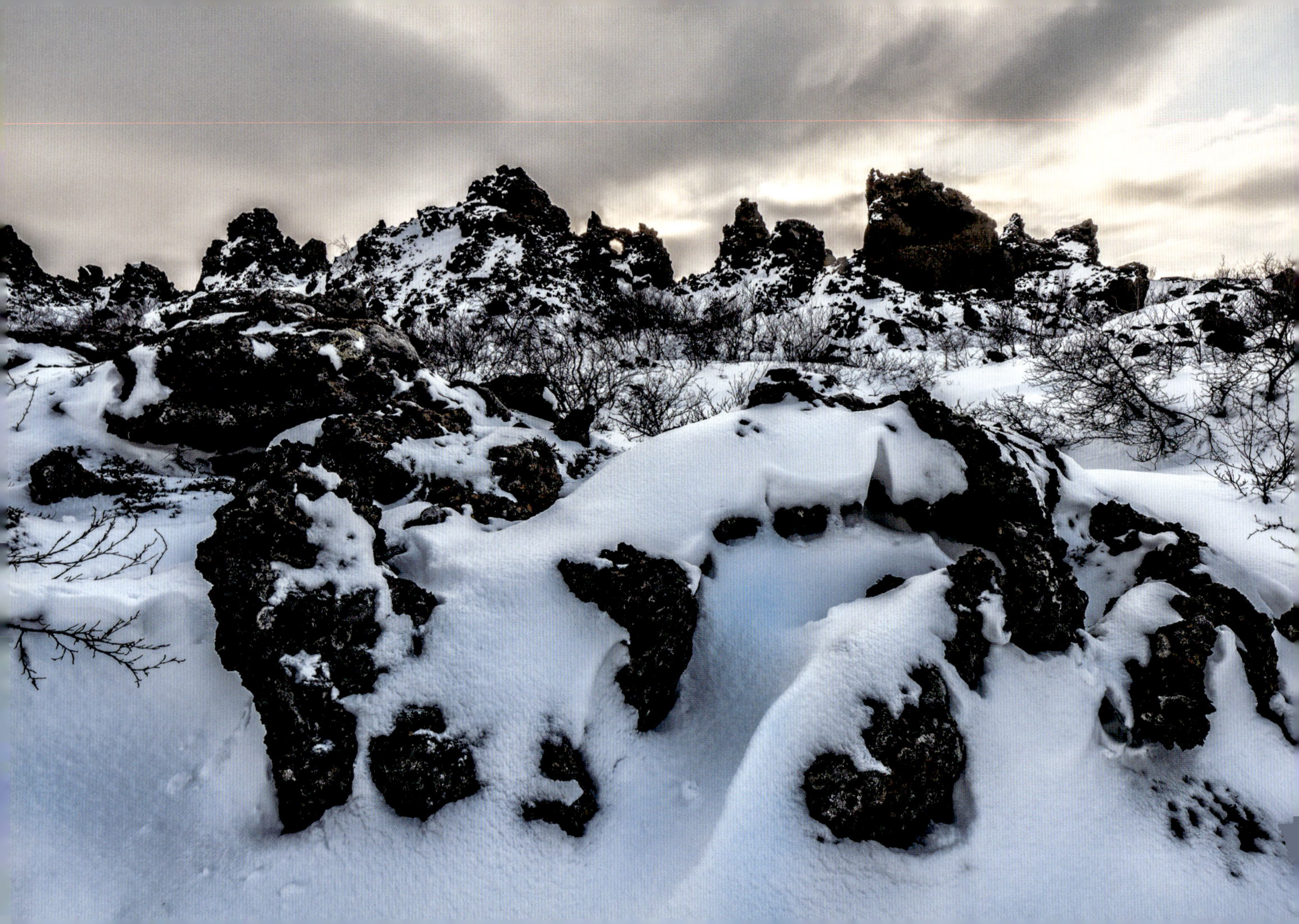

Dimmuborgir in thick winter snow
(f/14 · 1/100 sec. · ISO 31 · 14mm · Filter: Soft GND16)

dam that formed the lava lake then broke, the remains of the liquid lava flowed out, and the petrified crust collapsed. The remains of this process are the formations you see today. Judging by their proportions, the lava lake must have been more than 30 feet deep. To prevent the area from silting up, the Icelanders planted a large number of birch trees that have grown to become a prominent feature of the landscape at Dimmuborgir.

The longest of the three marked paths offers a great circular tour with plenty of photo opportunities. This area is very impressive in winter too, but the snow can make it difficult to visit all of the formations. On occasion, I have had to wade through waist-high snow at Dimmuborgir.

Parking Area

Photo Location

5 HVERARÖND AND HVERIR

Distance: 15 minutes from Dimmuborgir, 45 minutes from Laugar
Best time of day: Any time—the more clouds, the better. Nighttime is great, too.
Best time of year: Summer, fall, or winter
Equipment: No special requirements
Tour type: Self-drive
Parking area coordinates: 65.641602, –16.806939
Location coordinates: 65.641071, –16.809407

Just 15 minutes away from Dimmuborgir is a completely different world, made up of a broad plain full of bubbling mud pools, solfataras (gas-emitting fumaroles), and a strong smell of sulfur. To get there, follow Route 848 until you hit Route 1 at Reykjahlíð. Turn right on Route 1 and then keep driving past the turnoff for Mývatn Nature Baths and past the bright blue lake on the left. The road will begin to get steeper and leads over the Námaskarð pass that crosses mount Námafjall. The word "náma" means "mine" and bears witness to earlier times when sulfur was mined in the area.

Continue on from the pass, take the first road to the right (Route 885, Námaskarðsvegur), and follow the signs to Hverarönd/Hverir. At the end of the road is a busy parking area located directly next to the geothermal area.

A network of paths and boardwalks cover the area, and you are free to move around as you wish. Don't ever leave the marked paths, as the ground is often brittle, especially where it is lighter-colored, and the temperatures beneath are sure to cause serious injury if you should fall through.

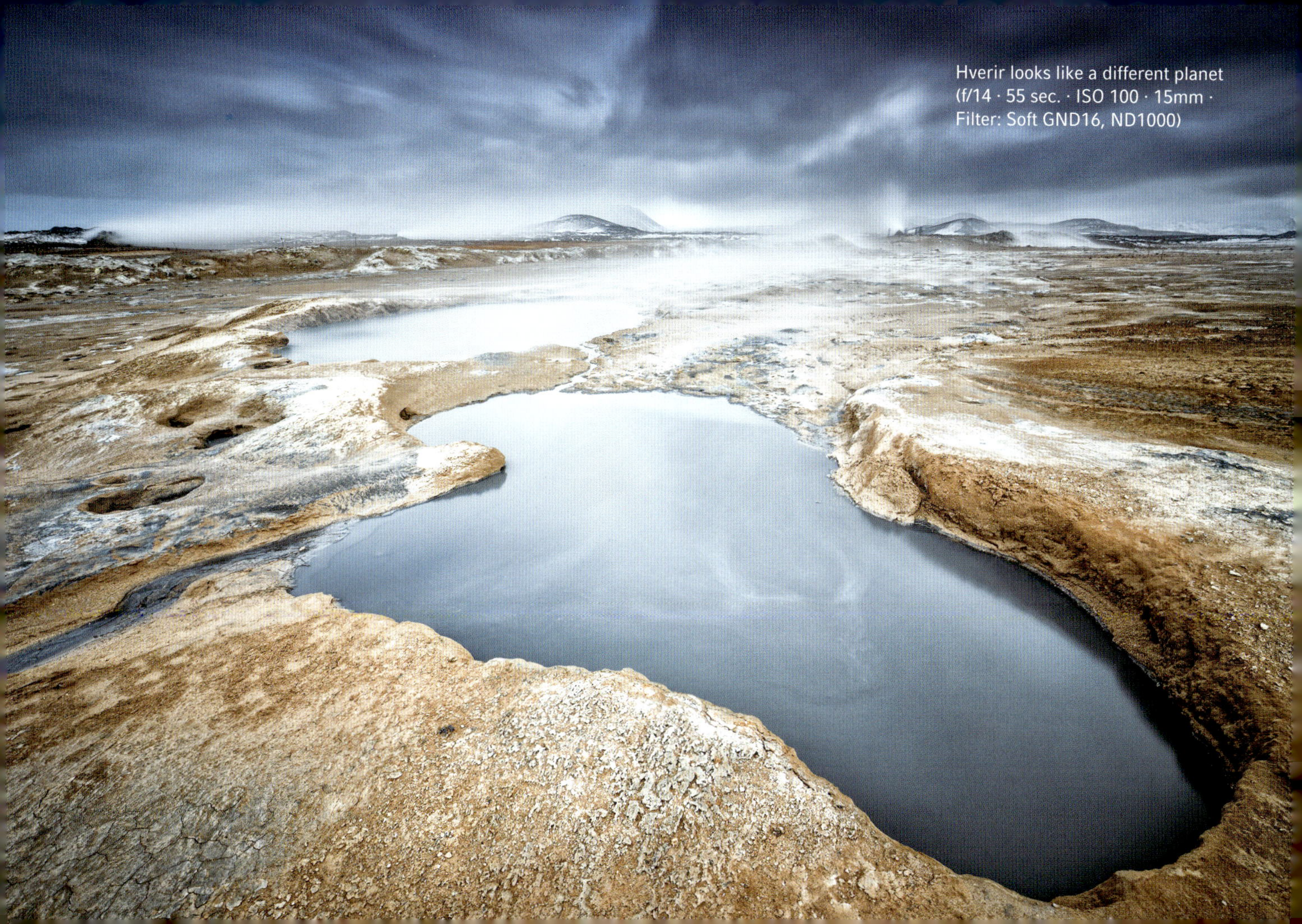

Hverir looks like a different planet (f/14 · 55 sec. · ISO 100 · 15mm · Filter: Soft GND16, ND1000)

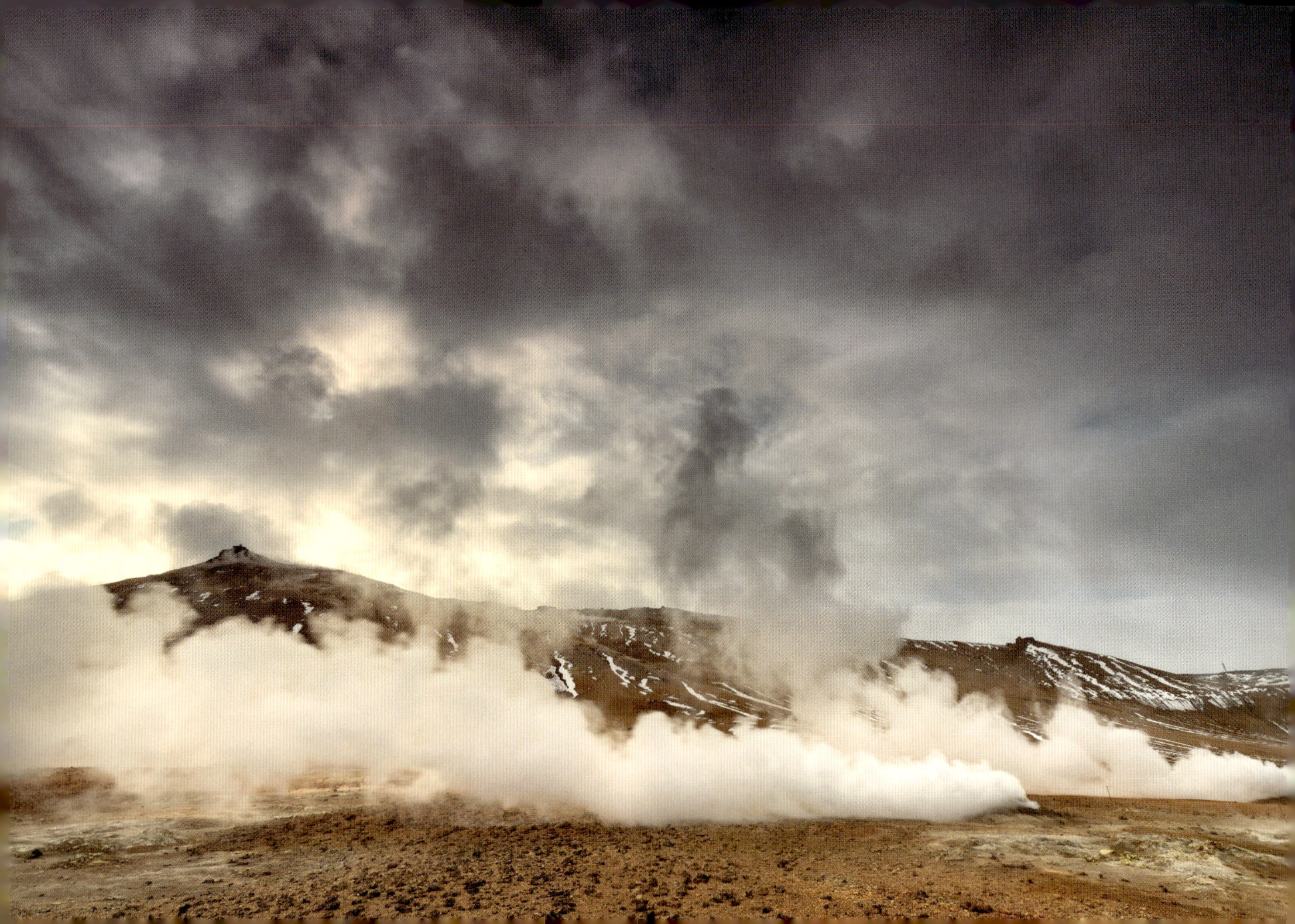

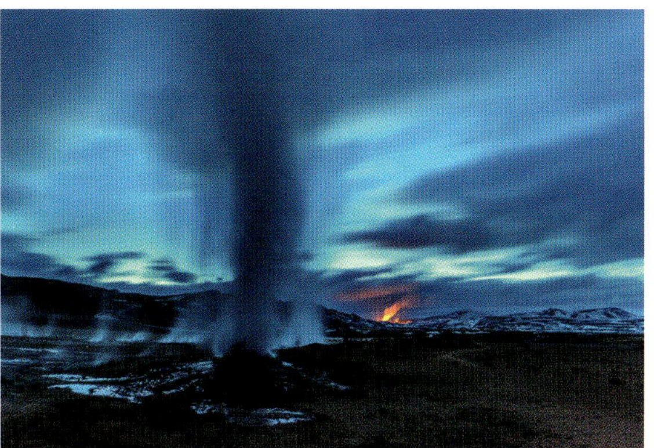

Northern Lights over the steam vents at Hverir
(f/2.8 · 30 sec. · ISO 500 · 16 mm)

TOP TIP

If you want to take a break from the rigors of photography, check out the Mývatn Nature Baths (*www.myvatnnaturebaths.is*). This natural geothermal spa is located at the foot of mount Námafjall and is similar to its more famous cousin, the "Blue Lagoon," which is in the south. However, the spa at Mývatn isn't nearly as busy and the price of admission is a lot lower.

Steam from underground and clouds become one (f/18 · 1/30 sec. · ISO 31 · 14mm · Filter: Soft GND16)

This area is extremely popular, so I have developed the habit of shooting here either using very long exposure times or during the night. During long exposures, the mist produced by the sulfur fumes is so intense that it often blocks the view of other visitors. The bubbling mud pools make for a dramatic foreground. The water levels in the pools varies depending on how much it has rained recently, so it is worth looking around to find the pools that look the best. Check out the two loudly hissing fumaroles close to the wooden platform at the main parking area, too. These are particularly impressive when backlit or at night, when the wind dies down and the steam rises almost vertically.

6 LEIRHNJÚKUR

Distance: 10 minutes from Hverir, about an hour from Laugar
Best time of day: Any time—the more clouds, the better
Best time of year: Summer, fall, or winter
Equipment: No special requirements
Tour type: Self-drive in summer and fall, guided in winter
Parking area coordinates: 65.713134, –16.774046
Location coordinates: 65.722786, –16.788653

Parking Area

Photo Location

Ten minutes away from Hverir, our next destination is another that shows just how active the Earth's crust is in Iceland. Leirhnjúkur is an active volcano that is part of the Krafla caldera. It played a significant role in the so-called "Mývatn Fire"—an eruption on the volcano's northern flank that lasted (with some interruptions) from 1975 through 1984. Although it hasn't erupted again since then, the ground in the area is still so hot that steam rises from it when it rains.

Leaving Hverir, turn right onto Route 1 and take the first turnoff to the left (Kröfluvegur, Route 863). You will soon see the enormous Kröflustöð Power Station and its awe-inspiring view of steam rising everywhere, and gigantic pipes and heat exchangers sprawled spread across the landscape. You will drive beneath an arch made of hot water pipes, and then the road gets rapidly steeper. Once you reach the top, a small parking area on your right gives you a great view of the entire site. Keep following the road until you see a sign on the left for Leirhnjúkur. Take this road until you reach a parking area, where you will also find restrooms and, in summer, a booth selling coffee and snacks.

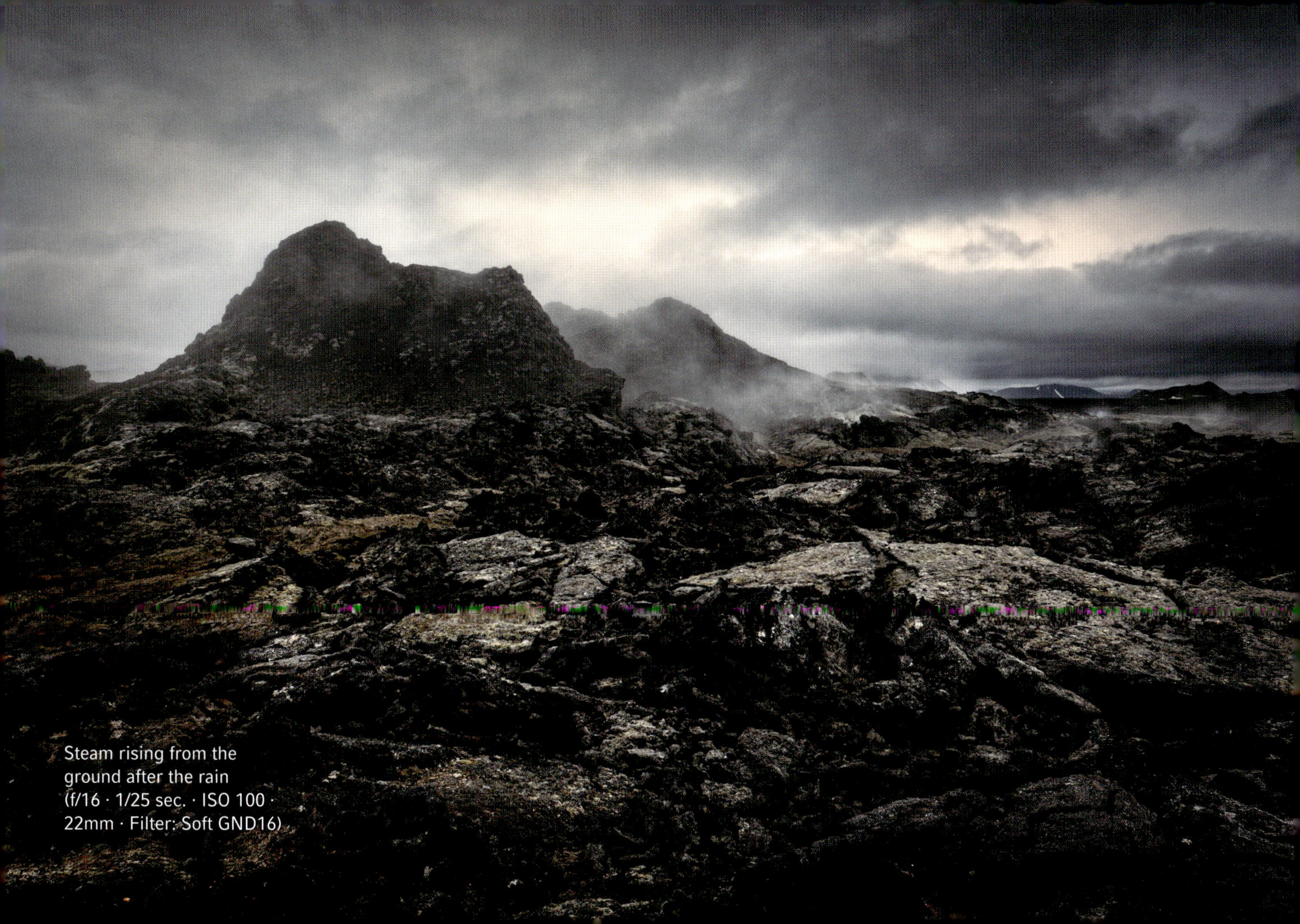

Steam rising from the ground after the rain (f/16 · 1/25 sec. · ISO 100 · 22mm · Filter: Soft GND16)

The path starts directly next to the restrooms and takes you through a bumpy field full of furrows caused by frost damage before it leads into the surrounding lava fields. If you look around, you will notice strange, technical-looking gear that is used to measure the volcanic activity in the area. Records show that a fresh eruption is long overdue. The closer you get to the volcano's cone, the more the landscape changes. On your left, you will see a yellow-colored slope with a lot of fumaroles, and a number of small solfataras line the route. After a small climb, you will reach a large lava field with numerous craters and a great view toward the parking area with large sulfur springs in the foreground. The boardwalk then forks, but, because it offers a circular tour, it doesn't matter which direction you choose. If you take the right-hand fork, you will soon reach a small upcropping that makes a great subject for a photo. This area is particularly attractive on cloudy days, and even with a little rain. Low clouds mix with the steam rising from the ground and create a mystical atmosphere

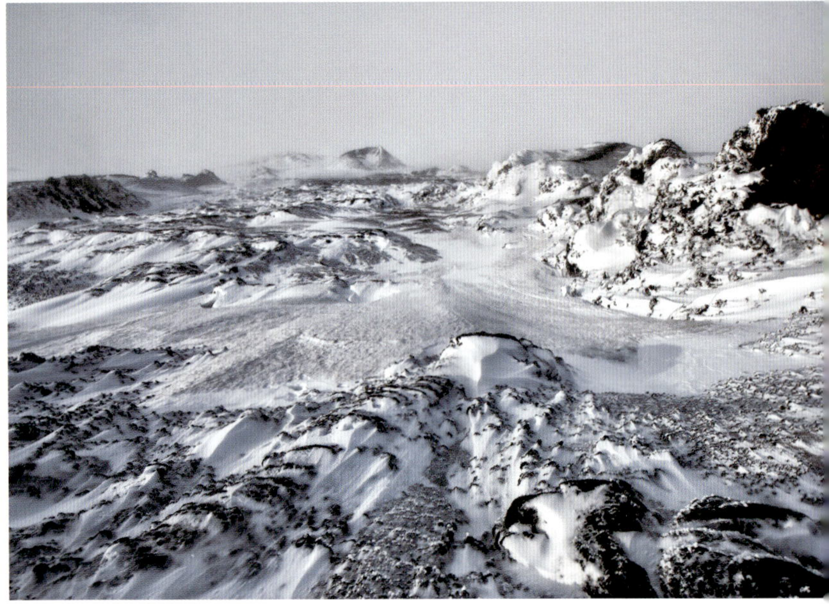

A snowstorm over the craters at Leirhnjúkur (f/20 · 1/50 sec. · ISO 31 · 14mm · Filter: Soft GND1

that makes it feel as if you have been transported back to the beginnings of life on Earth.

The area makes a great shooting location in winter too, but the climate can be severe, with huge amounts of snow and lots of storms, so it's not a trip you should attempt on your own in winter. I once experienced what it is like to completely lose my way in an area that I actually know very well, and it was only our guide who prevented the situation from becoming quite dangerous. As things turned out, my wife and I had a fantastic time. Even in the middle of winter, subterranean steam escapes from some of the craters and you can still feel the warmth from below (in my case, the steam ended up freezing in my beard!). Once again, *IceAk* (*www.iceak.is*) is recommended for guided tours. I took a private tour to the Leirhnjúkur area in combination with a waterfall tour to Aldeyarfoss, and enjoyed an adventurous and highly productive day of photography.

TOP TIP

For the inquisitive, the Krafla Power Station (Kröflustöð) is open to visitors in summer. However, the opening times are not particularly regular, so you simply have to stop at the main building and ask. If you want to learn more about this amazing piece of engineering, visit *www.landsvirkjun.com/company/powerstations/kraflapowerstation*.

Parking Area

Photo Location

7 DETTIFOSS

Distance: About an hour from Hverir, two hours from Laugar
Best time of day: Sunset, or any other time if cloudy
Best time of year: Summer, fall, or winter
Equipment: No special requirements
Tour type: Self-drive in summer and fall, guided in winter
Parking area coordinates: 65.819144, –16.379198
Location coordinates: 65.815189, –16.384057

An hour from Hverir is Dettifoss, reputedly Europe's most powerful waterfall. This thrilling sight plunges 150 feet into a gorge that is almost 330 feet wide. If you stand at the edge and look over into the mass of gray water as it rushes downward, you get a real feeling for the awe-inspiring power of the Icelandic environment. These moments never lose their appeal and underscore not only how beautiful our planet is, but also how insignificant we humans are in the grand scheme of things.

You can get to Dettifoss either along the western or the eastern bank of the Jökulsá river. The road to the west is in better condition, but the one to the east, although tougher and longer to drive, is my personal favorite. Because it is paved, the road to the west attracts countless busloads of tourists, so the western side of the falls is correspondingly busy. Furthermore, the view to the falls over the river from the east is much more interesting and photogenic.

The final 18 miles on the eastern road are rutted and graveled, so, depending on the car you have and your off-road driving experience, you will need to plan more time for this particular route.

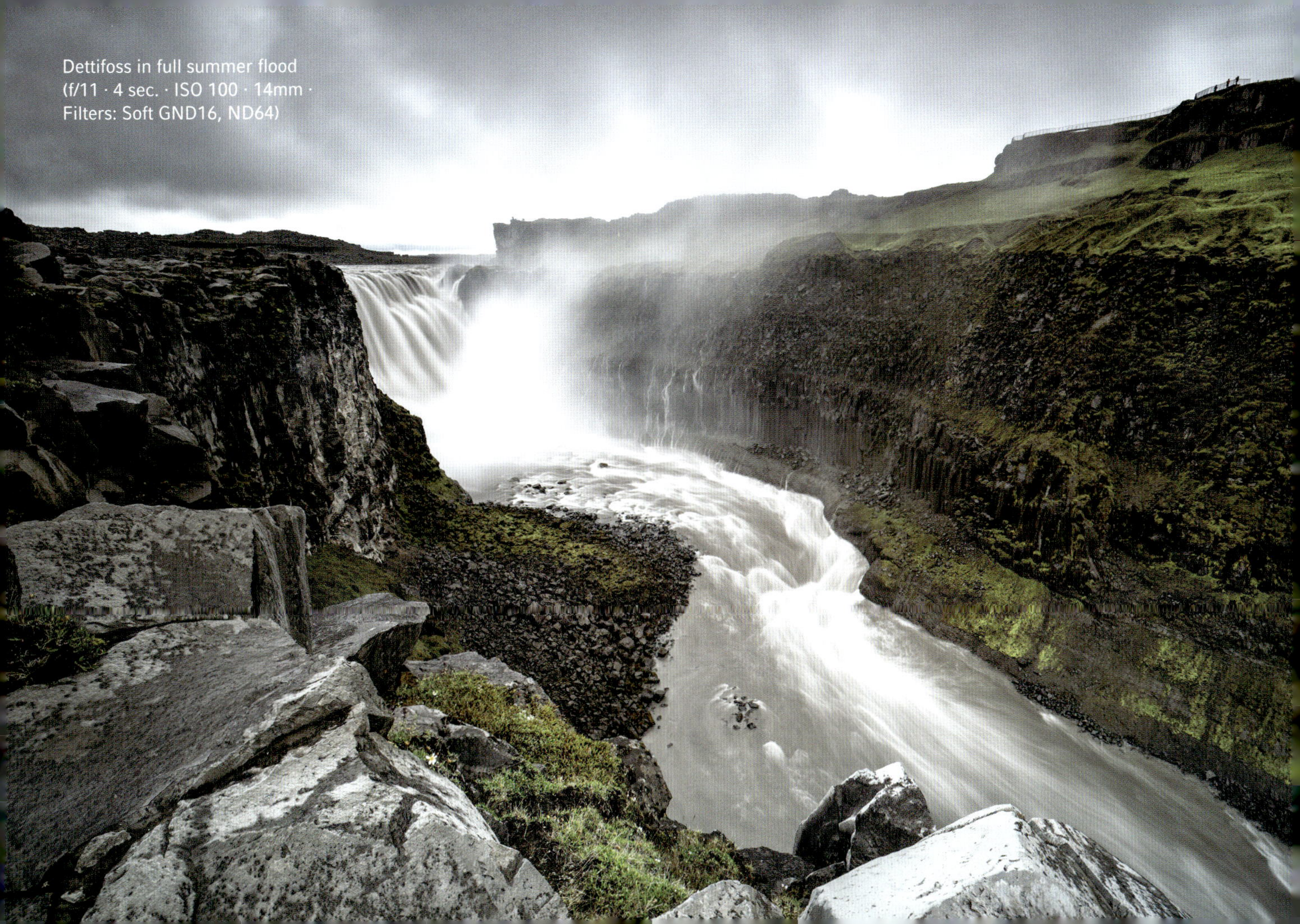

Dettifoss in full summer flood
(f/11 · 4 sec. · ISO 100 · 14mm ·
Filters: Soft GND16, ND64)

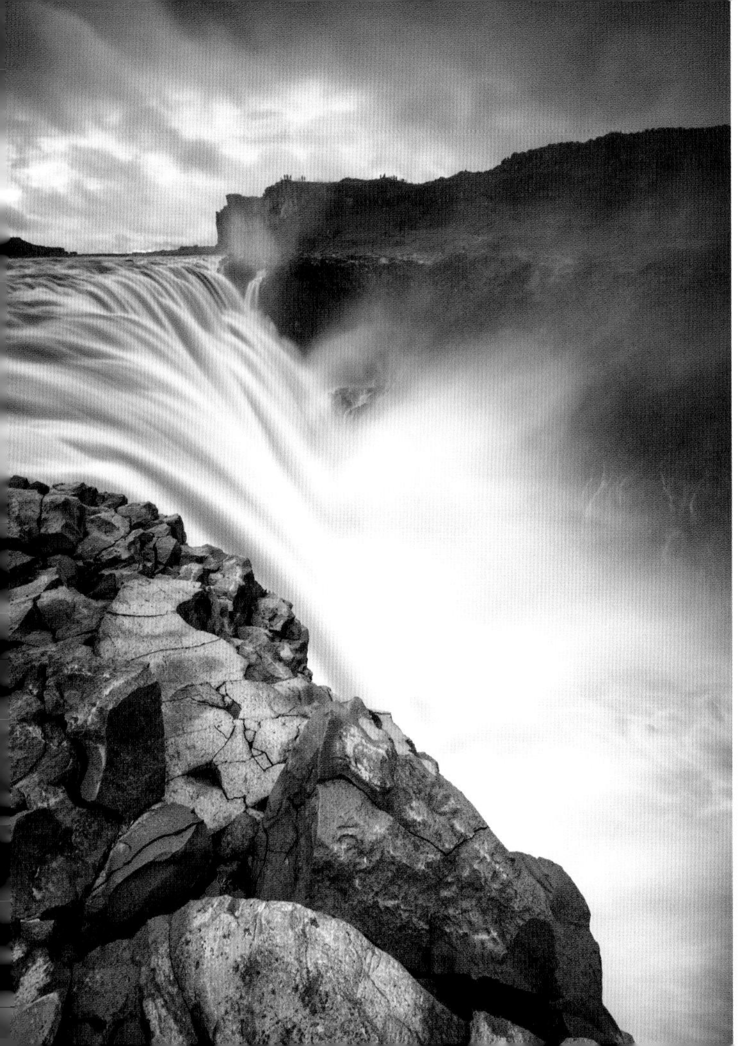

To reach Dettifoss, take Route 1 to the east. Once you have crossed a large bridge over the Jökulsá á Fjöllum (the river that feeds Dettifoss), the next turnoff to the left (Route 864 toward Hólsfjallavegur) heads north to Dettifoss. The next section is easy to negotiate with a decent 4WD vehicle. However, keep an eye out for some very deep potholes, but remember to keep your speed up somewhat if you want to avoid plunging into every rut. It takes about 45 minutes to reach the turnoff to Dettifoss; you will find a sign where you turn off to a busy parking area.

There is a path to the waterfall on the south side of the parking area. Large stone steps lead down into the canyon. These are easy to negotiate, but can be slippery in wet weather. Keep

Close to the edge at Dettifoss
(f/11 · 4 sec. · ISO 100 · 14mm ·
Filters: Soft GND16, ND64)

WARNING!
Take special care at the edge of the canyon. The ground is crumbly and many of the stones have been loosened or undercut by the water. The ground is slippery when wet and there are no barriers to guide you or to prevent you from slipping. Always put your own safety before your desire to capture a great photo!

to the right if you want to get as close as possible to the deep river gorge. There are plenty of places where you can capture photos of the plunging water. I like to use the basalt rocks as a foreground detail because they make the waterfall look even more gray and powerful.

If you continue along the riverbank toward the falls, there is a small dip in the rocks just before the edge that gives you a superb view of the entire waterfall.

The increasing numbers of tourists in the area also pose risks, and you need to keep an eye on what those around you are doing while you work. Many tourists don't keep their distance and trample around with no idea of the risks involved. Last year, just a few minutes after I had set up my camera in a good spot, I found myself surrounded by jostling tourists who wanted to capture the same shot. They were rude and reckless—behavior that can quickly put you in danger if you are concentrating on operating your camera.

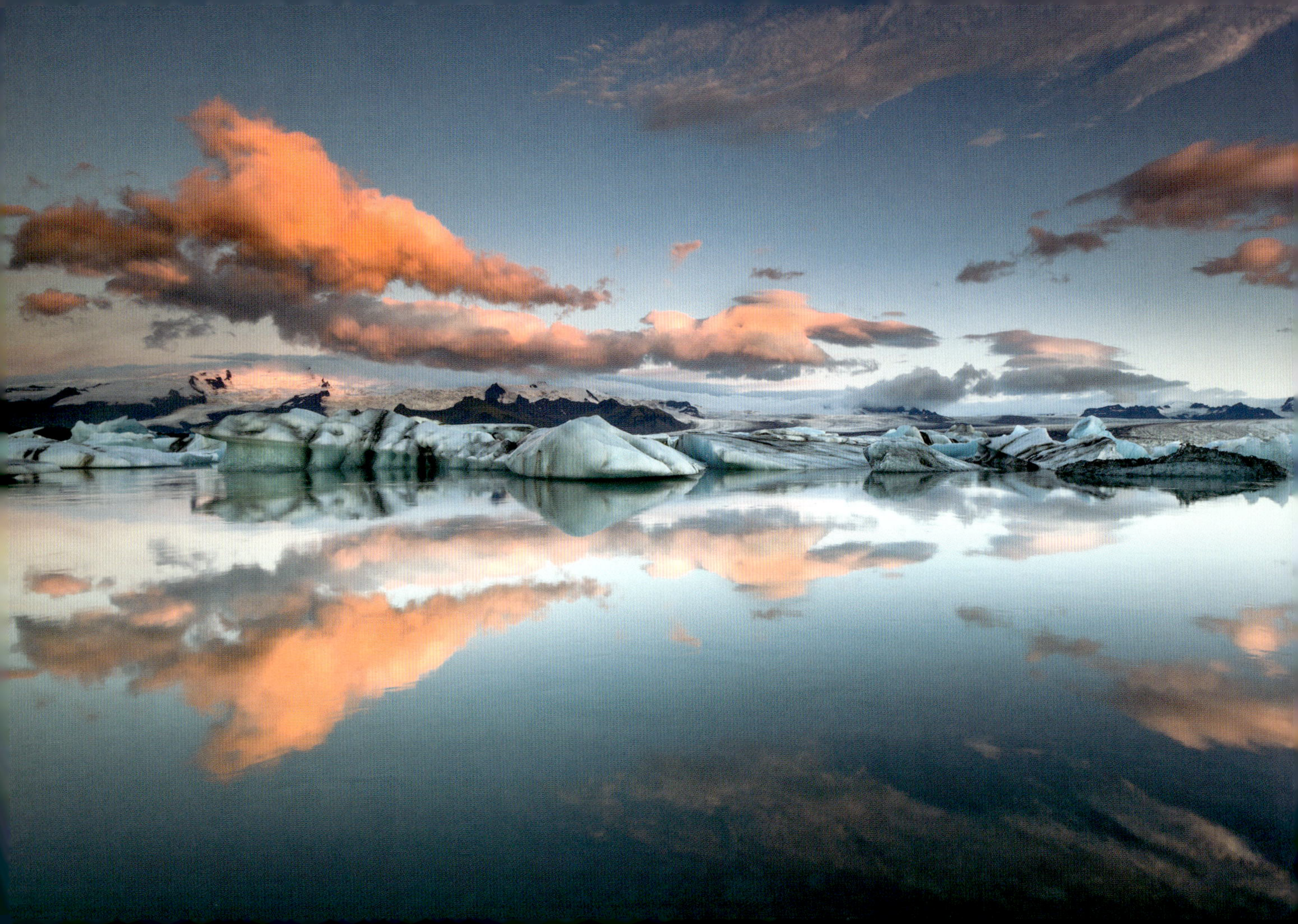

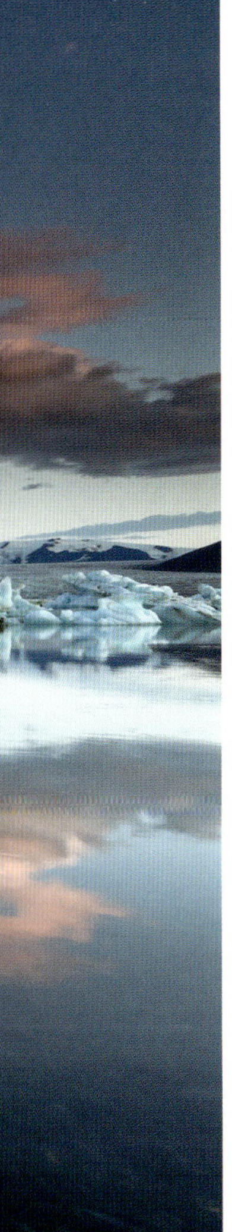

TOUR 3

ICELAND'S SOUTHERN COAST

This ultimate tour takes you along the southern coast to some of Iceland's best-known and most exciting photo locations. Huge waterfalls, a hidden airplane wreck, and perfect black beaches are just some of the things you will encounter on the two stages of this coastal trip to the world-famous glacial lagoon at Jökulsárlón.

The journey begins in Reykjavík, where you take Route 1 to the south toward Selfoss. Soon after you leave the city, the road climbs steeply up to the Hellisheiði highland plateau. The road is easy to drive, but look out for snow hazards and take special care in winter when visibility is reduced. Passing Hveragerði and Selfoss presents a great opportunity to visit four beautiful waterfalls (all close to the road) before you continue on to your first stopover in the town of Vík í Mýrdal. You will need to book one or two nights here, depending on which of the attractions you want to visit. The next stage takes you to a stopover in the Höfn region. Here, too, you should plan to stay for two nights. The return journey takes you along the same route, so you can stay in Vík on the way back, too, and perhaps take a look at some of the things you missed on the way.

TOUR 3 BASICS

Overall time required: 6 days or more

Travel time: Approx. 2–3 hours from Reykjavík to Vík í Mýrdal

Lodging: There are plenty of places to stay in and around Höfn. Hali Country Hotel (*www.hali.is*) is a favorite of mine that is only a 15-minute drive to the glacial lagoon at Jökulsárlón.

TOP TIP

Höfn is famous for its lobster, and their great taste is well known locally and outside of Iceland. They are definitely a treat for anyone who likes seafood. In addition to the traditional (and expensive) restaurants at the harbor, one great alternative eatery is Kaffi Hornið (*www.kaffihornid.is*), which you will find in a small wooden building in the center of town. The café is cozy and offers traditional food and various lobster dishes at reasonable prices. The lobster pasta is one of my favorites!

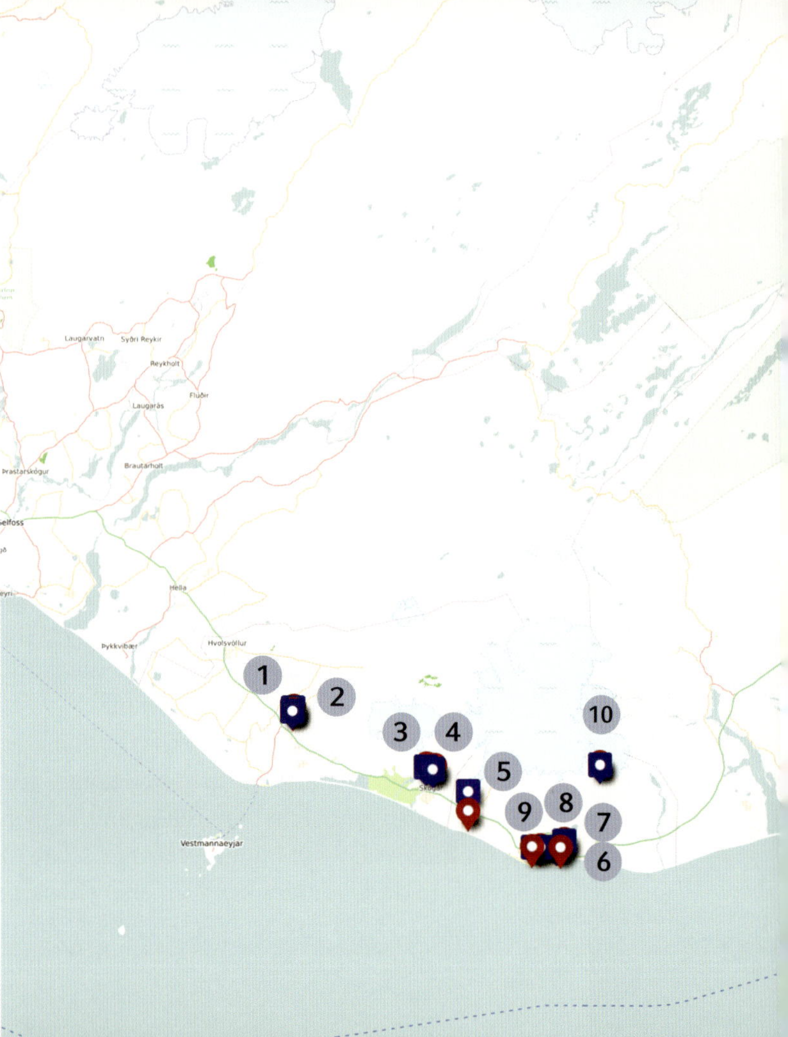

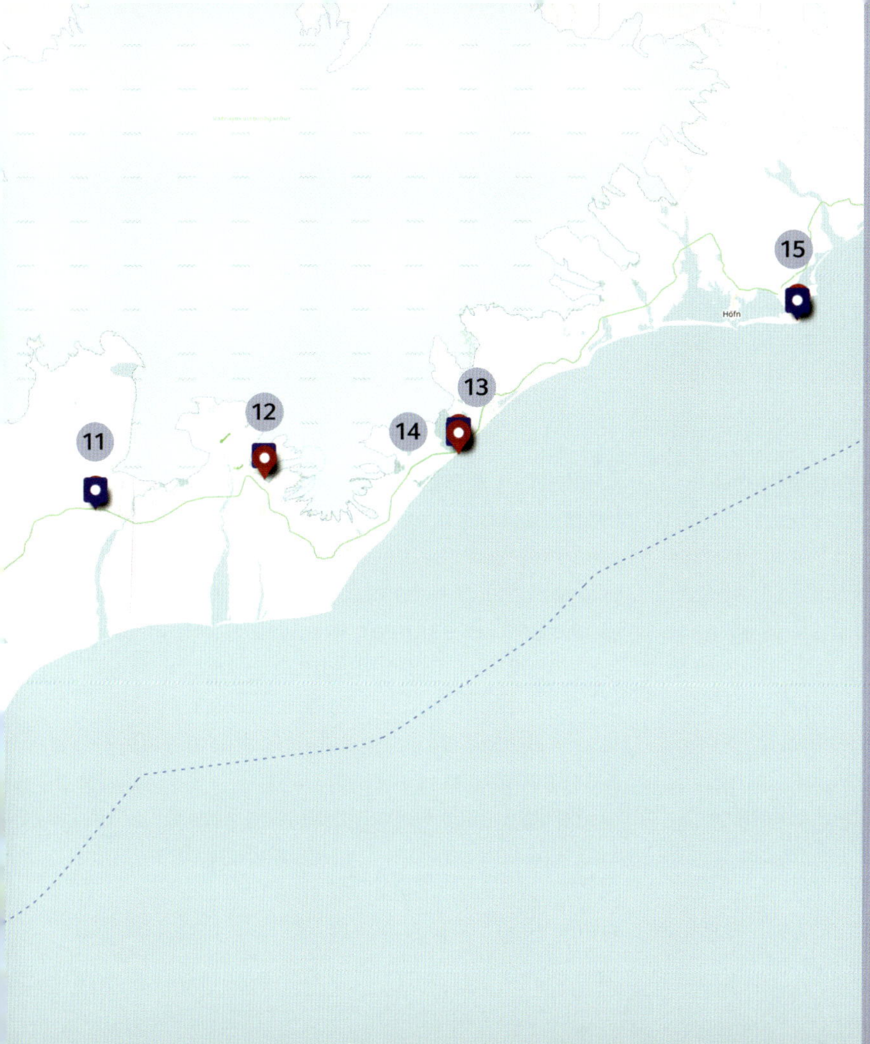

ICELAND'S SOUTHERN COAST

TOUR 3

1. SELJALANDSFOSS
2. GLJÚFURÁRFOSS
3. SKÓGAFOSS
4. KVERNUFOSS
5. THE AIRPLANE WRECK AT SÓLHEIMARSANDUR
6. THE BLACK BEACH AT VÍK
7. REYNISDRANGAR AND REYNISFJARA
8. KIRKJUFJARA VIEWS AND PUFFIN WATCHING
9. DYRHÓLAEY
10. ÞAKGIL
11. LÓMAGNÚPUR
12. SVÍNAFELLSJÖKULL
13. JÖKULSÁRLÓN
14. BREIÐAMERKURSANDUR
15. VESTRAHORN AND KLIFATINDUR

Parking Area

Photo Location

1 SELJALANDSFOSS

Distance: Less than 2 hours from Reykjavík
Best time of day: Sunset on a cloudy day
Best time of year: Summer, fall, or winter
Equipment: Rain jacket, spikes in winter, a towel for your camera
Tour type: Self-drive
Parking area coordinates: 63.615958, –19.992567
Location coordinates: 63.615473, –19.989555

The Seljalandsfoss waterfall is one of southern Iceland's biggest tourist attractions. This 220-foot monster is located below the Eyjafjallajökull glacier close to Route 1, about 1¾ hours from Reykjavík, and there is signage at the turnoff to direct you. The falls flows over a wide area into the river Markarfljót, and its special highlight is a path that enables you to walk behind the cascade. This is, of course, a photo opportunity that must not be missed, and you should take your time exploring it. The only issue here is the spray from the waterfall, which can soak your camera in no time at all. In summer, it is not unusual to find up to 15 buses in the parking area and a long line of tourists along the path behind the falls. The best way to avoid the crowds is to shoot in the evening or at night. In summer, it is well worth waiting for sunset (around midnight) to capture a few shots. Personally, I prefer the smaller Kvernufoss waterfall, which I will describe in more detail later in this section.

Parking fees were introduced here in 2017, and you can pay the 700 Icelandic Krone (about $6.75) at a basalt-shaped machine using a credit card. The owner of the land has said that the fees are necessary for the upkeep of the area and to keep the infrastructure (especially the restrooms) up and running.

If you don't want to pay to park, simply drive on to Gljúfurárfoss and park there. It takes about 10 minutes to walk back to Seljalandsfoss. It's anyone's guess how long parking at Gljúfurárfoss will remain free of charge.

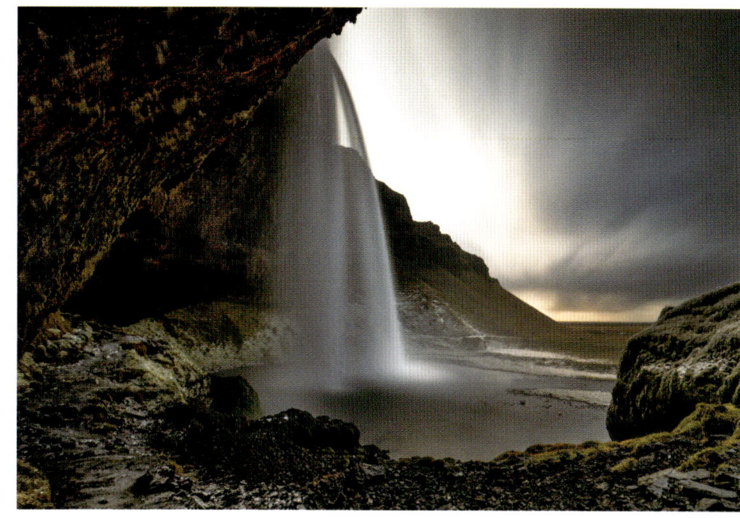

The mighty Seljalandsfoss in winter, captured using an extremely long exposure time. Shots like this are only safe to shoot if have spikes for your boots.
(f/11 · 137 sec. · ISO 31 · 14mm · Filter: Soft GND16, ND1000)

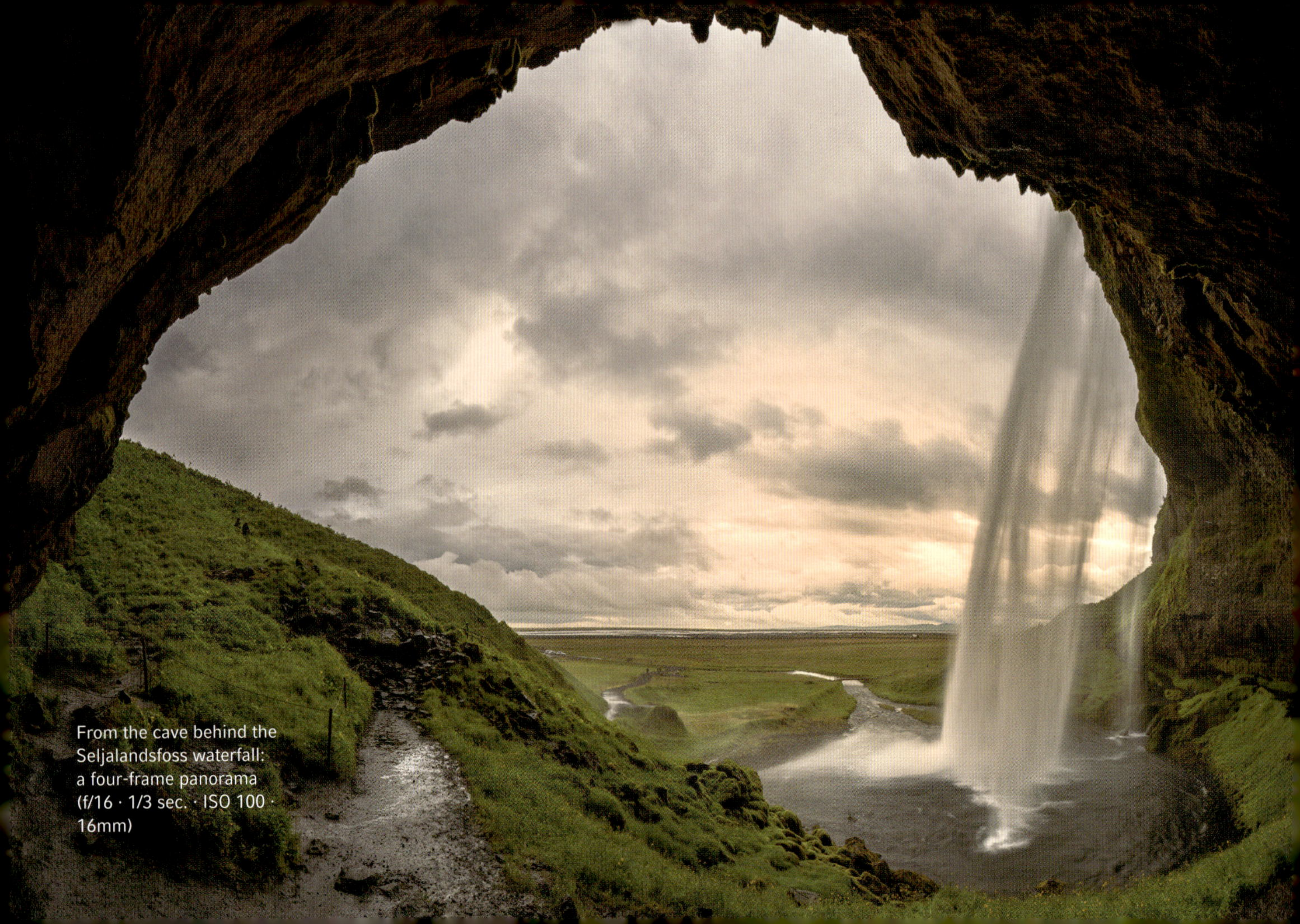

From the cave behind the Seljalandsfoss waterfall: a four-frame panorama (f/16 · 1/3 sec. · ISO 100 · 16mm)

2 GLJÚFURÁRFOSS

Distance: Less than 2 hours from Reykjavík, 2 minutes from Seljalandsfoss
Best time of day: Any time
Best time of year: Summer, fall, or winter
Equipment: Rain jacket, rubber boots, spikes in winter, a towel for your camera
Tour type: Self-drive
Parking area coordinates: 63.620813, –19.989280
Location coordinates: 63.620918, –19.986644

Parking Area

Photo Location

The next waterfall is only a couple of minutes drive from Seljalandsfoss and is one of the most interesting and wettest in Iceland. Gljúfurárfoss is hidden in a cave that can be reached only via the river it flows into. The spray from the falls will soak you on your way through the canyon before you even reach the cave. A high-end rain jacket is a must here, and you can edge your way along the rocks at the right-hand wall of the canyon to avoid getting wet from below too. Some of the rocks are below water level, so you need sturdy shoes or rubber boots to avoid getting your feet wet. I have ankle-high trekking boots that I treat with a waterproofing spray.

To get to the parking area closest to Gljúfurárfoss, take the turnoff from Route 1 toward Seljalandsfoss and drive past the main parking area. Follow the road until you see a campsite on the right. Turn into the campsite and drive straight ahead up a slight slope. There is a small parking area at the top where you can leave your car. If the road through the campsite is closed, you can park on the grass next to the main road. From there, looking toward the glacier, you can see the river leading

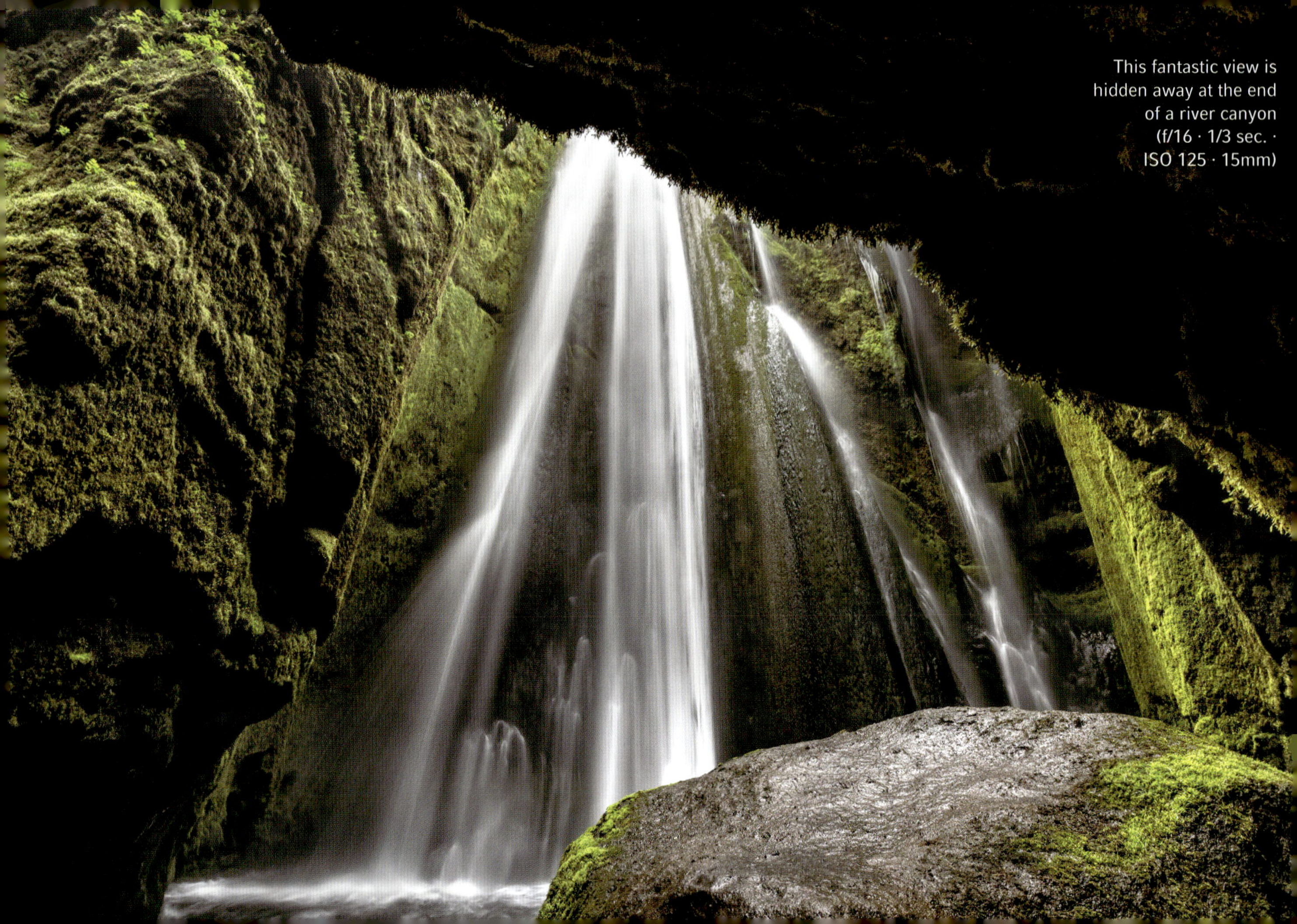

This fantastic view is hidden away at the end of a river canyon (f/16 · 1/3 sec. · ISO 125 · 15mm)

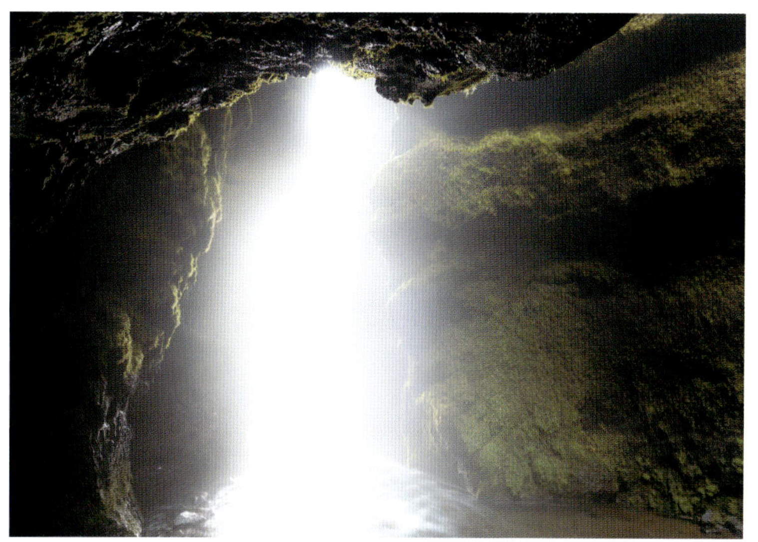

The view back along the gulley is impressive, too (f/8 · 2.5 sec. · ISO 100 · 14mm)

to Gljúfurárfoss and part of the falls peaking out from behind a cliff that is part of the cave the falls flow into. Following the riverbank takes you directly to the entrance of the canyon, which is easy to wade through.

Once you reach the cave, it is better to stick to the right-hand side and find a place under the overhanging rocks, which is by far the driest place around. Although I've been there many times, I am still fascinated every time by the spectacle of the waterfall flowing down the mossy cliff wall and hitting the ground behind a huge rock. My best shots of Gljúfurárfoss include the lone rock and the moss-covered

TOP TIP

Take special care of your camera. The tiny water molecules in the omnipresent spray makes everything wet all the time. I take a small towel with me and use it to wrap my camera, which I only uncover when I am ready to capture a shot. A cloth for wiping the lens after every shot is essential, too.

If you take your first shot using autofocus and then switch autofocus off, the lens will be correctly set and the lens won't waste time focusing once you have wiped it clean after each subsequent shot. In a place with so much condensation in the air, every microsecond counts if you want to capture photos with no water droplets on the lens. Always take multiple shots in situations like this—you never know whether there was water on the lens until you check your images later.

overhang. Lots of people like to grab a shot of themselves or a friend on the rock. This is a sure-fire way of getting soaked to the skin, but the closeness to the waterfall and the resulting images are easily worth it!

Heading back along the river, the bright backlight that shines through the entrance to the canyon and diffuses in the spray from the waterfall makes a great subject too—a wet, but picturesque view.

Parking Area

Photo Location

3 SKÓGAFOSS

Distance: About 30 minutes from Seljalandsfoss
Best time of day: Any time, especially with cloudy skies
Best time of year: Summer, fall, or winter
Equipment: No special requirements
Tour type: Self-drive
Parking area coordinates: 63.529271, –19.513321
Location coordinates: 63.531294, –19.512109

The 200-foot high by 80-foot wide Skógafoss is located between the Mýrdalsjökull and Eyjafjallajökull glaciers, and is visible from Route 1. A well-known hiking trail over the Fimmvörðuháls pass, between the two glaciers and into the sheltered Þórsmörk valley, begins beside Skógafoss. Coming from Seljalandsfoss, follow Route 1 eastward. Take the turnoff at the sign for Skógafoss, and turn left at the next junction. Drive on until you see a campsite located at a bend in the road, and then cross the campsite to reach the parking area.

Most of the well-known images of this location are taken right next to the parking area at the foot of the great waterfall, but here, too, increasing numbers of tourists make it almost impossible to capture an uncluttered image from this viewpoint. To get better pictures, take the steps to the right of the falls. About halfway to the top you will find a narrow path that (last time I was there) leads to the edge of the cliff that frames the waterfall. You won't be alone on the path, but from there you can capture people-free images of the falls surrounded by the cliffs. If you look carefully at the left-hand cliff-face, you should see the famous Skógafoss troll staring out at the water.

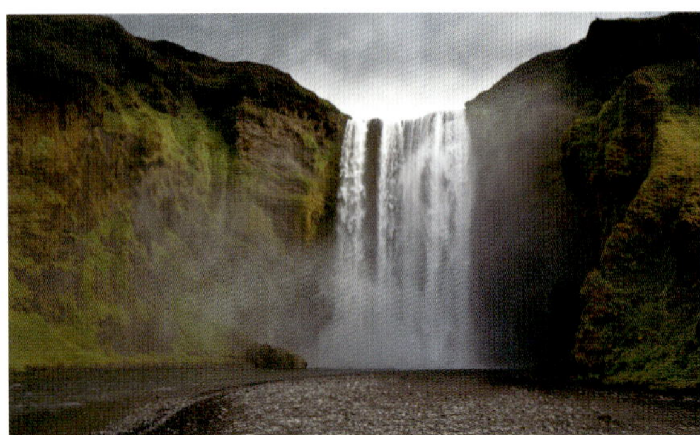

A classic Skógafoss photo. The trickiest part of shooting here is to capture a photo with no people in it.
(f/9 · 1/320 sec. · ISO 320 · 28mm · Filter: Soft GND8)

Shot from halfway up, this image clearly shows the troll who watches over the falls (f/16 · 1/5 sec. · ISO 100 · 19mm · Filter: Soft GND8)

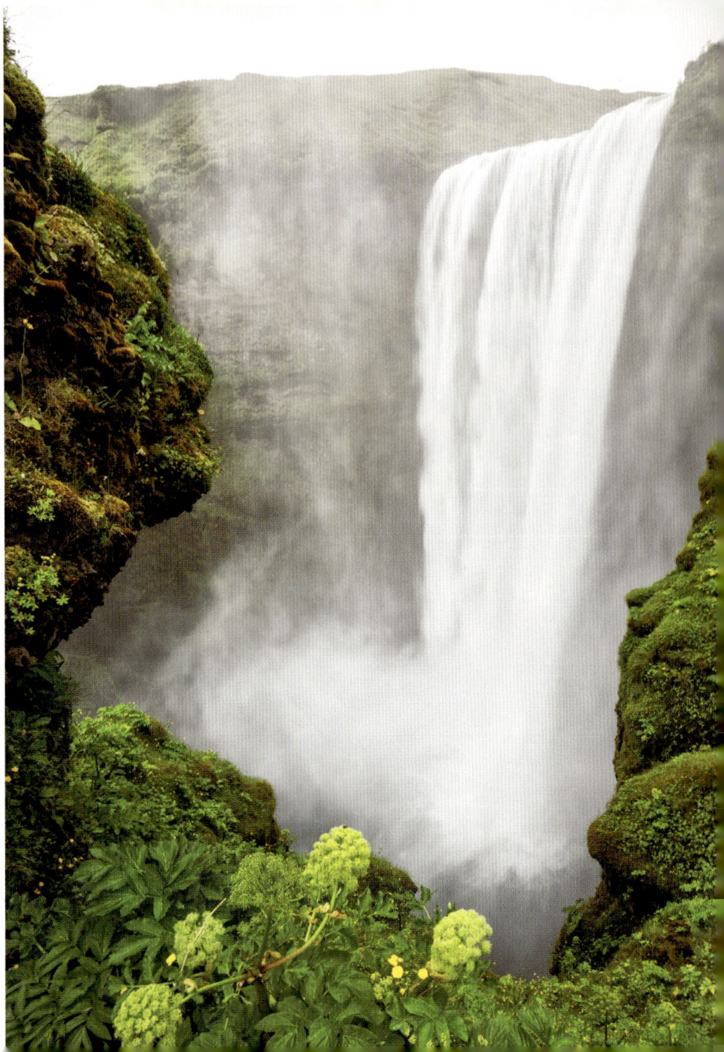

KVERNUFOSS

Distance: About 30 minutes from Seljalandsfoss, or 5 minutes from Skógafoss
Best time of day: Any time, especially on cloudy skies
Best time of year: Summer, fall, or winter
Equipment: Rain jacket, sturdy shoes, a towel for your camera, spikes in winter
Tour type: Self-drive
Parking area coordinates: 63.525226, −19.489321
Location coordinates: 63.528397, −19.481022

Parking Area

Photo Location

The next waterfall on our tour, Kvernufoss, is only 5 minutes away from Skógafoss, just past the Skógar Museum. Like its better-known big brother Seljalandsfoss, Kvernufoss is hidden away and also lets you walk behind the cascade. It is not as big as Seljalandsfoss, but I think it is just as impressive and it's not swarming with tourists. For some reason, not many visitors come here, even though the walk to the site takes just 10 minutes. Kvernufoss has an idyllic location in a small valley, and the walk to the site itself is a wonderful, tourist-free Icelandic nature experience.

To get there, drive back on the road that you took to Skógafoss from Route 1. Instead of turning right onto Route 1, turn left. At the next junction, turn right and head toward the Skógar Museum. At the museum, drive across the parking area and past a storehouse. There is a small parking area behind the storehouse. If you stand with the storehouse behind you and look over the fields, you will see a narrow path to the left that heads toward the mountains that frame the glaciers. Follow the path until you reach a fence, climb over the fence and follow the rough trail to the bank of the river fed by

Kvernufoss. Follow the path along the left-hand riverbank. About halfway along, you will encounter a steep, rocky patch that requires some climbing. There are plenty of great views of the waterfall along the way.

My favorite view is an unusual one from behind the waterfall. Simply follow the path until you find yourself behind the cascade. If it is windy, you will get pretty wet, so be sure to take a rain jacket along. Once you scout around the area, it is relatively easy to find a position away from the spraying water. On cloudy days, the cascade contrasts particularly well against the sky and provides a wealth of unforgettable compositions.

Shot from a semi-dry spot behind the waterfall. From this viewpoint, the mouth of the cave looks like a gigantic head. (f/20 · 1/100 sec. · ISO 31 · 14mm)

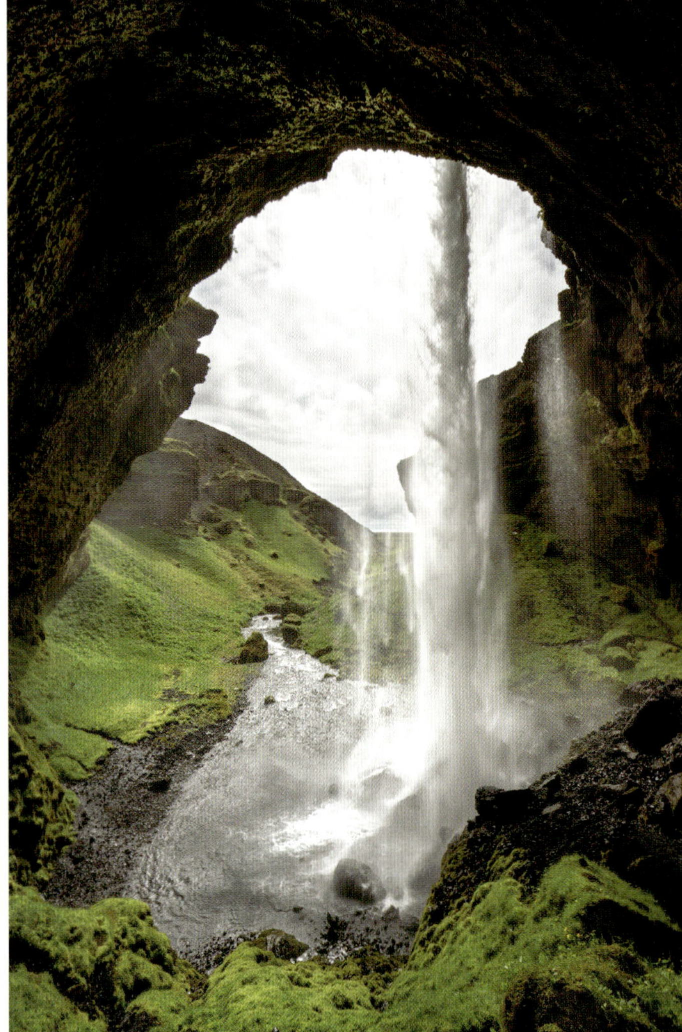

TOP TIP

If you aren't in a hurry, visit the Skógar Museum on your way back. The museum's mission is to preserve the country's cultural heritage, and it exhibits thousands of fascinating artifacts in a total of six historical buildings.

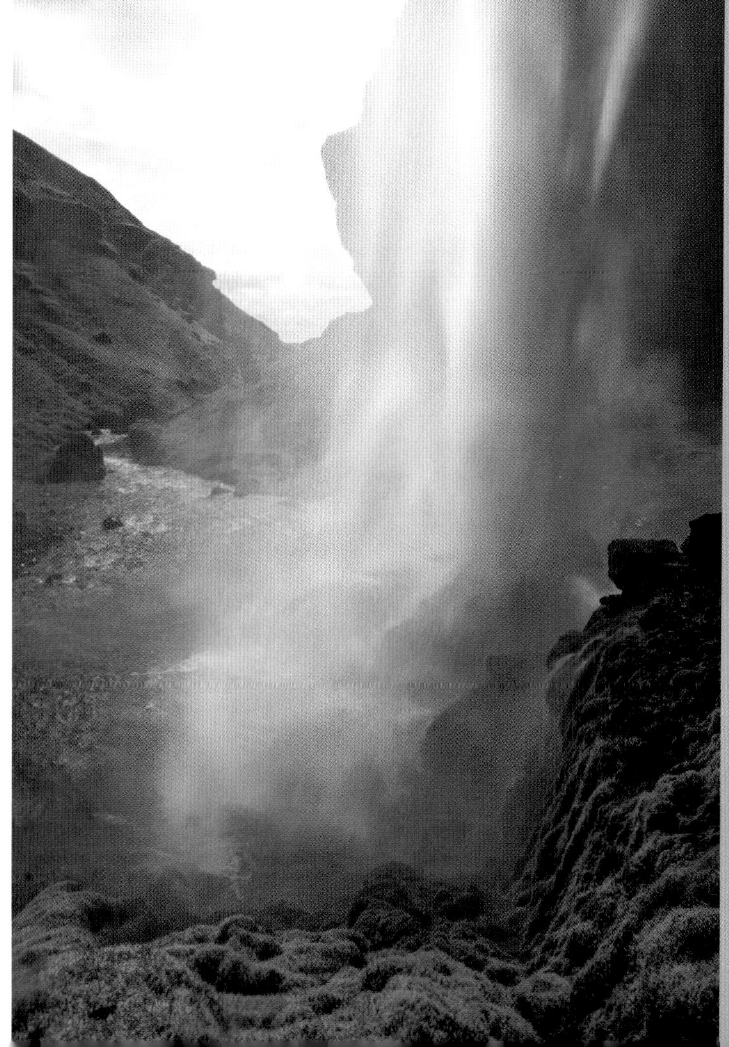

If you are prepared to get wet, there are plenty of great views close to the cascade (f/20 · 1/20 sec. · ISO 31 · 24mm)

Parking Area

Photo Location

5 THE AIRPLANE WRECK AT SÓLHEIMARSANDUR

Distance: 15 minutes from Skógafoss or 20 minutes from Vík, plus a 1-hour walk from the parking area
Best time of day: Sunset or nighttime with clear sky
Best time of year: Summer, fall, or winter
Equipment: Sturdy shoes, headlamp or flashlight for nighttime visits
Tour type: Self-drive
Parking area coordinates: 63.490785, –19.362765
Location coordinates: 63.459175, –19.364657

The U.S. Navy DC-3 that made an emergency landing on the black sand at Sólheimarsandur is a subject that has become increasingly popular in recent years. The crash landing occurred in 1973 and there are various rumors about what actually happened, although the most likely explanation is that the plane simply ran out of fuel. Whatever happened, we know that everyone on board survived.

The wreck is incredibly well preserved, especially when you consider that it has been exposed to the harsh Icelandic climate for over 40 years. Sand and wind have removed all the paint but the aluminum fuselage is still pretty much intact. Humans, too, have made their mark on the wreck, and the engines, the tail, and the nosecone were all removed and sold soon after the crash. There are also plenty of bullet holes that suggest it has been used for shooting practice. In addition, many visitors have immortalized themselves by scratching their names or random proverbs into the metal. It's a shame that people don't treat this memorial to bygone technology with due respect. Pictures of Justin Bieber on a skateboard on the roof of the plane have only boosted its fame.

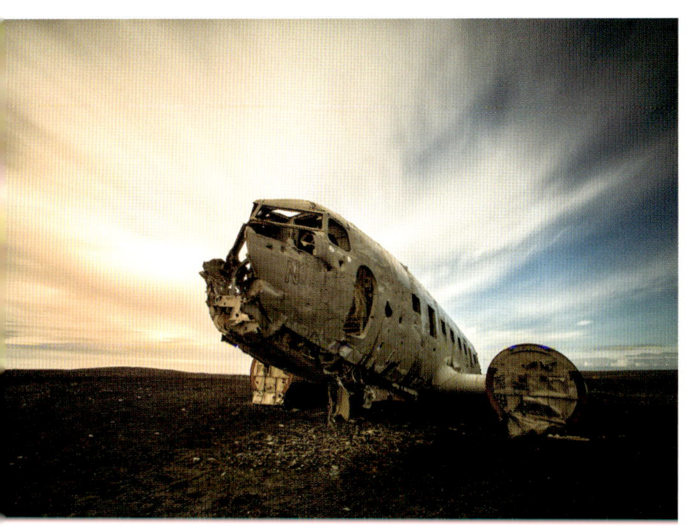

Sunset at the black sands illuminates the wreck in a wonderful way (f/14 · 80 sec. · ISO 160 · 16mm · Filter: Soft GND16, ND1000)

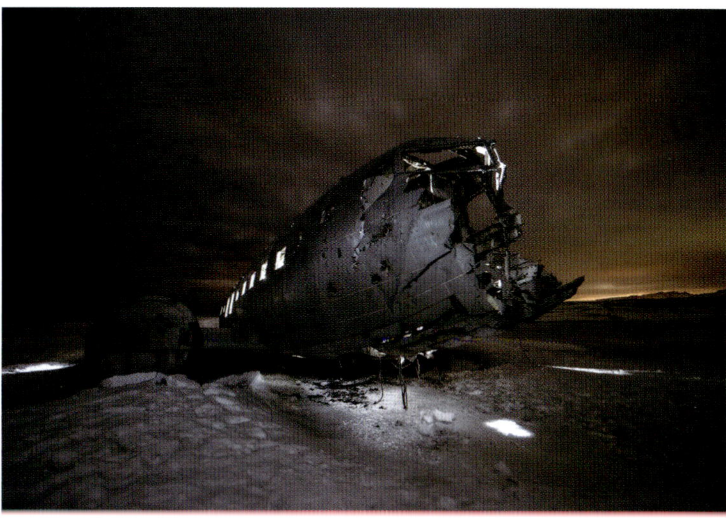

Shooting at night with a flashlight produces a totally different look (f/28 · 30 sec. · ISO 2000 · 15mm)

The wreck is located on private land, and visitors have caused a lot of damage to the property by driving right through it to get to the plane. The owner has responded by closing the access roads. There is a new parking area on Route 1, and anyone who wants to view the plane has to park there and take a one-hour hike to the site (and, of course, a one-hour hike back).

You can visit the site either on your way to Vík í Mýrdal, or after you have found somewhere to stay in Vík. I recommend the latter approach, as the site is most spectacular (and much less busy) in the evening or at night. If you do go there in the dark, make sure you save the coordinates of the site and the parking area in your phone or GPS device, and pack a reliable headlamp or flashlight. It is all too easy to get lost in a black desert in the dark!

Photos captured around sunset bathe this strange sight in a special kind of light and, on one my visits, I came up with the idea of visiting the plane at night. My original plan was to photograph the plane together with the Northern Lights. However, there were no Northern Lights on the day, so instead, my wife climbed into the plane with a powerful light to add some life to the scene. The result turned out to be my favorite shot of this location.

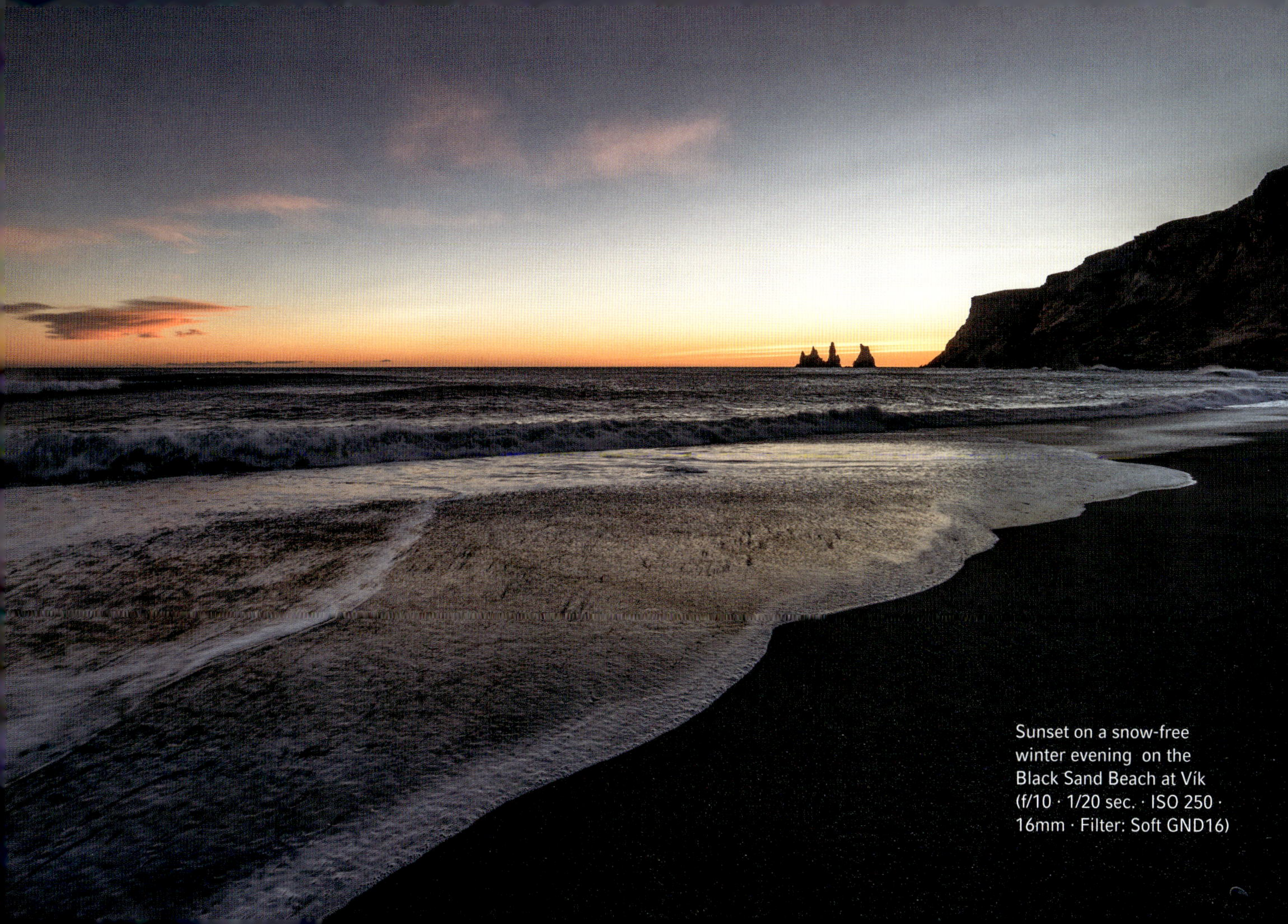

Sunset on a snow-free winter evening on the Black Sand Beach at Vík (f/10 · 1/20 sec. · ISO 250 · 16mm · Filter: Soft GND16)

Parking Area

Photo Location

6 THE BLACK SAND BEACH AT VÍK

Distance: 5 minutes on foot from Vík
Best time of day: Sunrise or sunset
Best time of year: Summer, fall, or winter
Equipment: No special requirements
Tour type: Self-drive
Parking area coordinates: 63.414161, –19.017902
Location coordinates: 63.413183, –19.017179

Vík í Mýrdal is famous for its beach of fine black lava sand. Many years ago, it was voted one of the 10 best beaches in the world, and it is still definitely worth a visit. If you are staying in Vík, it is only a short walk to the beach. The quickest route begins behind the gas station/shop, where you will find a wide, well-maintained path that takes you to a small crossing. Turn right at the crossing, cross over a small bridge, and then keep left, heading directly toward the coast. If you walk westward along the beach, you can get closer to the striking Reynisdrangar basalt sea stacks that rise out of the ocean. Legend has it that the stacks are the remains of three trolls called Skessudrangur, Landdrangur, and Langsamur who tried to land a ship there and were turned to stone by the rising sun.

If you shoot from close to the water's edge, it's easy to capture a classic shot of this scene with the cliffs and the stacks in the background. But take care, as the powerful waves are unpredictable and can be dangerous when they break higher up the beach than you expected.

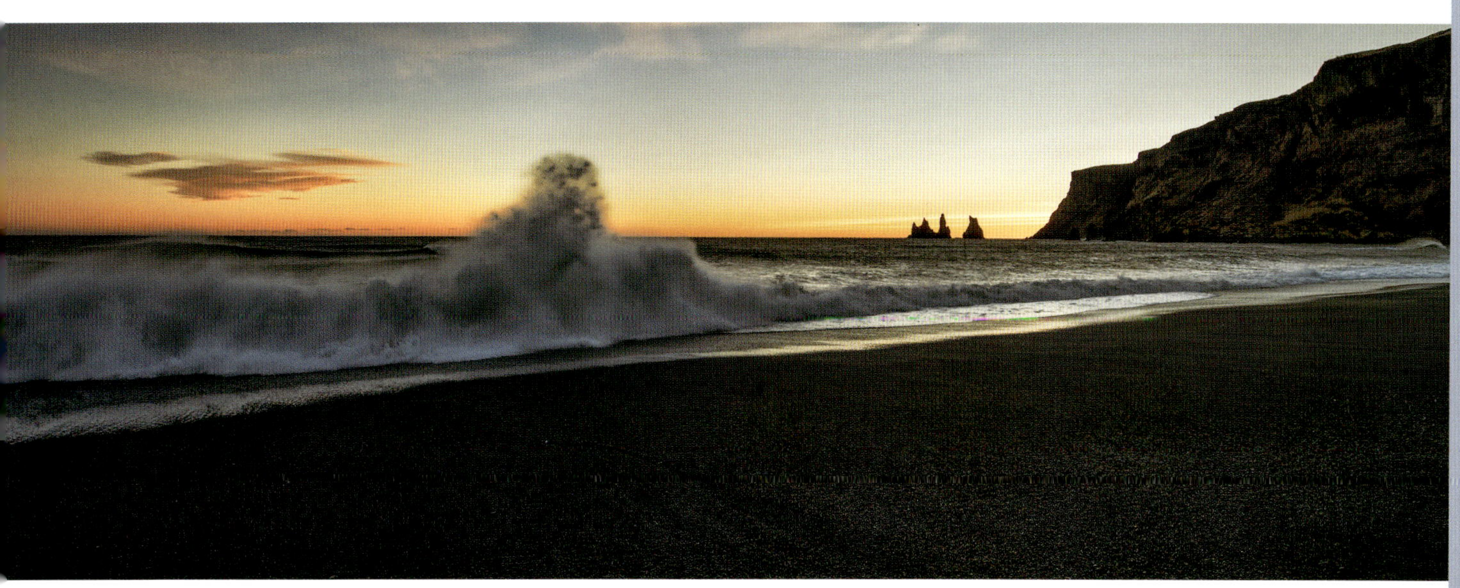

The waves often break high up the beach
(f/10 · 1/40 sec. · ISO 250 · 17mm · Filter: Soft GND16)

THE REYNISDRANGAR AND REYNISFJARA

Distance: About 15 minutes from Vík
Best time of day: Sunset on a cloudy day (between midday and afternoon in summer if you want to see the secret beach)
Best time of year: Summer, fall, or winter
Equipment: No special requirements
Tour type: Self-drive
Parking area coordinates: 63.404300, –19.045438
Location coordinates: 63.401796, –19.032031

Parking Area

Photo Location

This tour takes you to the next black lava beach near Vík and even closer to the Reynisdrangar sea stacks. Leave town heading west along Route 1 as it climbs and circumnavigates Mount Reynisfjall. About halfway, take a left onto Route 215 (Reynishverfisvegur) and follow the road to the end, where you will find a busy parking area and a café. A path with a veritable forest of warning signs begins next to the café and leads to the beach directly in front of the sea stacks. The warning signs are there to prevent serious or fatal accidents caused by the powerful waves and strong undertow. People still choose to ignore the signs and endanger their lives, and some even play in the water with their kids despite warnings from the locals. Please take these warnings seriously and take care at all times.

If the season and the weather permit, you can safely walk along the beach toward the sea stacks and get some shots of the waves as they hit the cliffs. At low tide in summer, when the waves are not whipped up by a storm, you can actually get to a small, hidden beach directly

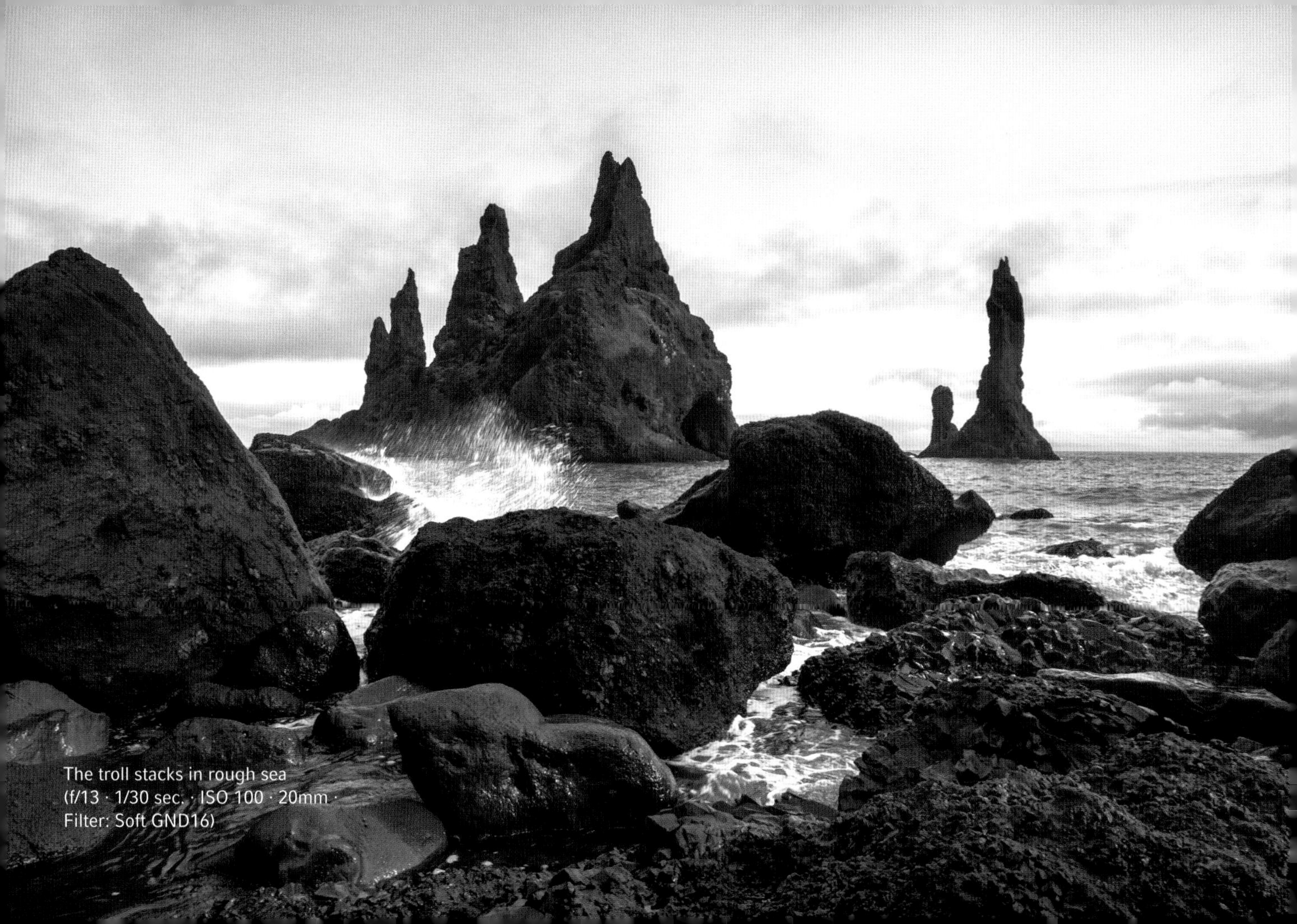

The troll stacks in rough sea
(f/13 · 1/30 sec. · ISO 100 · 20mm ·
Filter: Soft GND16)

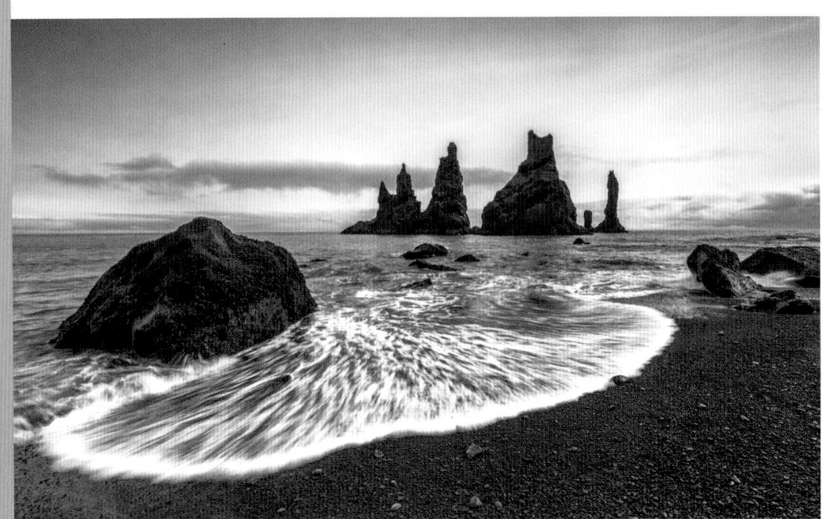

The hidden beach with its uninterrupted view of the Reynisdrangar (f/16 · 1/5 sec. · ISO 31 · 14mm · Filter: Soft GND16)

opposite the Reynisdrangar. You still need sturdy shoes and a sure foot, and you definitely need to keep an eye on the waves, but the walk itself is easy. Simply head to the left along the coast toward the stacks. At the end of the beach, a heap of rocks bar your way. If you climb over these, you will find a secluded beach that is only there at low tide. It offers a perfect view of the stacks with plenty of photogenic rocks in the foreground.

WARNING!

If you want to visit the hidden beach, take great care and make sure you know exactly when the tide is out (you can ask in the Visitor Center in Vík), and always keep an eye on the waves. You should head back as soon as you see the water beginning to rise. Never climb over the rocks in winter or during a storm—the swell here is simply too dangerous.

Parking Area

Photo Location

8 THE VIEW AT KIRKJUFJARA AND PUFFIN WATCHING

Distance: About 20 minutes from Vík or 5 minutes from Reynisdrangar
Best time of day: Sunrise
Best time of year: Summer, fall, or winter
Equipment: No special requirements
Photo gear: Long telephoto or telephoto zoom
Tour type: Self-drive
Parking area coordinates: 63.403634, –19.103577
Location coordinates: 63.404006, –19.103489

There is another view of the sea stacks and of the beach you have just visited farther to the west. Five minutes down the road is a natural lookout with a great view toward Vík and the Reynisdrangar. There is also an imposing lava column in the sea and, in summer, you can watch and photograph nesting puffins ("Lundi" in Icelandic) from up close.

Driving from Vík, take the Ring Road to the west and drive past the turnoff for Reynisdrangar. A couple of minutes later, you will come to a turnoff onto Route 218 (Dyrhólavegur). Follow the signs to Dyrhólaey along a paved road. Drive past a large lagoon on your left, over a cattle guard, and past the next turnoff to Dyrhólaey (which we will visit on the next tour). A few minutes later, you will reach a newly built parking area. Drive straight through and follow the road to the end, where you will find an older parking area and the cliffs with the view mentioned above. Follow the cliff path to the first corner, where you can get right up close to the edge. From there, you will have a wonderful view toward Reynisdrangar, with the

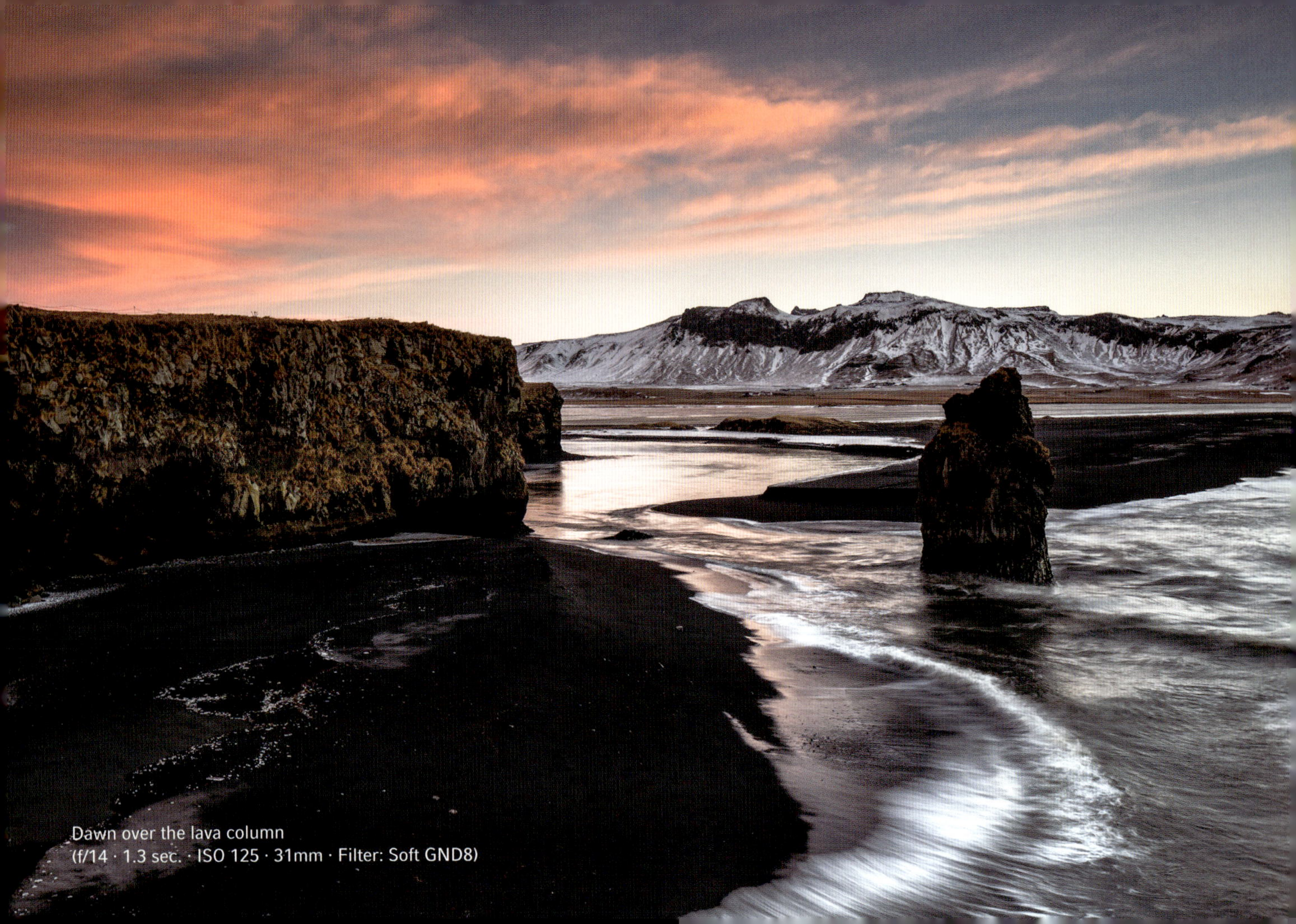

Dawn over the lava column
(f/14 · 1.3 sec. · ISO 125 · 31mm · Filter: Soft GND8)

waves breaking on the black sand and the lava column in the foreground.

In summer, this is where you can watch nesting puffins. These cute and sometimes rather ungainly birds make ideal photo subjects when they land or fly out to sea to look for food. I have captured loads of images there using my 100–400mm zoom lens. If you follow the path farther along the cliff top, you will find more puffins, but the place described above seems to offer the best views.

If you head to the beach next to the parking area, take great care there, too. In 2017, a German tourist was killed when she underestimated the power of the waves and was dragged out to sea.

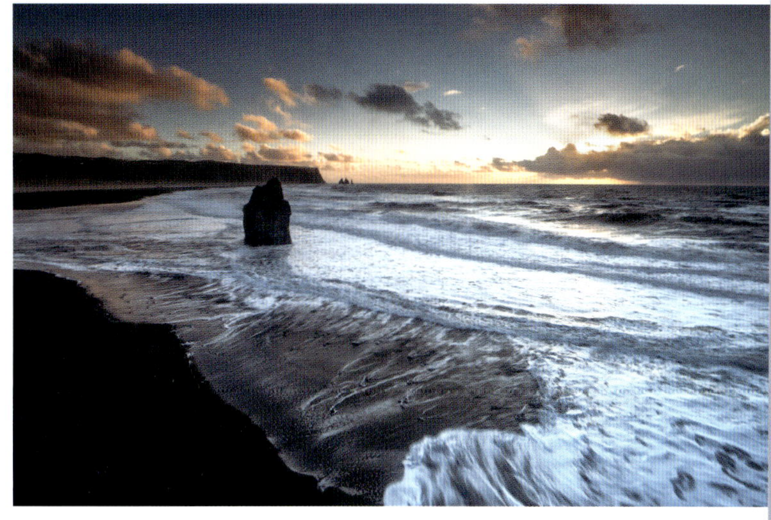

A sunrise view with the Reynisdrangar on the horizon
(f/13 1/4 sec. ISO 40 16mm Filter: Soft GND16)

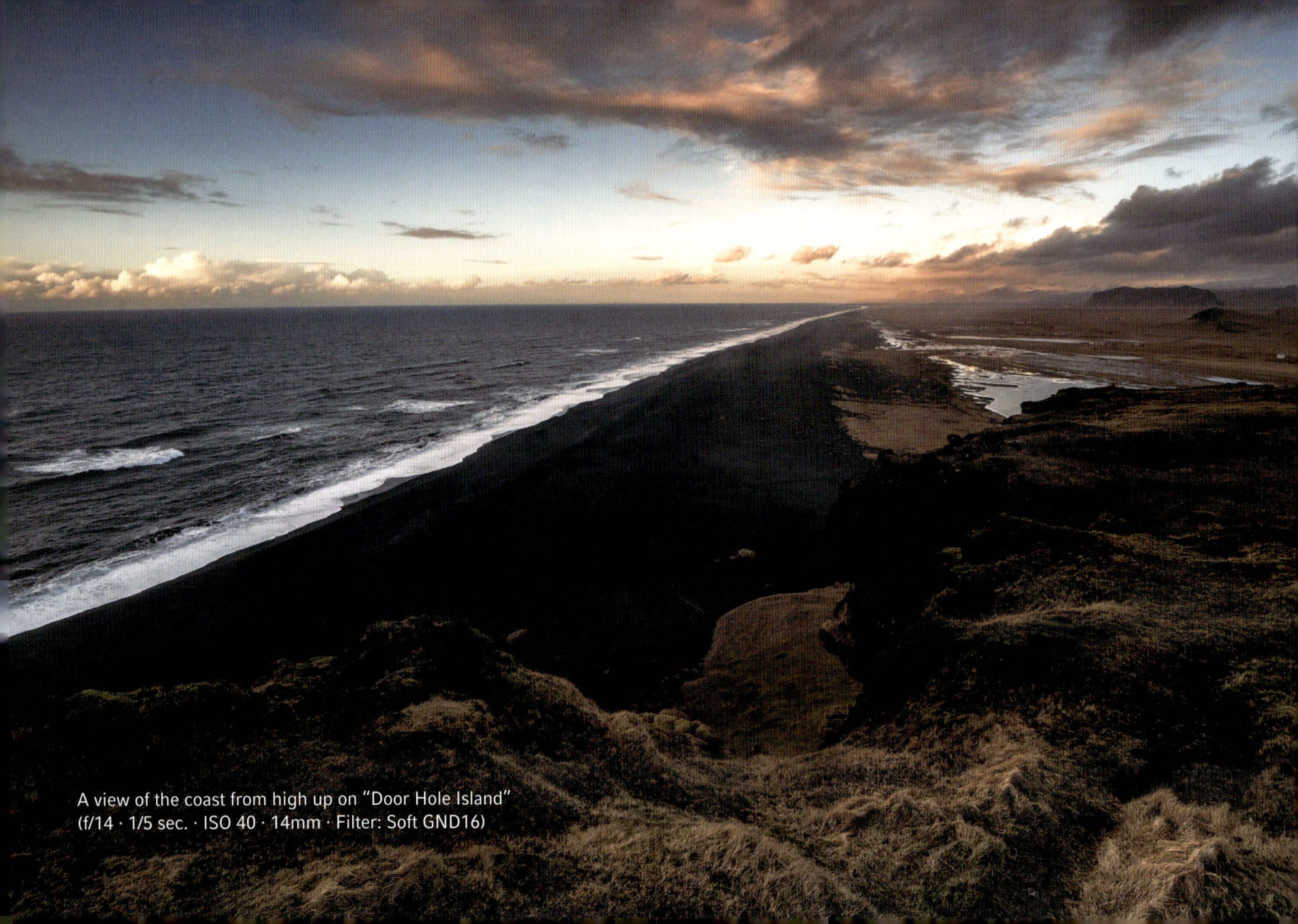

A view of the coast from high up on "Door Hole Island"
(f/14 · 1/5 sec. · ISO 40 · 14mm · Filter: Soft GND16)

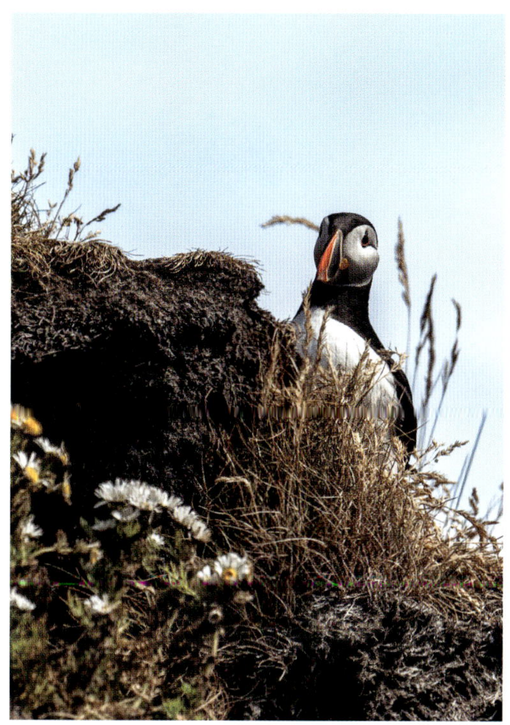

An inquisitive puffin
(f/10 · 1/800 sec. · ISO 250 · 400mm)

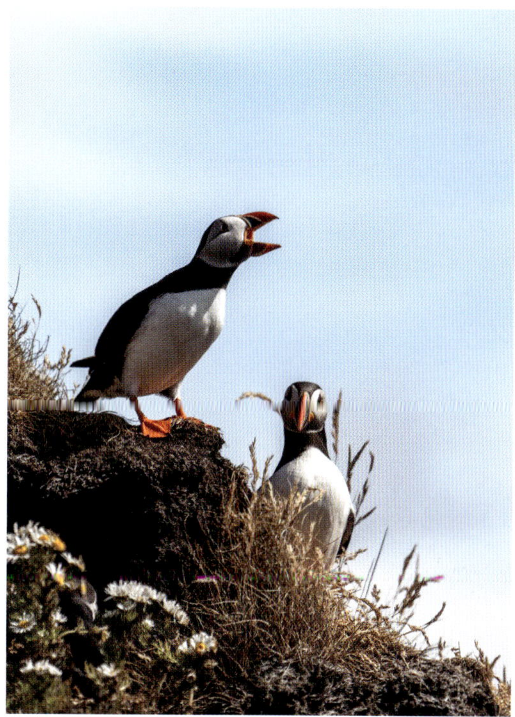

Puffins offer endless wonderful photo opportunities
(f/10 · 1/1000 sec. · ISO 250 · 400mm)

Parking Area

Photo Location

9 DYRHÓLAEY

Distance: About 20 minutes from Vík or 5 minutes from Reynisdrangar
Best time of day: Sunrise
Best time of year: Summer, fall, or winter
Equipment: No special requirements
Tour type: Self-drive
Parking area coordinates: 63.404347, –19.128818
Location coordinates: 63.403199, –19.131399

Dyrhólaey means "Door Hole Island" and is the name of a 380-foot promontory that developed thousands of years ago during a volcanic eruption. From the cliff top you can view a lighthouse built in 1927 and enjoy a fantastic view toward Mýrdalsjökull in the west, as well as a view of the promontory itself. The huge arch in the rocks (the "door hole") has been carved out over the centuries by the waves, and is large enough to sail a 30-ton boat through.

Take the same route as described for the previous tour and take the turnoff to the left onto Route 218 (Dyrhólavegur). This time, instead of heading straight ahead to the puffin cliffs, take a right after the lagoon. The road is steep and rocky, but can be driven in a regular car (although allowing oncoming traffic to pass can be quite tricky). Follow the road to a parking area on the cliff top. If you are facing the lighthouse, keep to the right and follow the path to the lighthouse itself. This path offers the best views of the seemingly endless beach to the west and of Mýrdalsjökull to the right. Sunrise in winter is a magical time to visit this location. If you have time, take a walk around the lighthouse and explore the whole

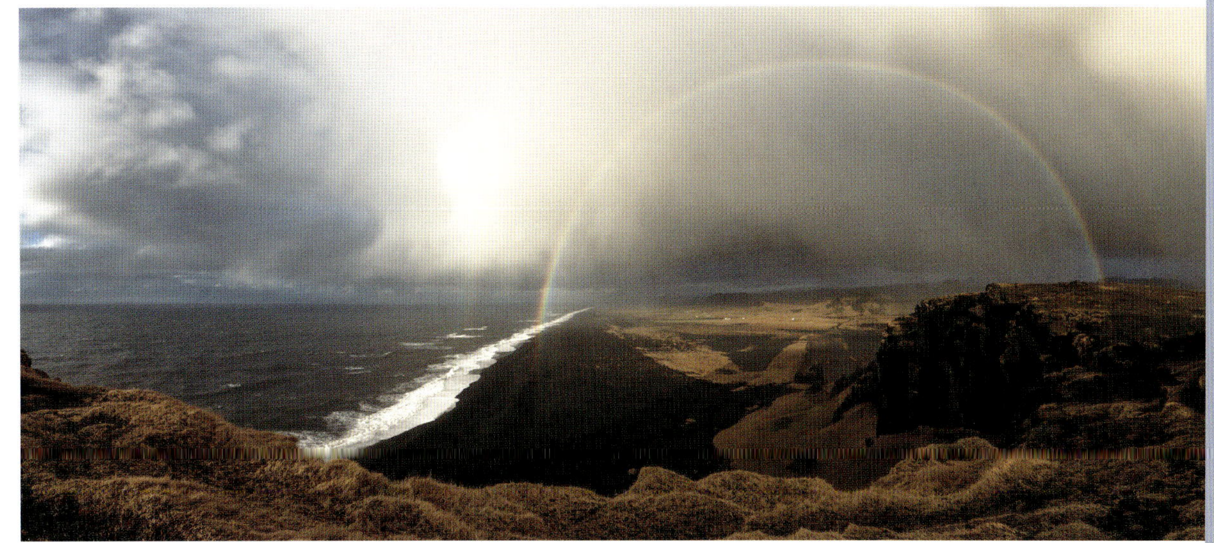

A double rainbow frames the breath-taking view (f/14 · 1/30 sec. · ISO 31 · 15mm · Filter: Soft GND8)

plateau. At the tip of the promontory, you have a great view of the rock formation that gives the area its name, and of the waves as they crash through the massive hole in the rock. There is a heavy-duty fence that prevents you from reaching the arch itself, and makes it difficult to get images of the arch with interesting foreground details. Generally, I prefer the view to the west.

10 ÞAKGIL

Distance: About 45 minutes from Vík í Mýrdal
Best time of day: Daytime, preferably cloudy
Best time of year: Summer, fall, or winter
Equipment: Rubber boots or waders
Vehicle: 4WD required
Tour type: Self-drive, or guided in winter (or if you don't have a jeep)
Parking area coordinates: 63.532626, –18.889299
Location coordinates: 63.534341, –18.888089

Parking Area

Photo Location

This tour takes you deep into Mýrdalsjökull glacier territory. Þakgil means "roof ravine" and is a hidden ravine close to the glacier itself. At the end of the ravine is a small stream with a rocky bed and a twin-peaked mountain in the background—in other words, a great subject for a photo. The journey to Þakgil offers just as many great views as the destination itself, either for photos or simply to enjoy.

The gravel road to Þakgil (Kerlingardalsvegur) is not actually an F-road, but is nevertheless not recommended unless you are driving a 4WD vehicle. The road is steep, winding, and heavily rutted. I have seen plenty of people turn around and go back rather than risk damaging the underside of their vehicles. If you don't have access to an SUV, the "Hidden Mountains" tour from Katlatrack Adventure Tours (*www.katlatrack.is*) takes you to Þakgil. The owner, Guðjón, also offers private tours—see the Top Tip below for more details.

To get to Þakgil, leave Vík heading east. About 5 minutes after you leave town, you will see a sign to Country Hotel Katla on the left,

Moss-covered rocks and rushing water make for a fantastic scene (f/10 · 1/10 sec. · ISO 400 · 14mm · Filter: Soft GND8)

and a sign to Þakgil right next to the entrance to the hotel. Turn off there, drive past the hotel (on your left), and follow the road up into an increasingly unreal landscape. The fields and plateaus that first dominate the view soon give way to green, moss-covered rock formations, black sand, and various views of the ice mass of the Mýrdalsjökull glacier. Signposts along the way confirm that you are still heading in the right direction. About 10 minutes before Þakgil, the road winds steeply downhill, giving you an incredible view of the huge sandy expanses of the Mýrdalsjökull—collectively known as Mýrdalssandur.

Rivers and streams flow this way and that across the dark sands, and you take a bridge over one of these to continue on between the

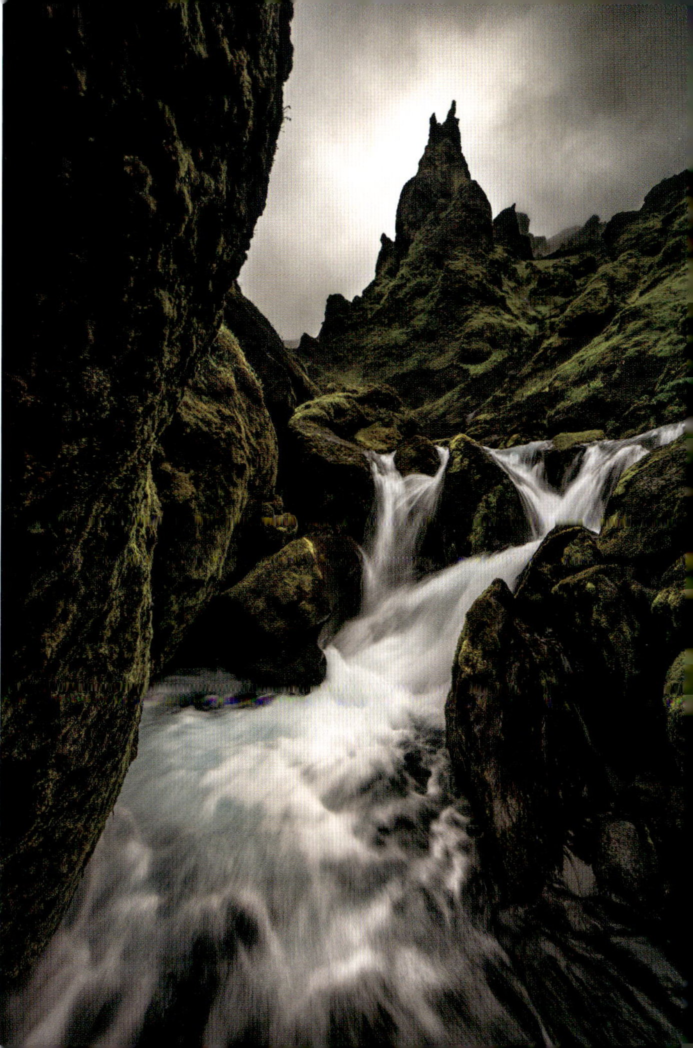

mountains to the campsite at Þakgil. The campsite used to be poorly maintained, but its owners have now recognized the area's potential and have installed nice restrooms and showers, making camping overnight a reasonable possibility for those who wish to spend more time in the area. To reach the next spot, drive past the campsite to the end of the road and park there.

There is a path over a bridge next to the parking area that takes you along the right-hand riverbank. The path, which is strewn with rocks that have slid down the surrounding slopes, takes you along the river and farther into the mountains. There are plenty of places to scramble down to the river, but I prefer to use one of the many waterfalls as my foreground when capturing photos of the surrounding countryside. If you have rubber boots or waders with you, it is worth getting into the water and shooting from there. I have captured some of my favorite images of this area from the middle of the stream, and taking this approach also makes you an interesting photo subject for the other tourists in the vicinity!

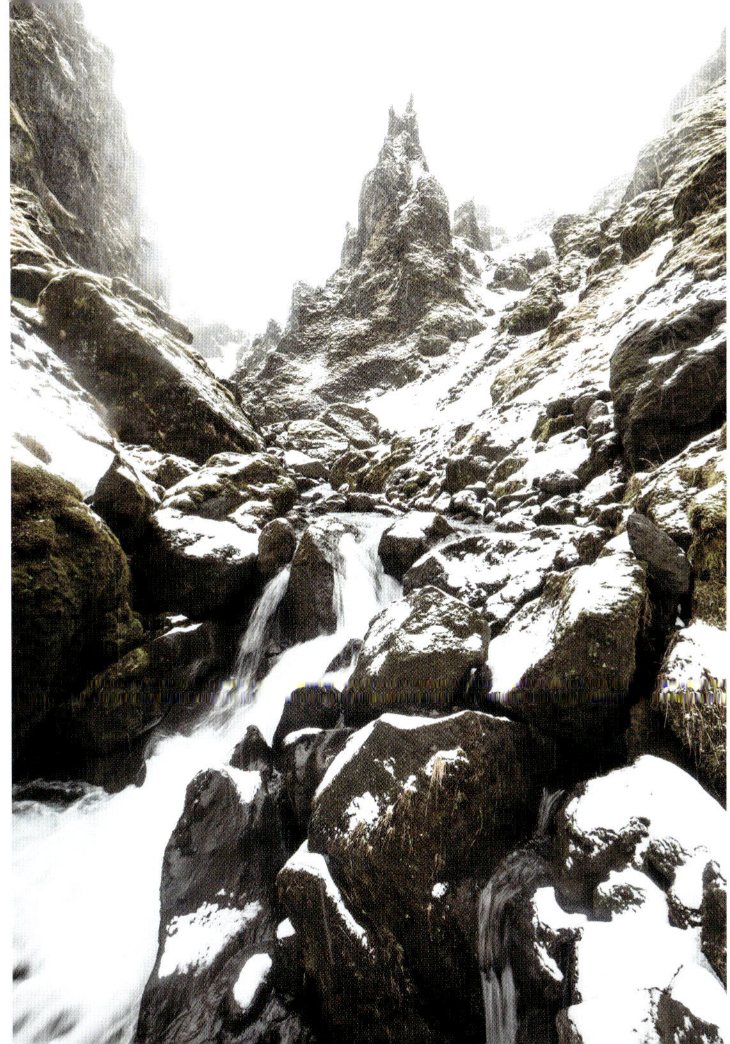

A snowstorm turns the sky white
(f/10 · 1/15 sec. · ISO 200 · 14mm ·
Filter: Soft GND8)

TOP TIP

The only way to visit this magical place in winter is on a guided tour. The snow masses and the steep, winding road often make it inaccessible, even for the local "superjeeps." Experienced tour operators drive you straight across the sand plateau through countless rivers and streams to the ravine. The view of the snow-capped mountains is truly unique, and you can combine a tour there with a trip to the ice caves of the Mýrdalsjökull glacier. This is an unforgettable experience and—unlike at the much more popular ice caves beneath the Vatnajökull glacier or at Jökulsárlón—you will usually be alone with your guide or group.

I can thoroughly recommend Katlatrack Adventure Tours (*www.katlatrack.is*) for this area. Guðjón and his guides know the area like the backs of their hands and are sure to provide an unforgettable adventure. As ever in Iceland, safety is key. The guides at Katlatrack take safety seriously, and they have even prepared meeting points with emergency supplies in case the Katla volcano that lies beneath Mýrdalsjökull should unexpectedly erupt.

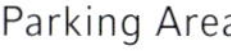
Parking Area

Photo Location

11 LÓMAGNÚPUR

Distance: About 90 minutes from Vík
Best time of day: Sunset, preferably cloudy
Best time of year: Summer, fall, or winter
Equipment: No special requirements
Tour type: Self-drive
Parking area coordinates: 63.956453, –17.482222
Location coordinates: 63.956634, –17.482187

This spot is right next to the Ring Road on the way to the next stopover in Höfn or Hali, so there is no reason to miss it. Lómagnúpur is a mountain located about 90 minutes from Höfn, and is easy to spot from the road due to its steep sides and unmistakable shape. This 2,500-foot beauty is one of Iceland's most captivating mountains. Although the mountain can be clearly seen from far away, the best place to shoot it is from the foot of the mountain itself. Follow the parking coordinates shown above to a small parking area on the left of the Ring Road (just before you get to the bridge). If it has rained recently, the plateau will be covered in puddles and tiny lakes, which are perfect for capturing reflections of the mountain. In winter, the water is mostly frozen over but still provides great foreground detail. My favorite shots include the patches of cotton grass that usually grow next to the lakes. These provide an ideal contrast to the towering Lómagnúpur in the background.

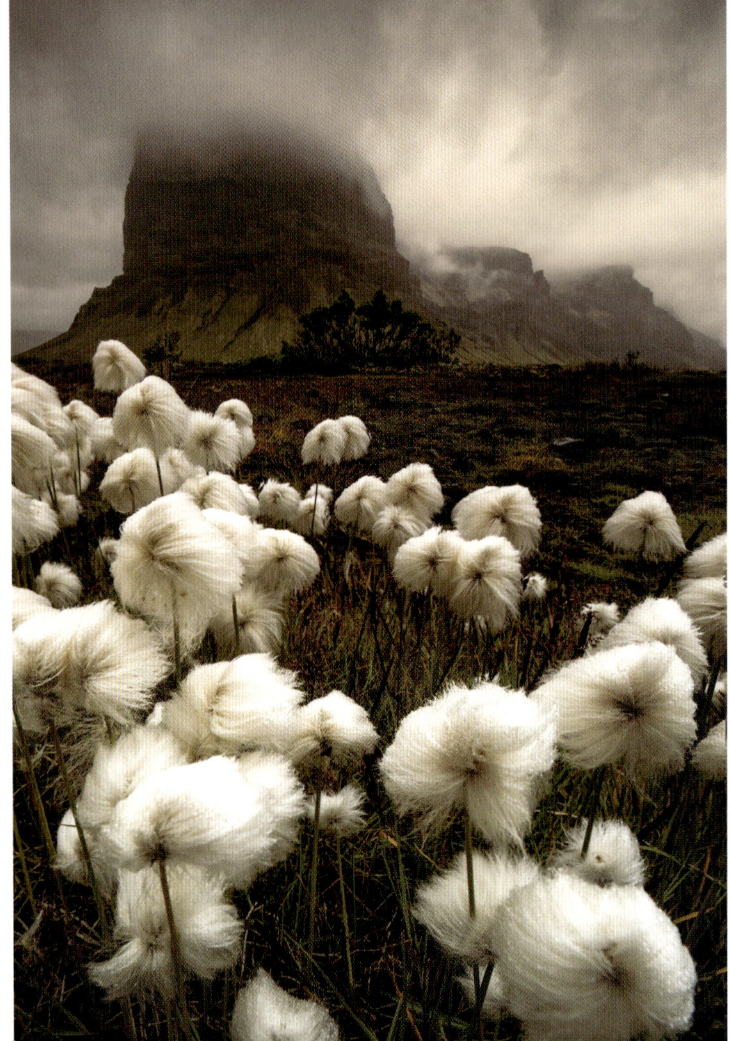

Cotton grass growing near the mighty Lómagnúpur
(f/14 · 1/13 sec. · ISO 100 · 16mm · Filter: Soft GND16)

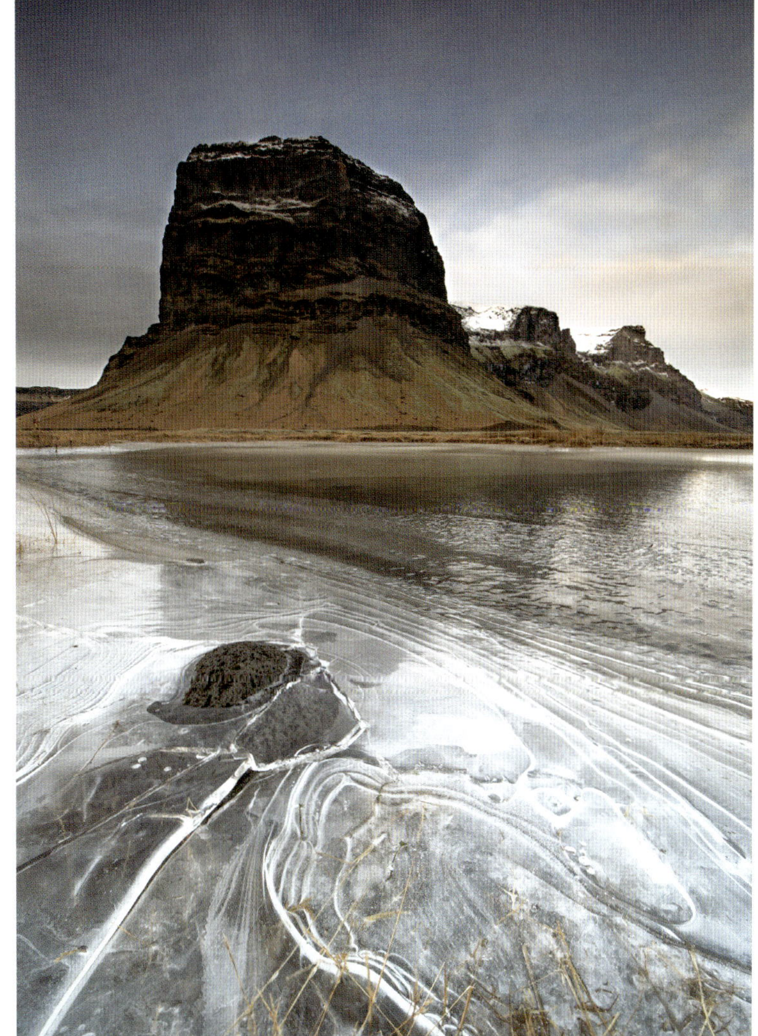

A frozen lake guides the viewer's eye into this image
(f/10 · 1/25 sec. · ISO 125 · 14mm · Filter: Soft GND16)

Parking Area

Photo Location

12 SVÍNAFELLSJÖKULL

Distance: About 30 minutes from Lómagnúpur
Best time of day: Sunset
Best time of year: Summer, fall, or winter
Equipment: No special requirements
Tour type: Self-drive
Parking area coordinates: 64.008435, –16.879988
Location coordinates: 64.002942, –16.878031

The mighty Vatnajökull, Europe's largest glacier, is now your constant companion as you journey eastward. Although the main body of the glacier is often hidden behind the surrounding mountains, you will see many of its glacial tongues along the way. One of the most impressive of these is Svínafellsjökull, which is located in what used to be the Skaftafell National Park. The park was founded in 1967 to protect Iceland's unique natural environment but became part of the larger Vatnajökull National Park in 2008.

The drive to Svínafellsjökull takes about 30 minutes from the previous stop in Lómagnúpur. Follow the sign to the left onto a worn-out gravel road, and drive straight ahead to the parking area near the edge of the glacier.

A well-surfaced footpath from the parking area leads directly to the glacier. A memorial plaque at beginning of the path tells of the power and peril of this strange, icy world. It tells the story of two tourists who went missing here in 2007. Their tents were found near Svínafellsjökull, and it is assumed they never made it back from a tour of the glacier. In 2010,

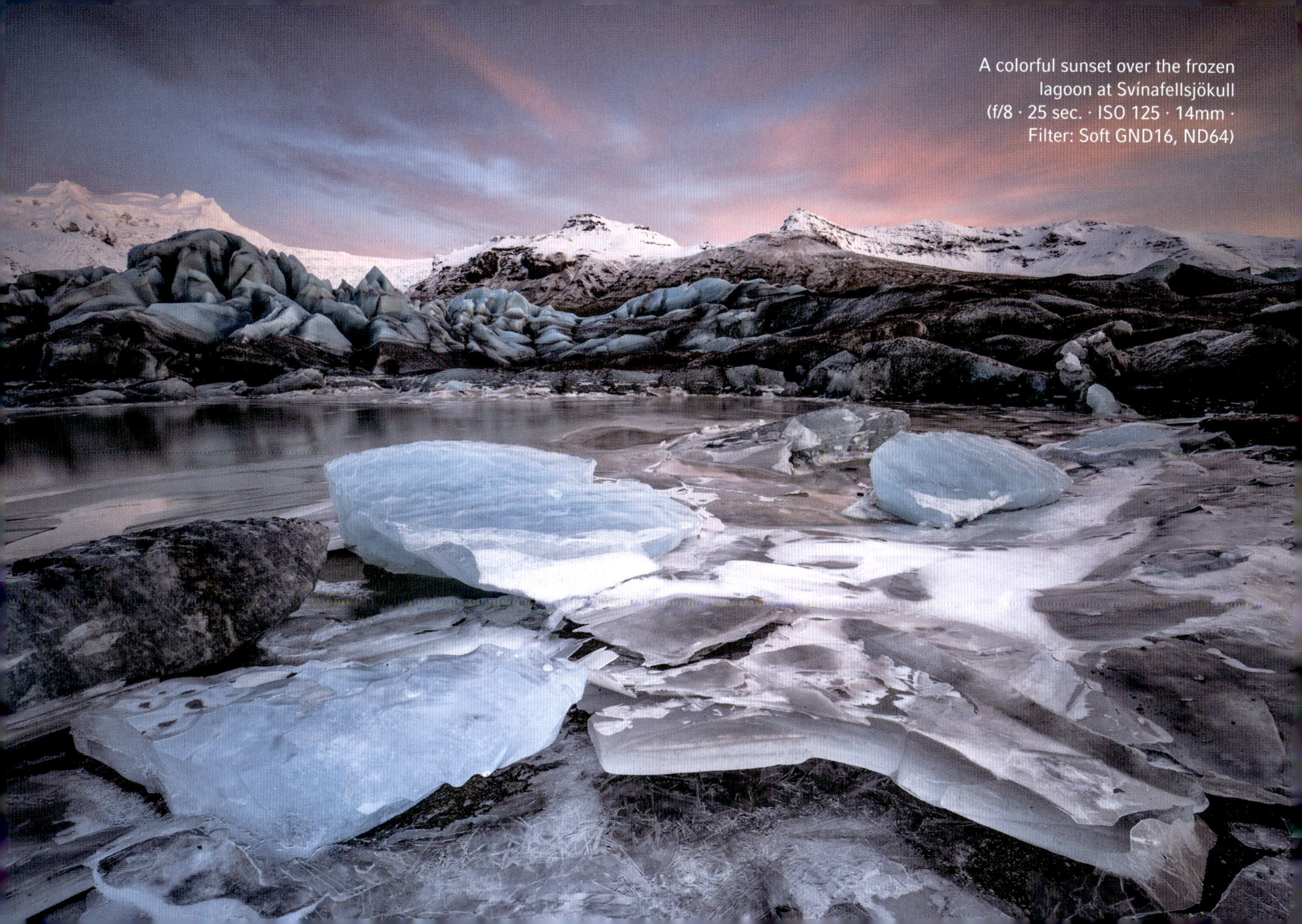

A colorful sunset over the frozen lagoon at Svínafellsjökull (f/8 · 25 sec. · ISO 125 · 14mm · Filter: Soft GND16, ND64)

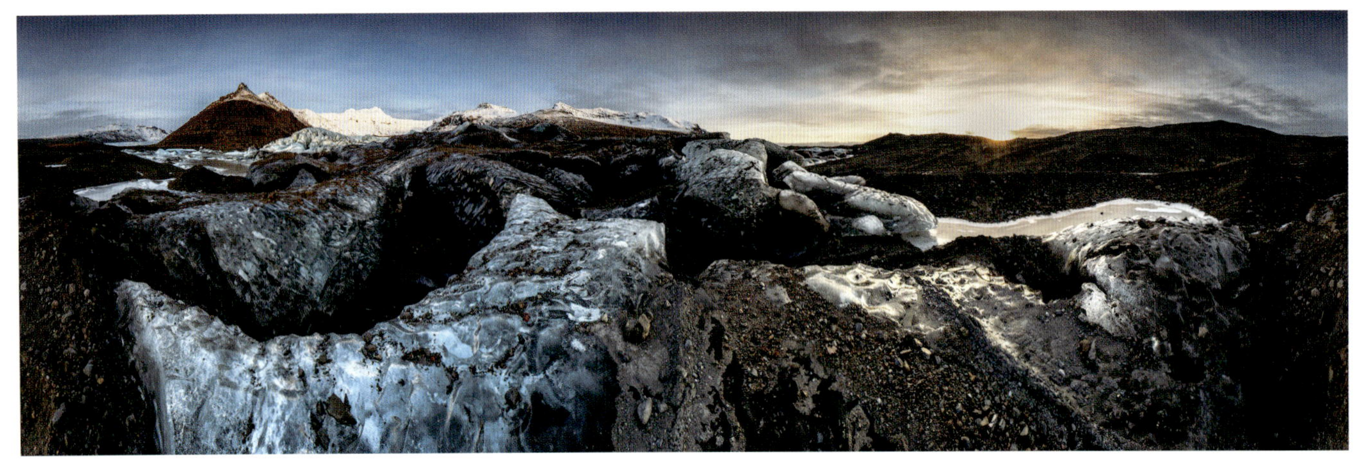

A panorama taken from the foot of this awe-inspiring glacier
(f/14 · 1/3 sec. · ISO 125 · 14mm · Filter: Soft GND16)

Icelandic mountaineers found the remains of a climbing rope, which indicated the missing pair had attempted to climb Hvannadalshnjúkur, east of Svínafellsjökull. The two tourists have still not been found.

Visiting Svínafellsjökull is an easy way to get right up close to the glacial ice. Never try to climb the ice on your own. It is only safe to do so with appropriate gear and an experienced guide, and you can sign on for a guided tour at the National Park Visitor Center.

If you take the footpath toward the glacier, this automatically leads you to the left, toward the mountains. Even though this offers a great view of Svínafellsjökull, there is a better place for taking photos that offers an even better view and takes you away from the horde of tourists that constantly sweep the area. To get

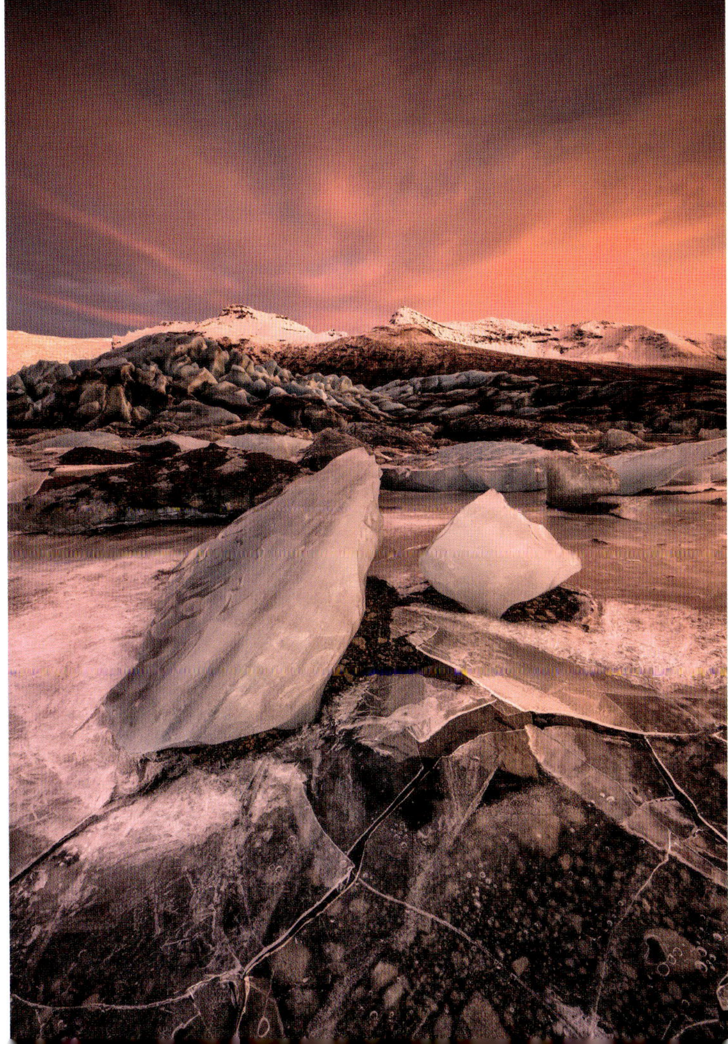

there, instead of following the path to the left, walk straight ahead over the graveled area that leads down to the lake.

At the lake, keep right along a well-worn trail that takes you in a loop to the end of the lake and to the very end of the glacial tongue. The view here is especially beautiful in winter, when great blocks of ice lie at the edge of the lagoon, which is often frozen over. Sheets of ice are thrust way up into the air by the brute force of the glacier, and this is the only place in Iceland where you can get so close, so easily, to active glacial ice.

Evening light in a world made of ice
(f/10 · 1/3 sec. · ISO 125 · 14mm ·
Filter: Soft GND16)

13 JÖKULSÁRLÓN

Distance: About 15 minutes from Hali
Best time of day: Sunrise, sunset, or at night
Best time of year: Summer, fall, or winter
Equipment: No special requirements
Tour type: Self-drive
Parking area coordinates: 64.048182, –16.179743
Location coordinates: 64.050914, –16.180129

Parking Area

Photo Location

Jökulsárlón—which means "glacial river lagoon"—is the most famous glacial lagoon in the world. At 820 feet in depth, it is also Iceland's deepest body of water. The glacial tongue Breiðamerkurjökull leads into the water, providing visitors with a constant stream of icebergs in an endless variety of colors. Blue-toned icebergs are made from layers of ice that were under great pressure and therefore contain very little air. Black and gray tones are caused by volcanic ash that rains down on the glacier and blends with the ice. Jökulsárlón is connected to the sea by the river Jökulsá á Breiðamerkursandi, which is the shortest river in Iceland. When it is in flood, the force of the flow carries a stream of icebergs out into the open sea. When the tide is coming in, the river sometimes reverses its flow and forces salt water into the lagoon, which is why the lagoon seldom freezes in winter.

I recommend that you find lodging in Höfn at the Hali Country Hotel. Drive from Hali toward the Westenzur lagoon. After about 15 minutes, you will come to a large and very busy parking area right next to a large bridge on the right.

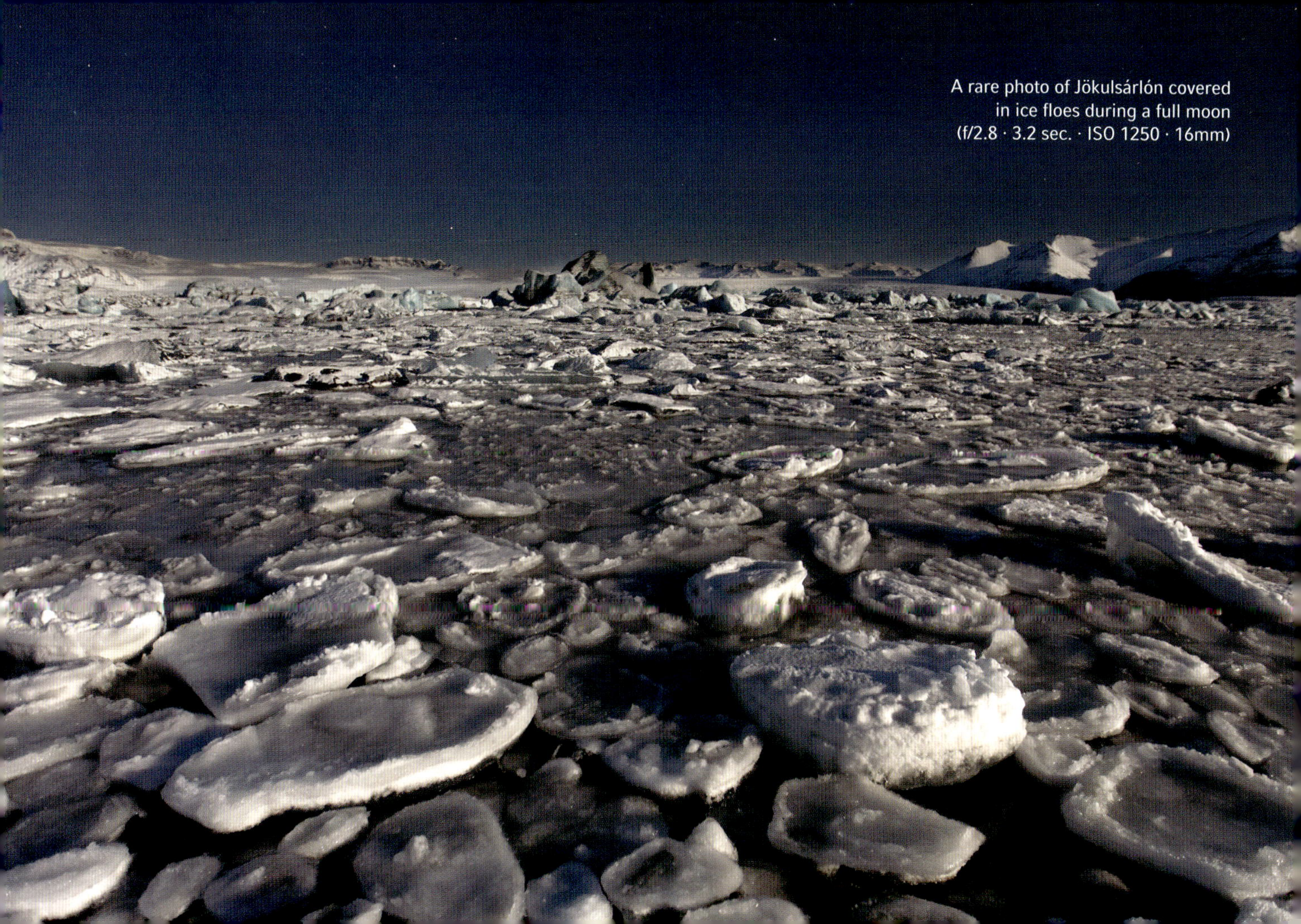

A rare photo of Jökulsárlón covered in ice floes during a full moon (f/2.8 · 3.2 sec. · ISO 1250 · 16mm)

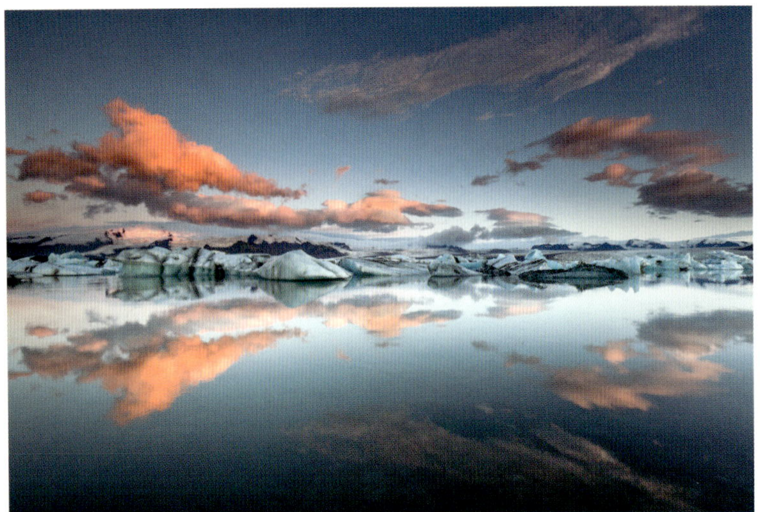

Sunrise over the famous glacial lagoon (f/13 · 1/3 sec. · ISO 250 · 16mm · Filter: Soft GND16)

TOP TIP

Jökulsárlón is great to visit at sunrise, at sunset, or during the day, but is also appealing at full moon (especially in winter). In addition to a chance of seeing the Northern Lights, the moonlight provides a completely different mood and unusual light to shoot by.

The lagoon is one of the best-known tourist attractions in southern Iceland, so it is always extremely busy during the day. I prefer to go there either very early in the morning or late in the evening when the light is much better and there are far fewer tourists around.

You can walk directly to the edge of the lagoon from the parking area and take the path along the bank. Sometimes, you only need to go about 100 yards to escape from most of the crowds and where you can listen to the peaceful crunching and cracking of the icebergs. On calm days, the icebergs are reflected in the still water while the sun climbs high in the sky.

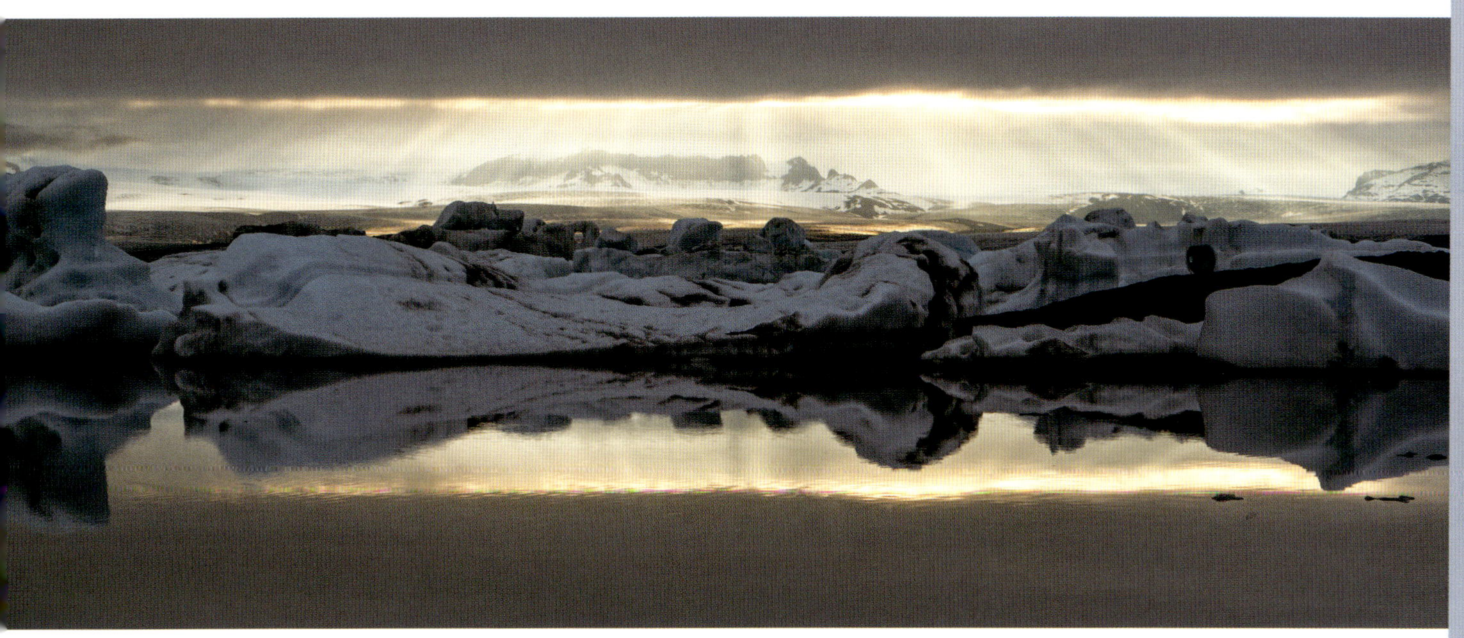

All is calm as the setting sun illuminates the lagoon
(f/16 · 1/15 sec. · ISO 100 · 59mm · Filter: Soft GND8)

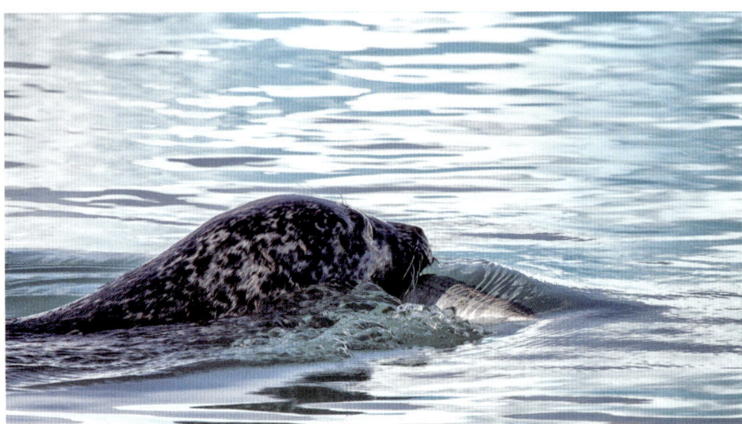

A seal on a successful hunt in the lagoon
(f/14 · 1/160 sec. · ISO 200 · 400mm)

TOP TIP

If you want to get up close and personal with icebergs, you would do well to visit the neighboring glacial lake Fjallsárlón. Though it is smaller than the lagoon at Jökulsárlón and has fewer icebergs, it is less busy and has a more relaxed atmosphere.

To get there, follow Route 1 just a few minutes farther to the west, and then turn right where you see the sign for Fjallsárlón and boat trips.

The farther you walk along the lagoon, the crowds of tourists thin out and you will encounter more interesting photographic subjects. Note, however, there are two amphibious vehicles that take visitors on a short trip from the parking area to the lagoon and back. These tend to go pretty fast and they seem to ignore other visitors, so keep an eye out for them and stay clear when they are about.

14 BREIÐAMERKURSANDUR

Distance: About 15 minutes from Hali, or 1 minute from Jökulsárlón
Best time of day: Sunrise or at night
Best time of year: Summer, fall, or winter
Equipment: Rubber boots or waders
Tour type: Self-drive
Parking area coordinates: 64.042643, –16.182492
Location coordinates: 64.040909, –16.180863

Parking Area

Photo Location

Our next highlight is on the opposite side of the road from Jökulsárlón. Many of the icebergs that float out to sea through the Jökulsá á Breiðamerkursandi end up floating back toward land on the black sandy beach at Breiðamerkursandur. Here, you can see anything from enormous icebergs to a multitude of tiny chunks of ice that glint like diamonds in the sun. Whatever size they are, the ice is often surrounded by the approaching waves and the contrast between the dark sand and the bright, twinkling ice offers an endless selection of photographic subjects.

You can reach the beach on the east or the west side of the bridge that crosses over the river. I prefer the west side with its greater variety of icebergs, and the beach is longer there, too. To get there, take a right from the parking area at Jökulsárlón, cross the bridge, and turn left directly after the bridge onto a gravel road that heads downhill. The broad, rutted road takes you to the coast, where you can park and walk along the beach. The farther you walk, the fewer people you will come across. Try capturing a few icebergs using long exposure times to give the water a soft, dynamic look.

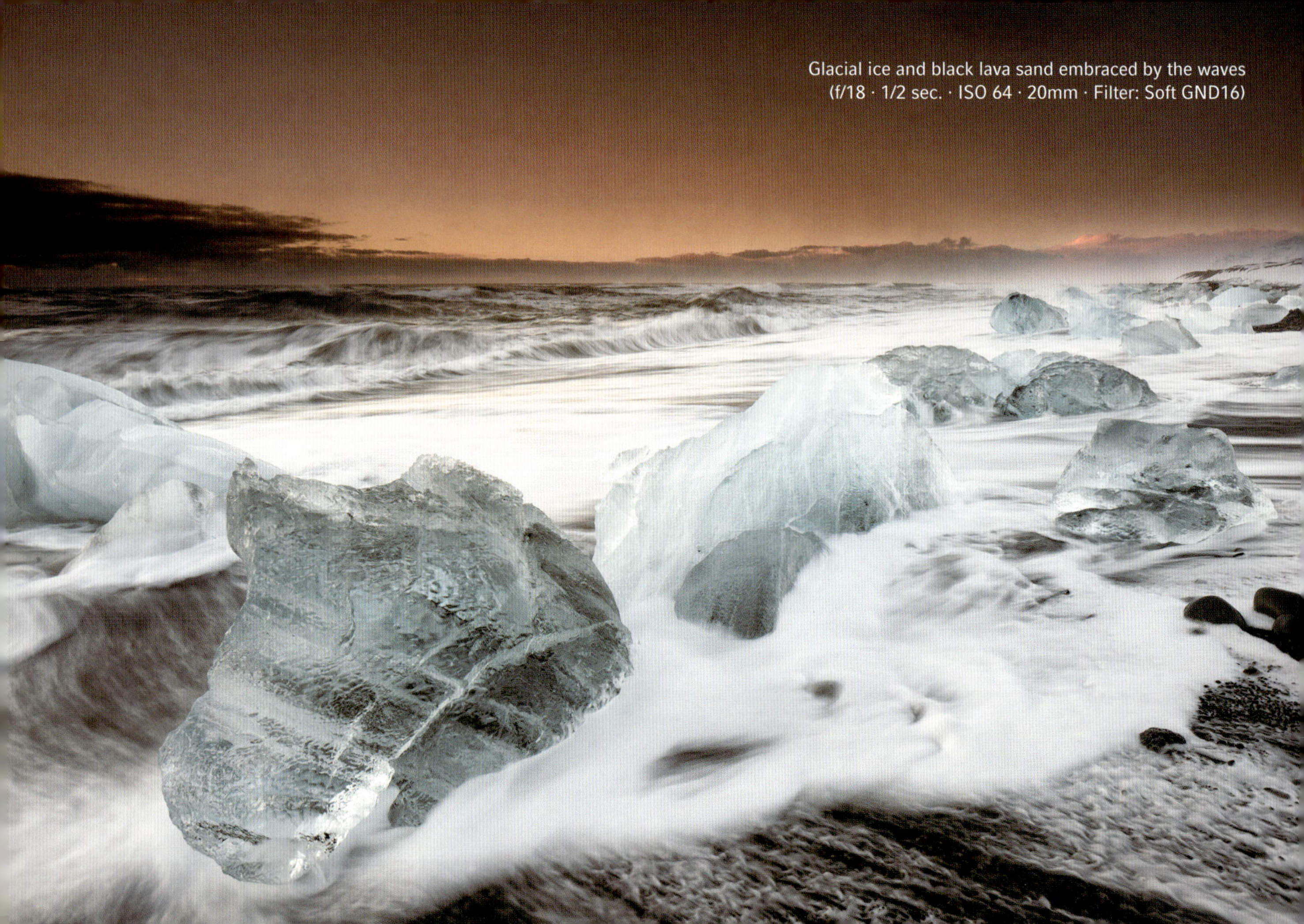

Glacial ice and black lava sand embraced by the waves
(f/18 · 1/2 sec. · ISO 64 · 20mm · Filter: Soft GND16)

WARNING!
Be sure to take either rubber boots or waders with you to Breiðamerkursandur. It is all too easy to get surprised by a wave if you are concentrating on your photography, and some waves are a lot bigger than others. It takes a while to dry out your shoes and pants once they are wet, and ice-cold feet don't make the excursion any nicer. Keep an eye on the surf and always keep safety in mind.

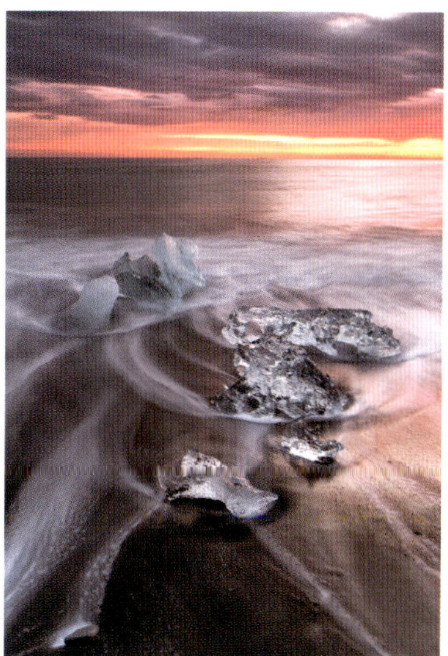

Glinting ice on black sand in the morning sun
(f/11 · 5 sec. · ISO 250 · 32mm · Filter: Soft Reverse GND8)

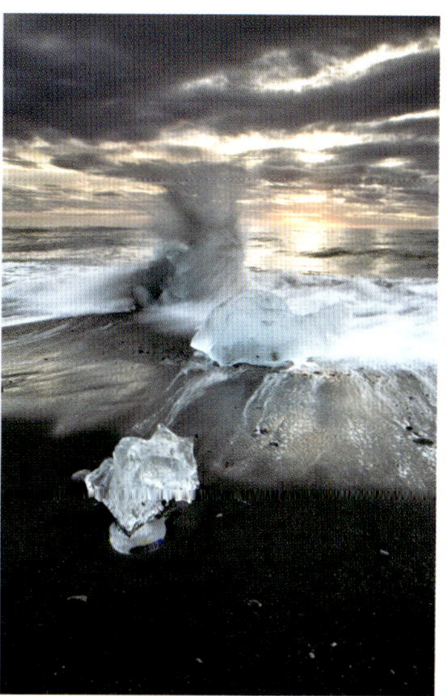

Unpredictable waves can make for wet feet, but they make spectacular action photos, too
(f/14 · 1/2 sec. · ISO 100 · 23mm · Filter: Soft GND16)

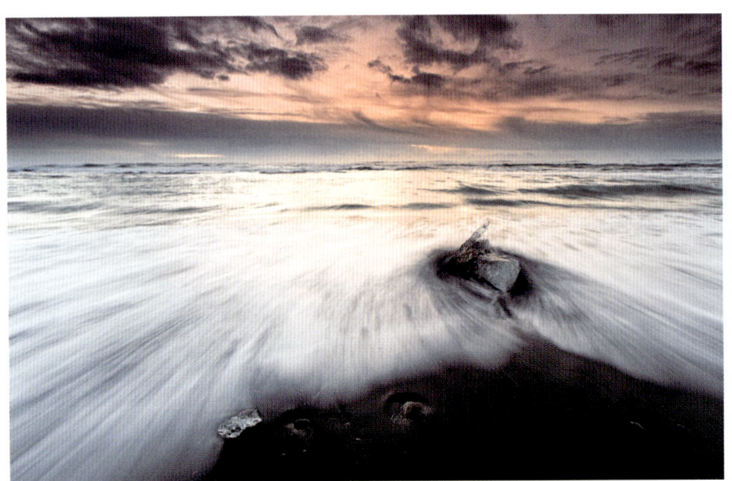

A wave breaking on glacial ice
(f/13 · 0.6 sec. · ISO 160 · 16mm · Filter: Soft GND16)

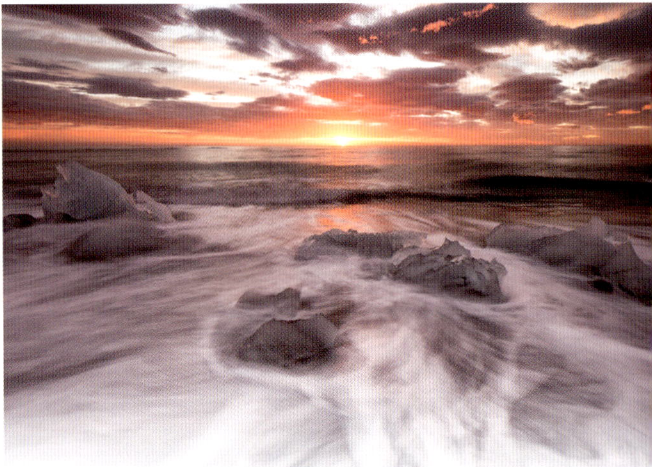

The red of the sunrise reflected in the approaching waves
(f/14 · 2 sec. · ISO 100 · 18mm · Filter: Reverse GND8)

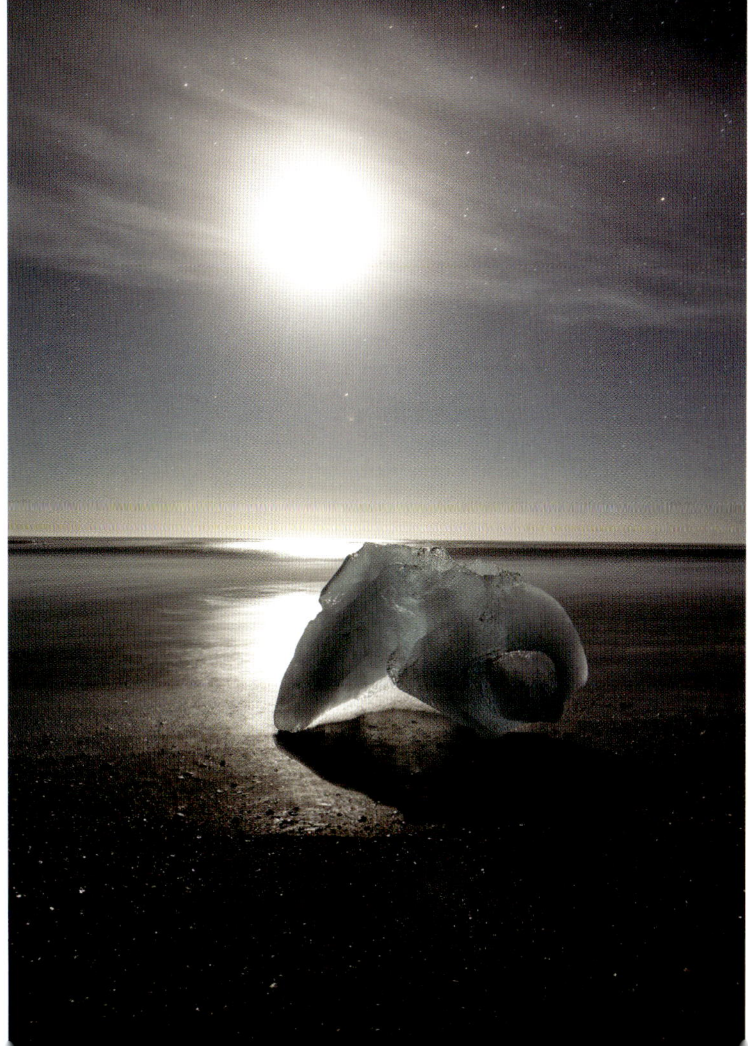

TOP TIP

This beach is especially picturesque at sunrise in winter. The sun rises directly over the sea's horizon and bathes the floating ice in unusually beautiful light. Shooting into the sun produces unique images that can't be found anywhere else. It is always a pleasure to see the sun rise at the darkest time of year, and to experience it in a place like this is an exquisite experience.

A magical moment during a full moon
(f/5 · 30 sec. · ISO 1600 · 23mm)

Parking Area

Photo Location 1

Photo Location 2

15 VESTRAHORN AND KLIFATINDUR

Distance: About 1 hour from Hali, or 20 minutes from Höfn
Best time of day: Sunrise or at night
Best time of year: Summer, fall, or winter
Equipment: Rubber boots or waders for shooting in the breakers
Tour type: Self-drive
Parking area coordinates: 64.244047, –14.971412
Location coordinates: 64.244593, –14.970678 and 64.248500, –14.969948
Additional Information: There is an entry fee at this site

Vestrahorn is one of the most popular spots near Höfn. Although it is extremely well known, it still hasn't lost its appeal and is definitely worth a trip, especially at sunrise. Vestrahorn is just a tiny part of a larger mountain range called Klifatindur; however, the locals refer to the entire range as Vestrahorn.

The area surrounding Vestrahorn is dominated by a broad, sandy plain that gently transitions into sand dunes. The tall dunes are covered in grass and make for a great foreground subject. The waves here break more gently than elsewhere and leave behind a layer of moisture that is ideal for capturing reflections.

To get there, take Route 1 to the east from Hali. After about 45 minutes, you will reach the Almannaskarðsgöng tunnel. Just before the tunnel, there is a sign for Vestrahorn to the right that takes you along a gravel road to a parking area with its own café.

Many of the most attractive subjects are on private land, and many of the owners now charge an entry fee. The fees are usually described as a contribution toward preserving the

Icelandic environment, but the infrastructure tells a different story. A few years ago, you paid at the café or, if it was closed, you left your money in a mailbox. Now, there is a pay-to-enter barrier like the ones in city carparks. There is also a credit card machine at the café that prints a ticket that is used to open the barrier. Personally, I don't think you need a barrier to levy an environmental fee.

Last time I was there, it cost about $8.00 for a single visit.

Once you are through the barrier, drive all the way to the end of the road, where you will find a fenced area with security cameras that belongs to the Icelandic Coast Guard. There you can park on either side of the road.

If you take the trail that follows the fence to the left, you will end up at the dunes. If you are lucky, you will find a tiny lake with a grass-covered island in its center, which makes a perfect mirror for shots of Vestrahorn. However, this only works if it is calm and has rained recently. Don't be disappointed if you can't capture this

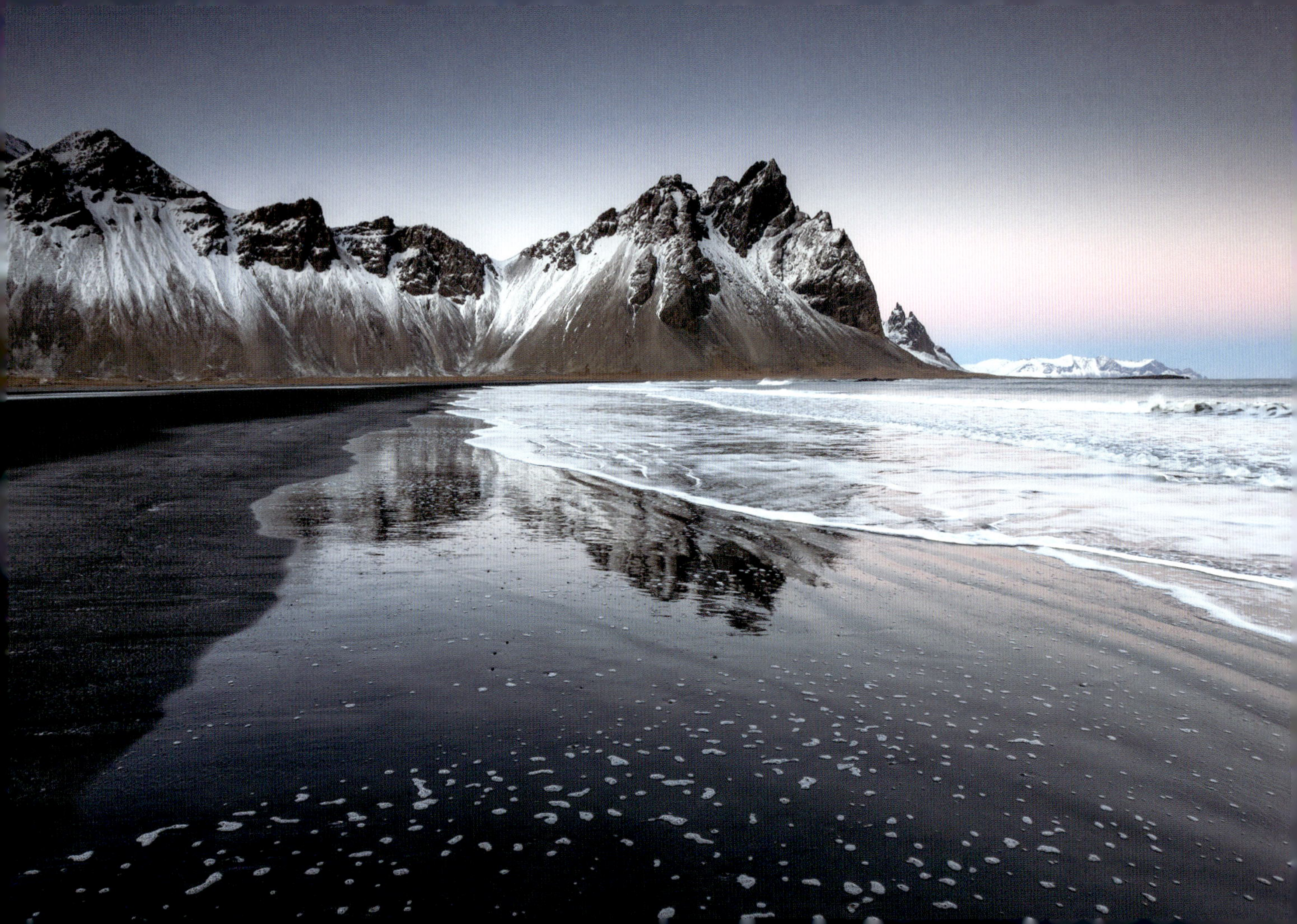

Vestrahorn captured in the fading evening light
(f/10 · 1/20 sec. · ISO 640 · 16mm · Filter: Soft GND8)

particular shot, as there are plenty of other things to look out for in the area.

From the pool, head directly into the dunes in front of Vestrahorn, where you will find loads of great views. It is worth taking a walk along the coast, too, and taking some pictures of the mountains reflected in the moisture left by the breakers on the beach. Be sure to wear waterproof boots if you want to concentrate on your photography without getting your feet wet. I have often ended up with my shoes and pants soaked, so don't do the same if you can avoid it. As well as the reflections, the approaching waves make a great subject, too, and using a long exposure time intensifies both effects.

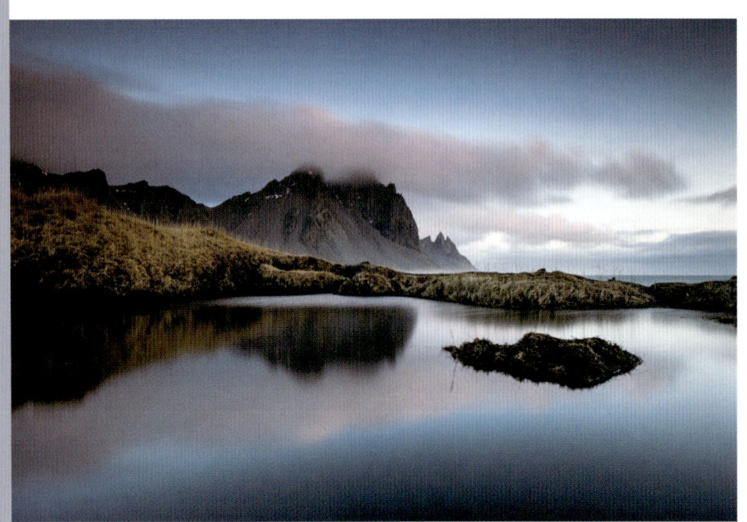

Pink clouds in the morning
(f/10 · 25 sec. · ISO 200 · 24mm · Filter: Soft GND16, ND1000)

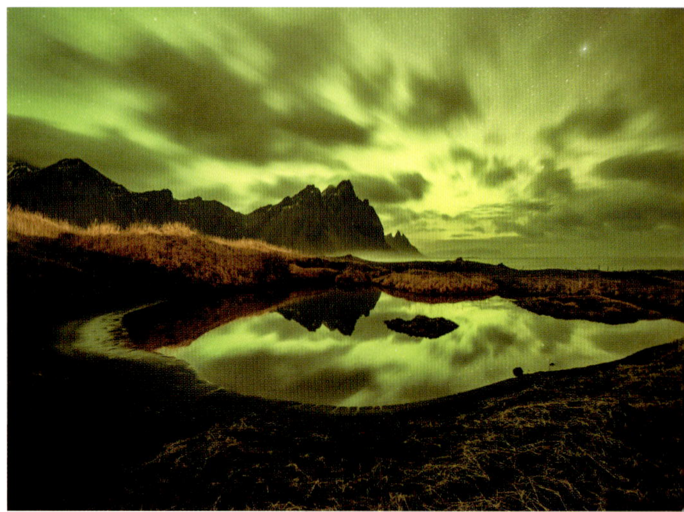

The Northern Lights color the sky green while the wind drives the clouds onward
(f/2.8 · 30 sec. · ISO 2000 · 15mm)

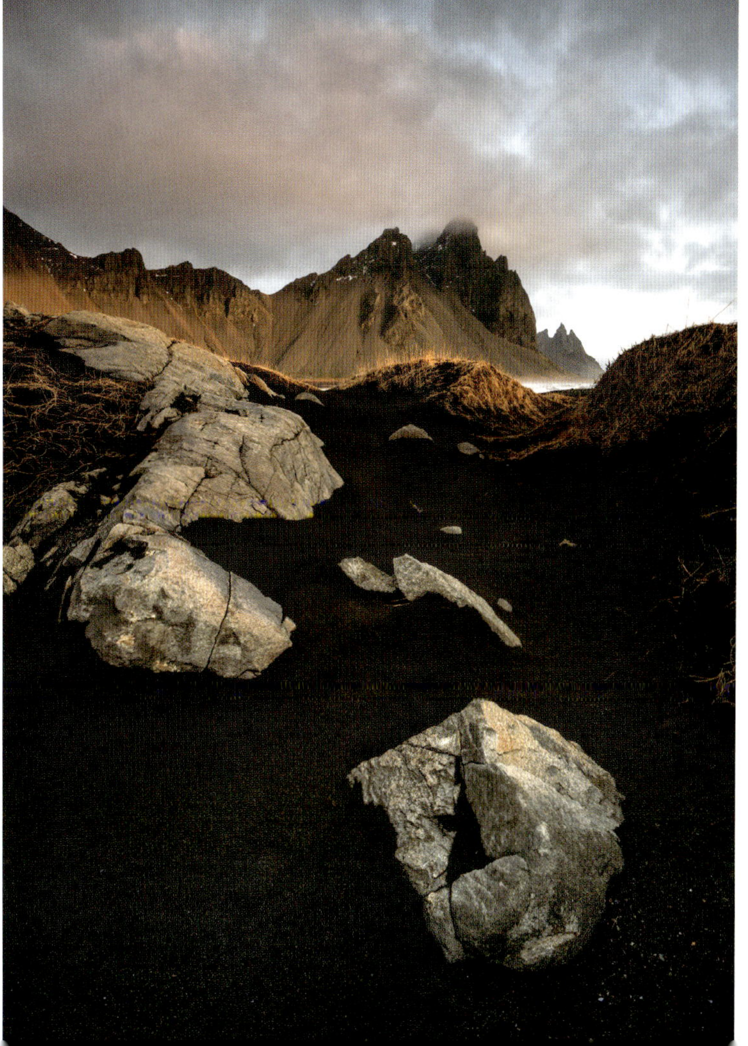

The dunes offer endless new views. This shot was captured in the early morning.
(f/10 · 1/8 sec. · ISO 100 · 19mm · Filter: Soft GND16)

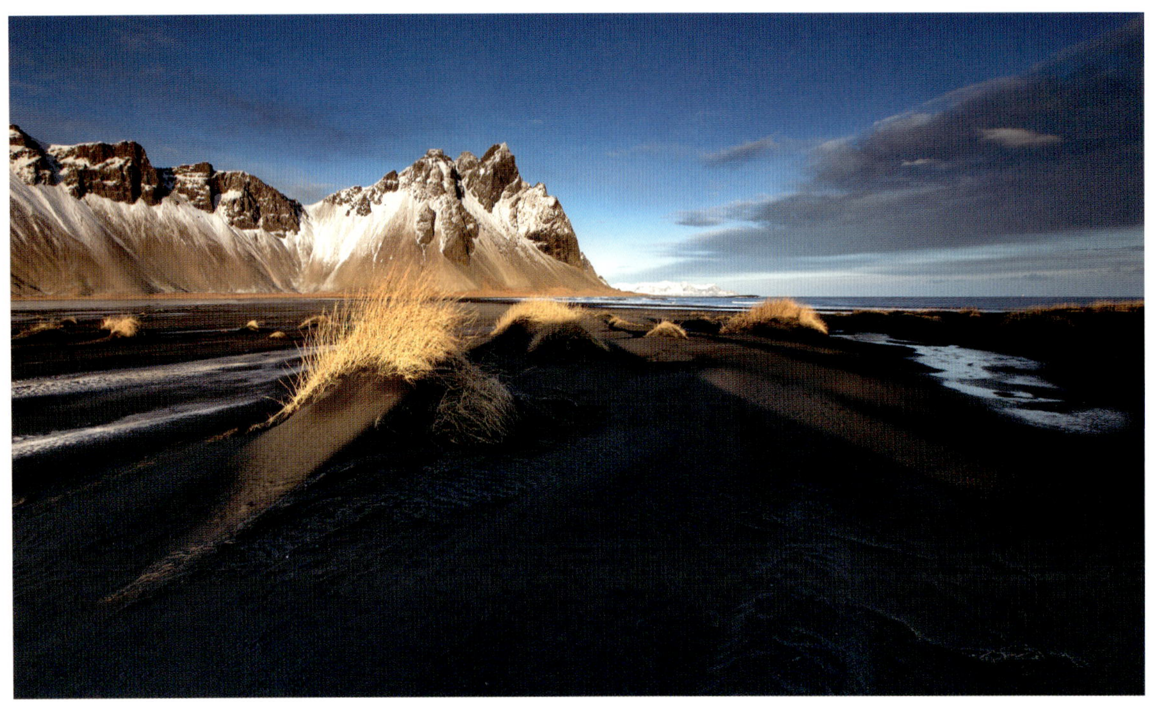

The grass glows golden in the evening light (f/14 · 1/10 sec. · ISO 125 · 19mm · Filter: Soft GND16)

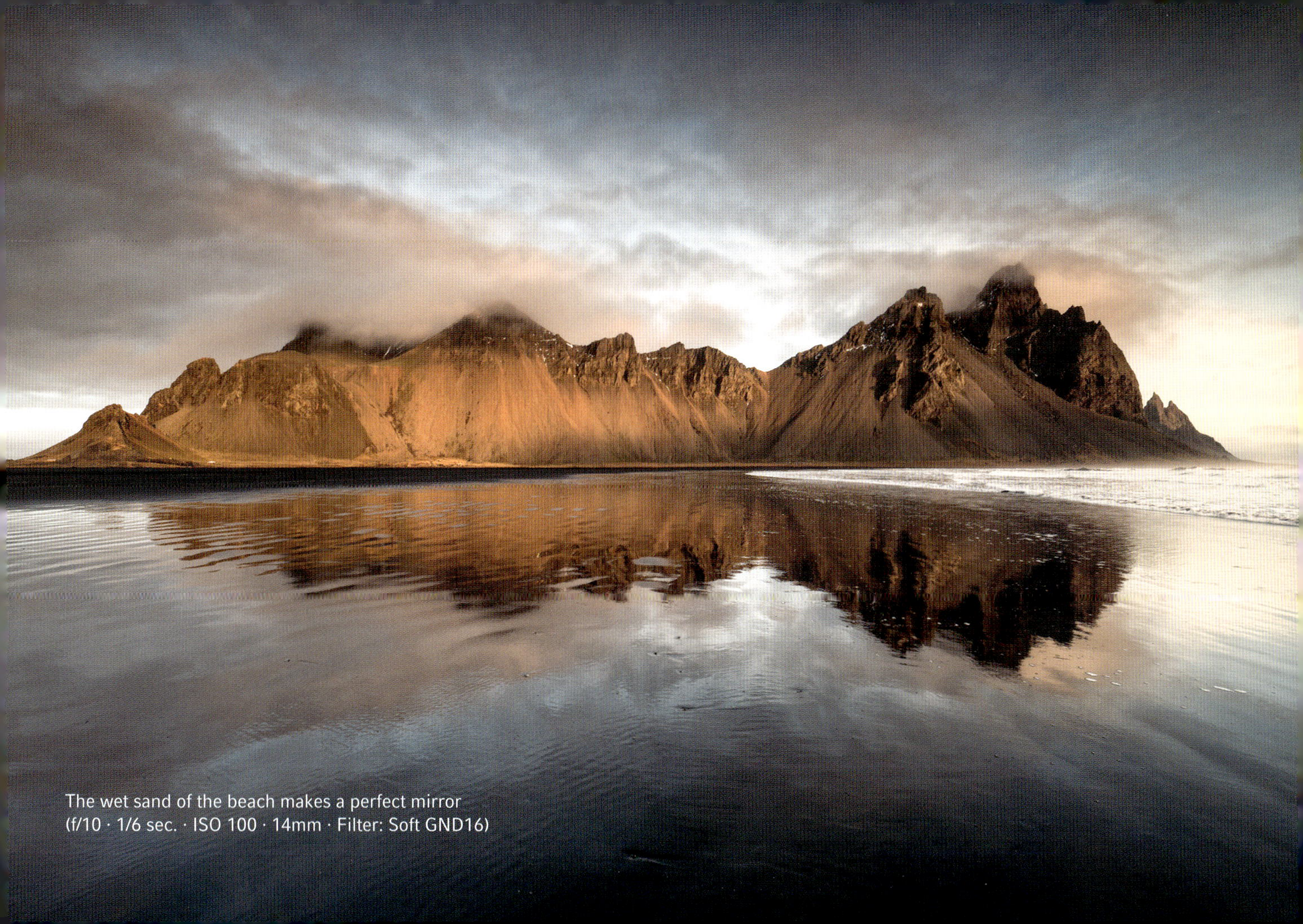

The wet sand of the beach makes a perfect mirror
(f/10 · 1/6 sec. · ISO 100 · 14mm · Filter: Soft GND16)

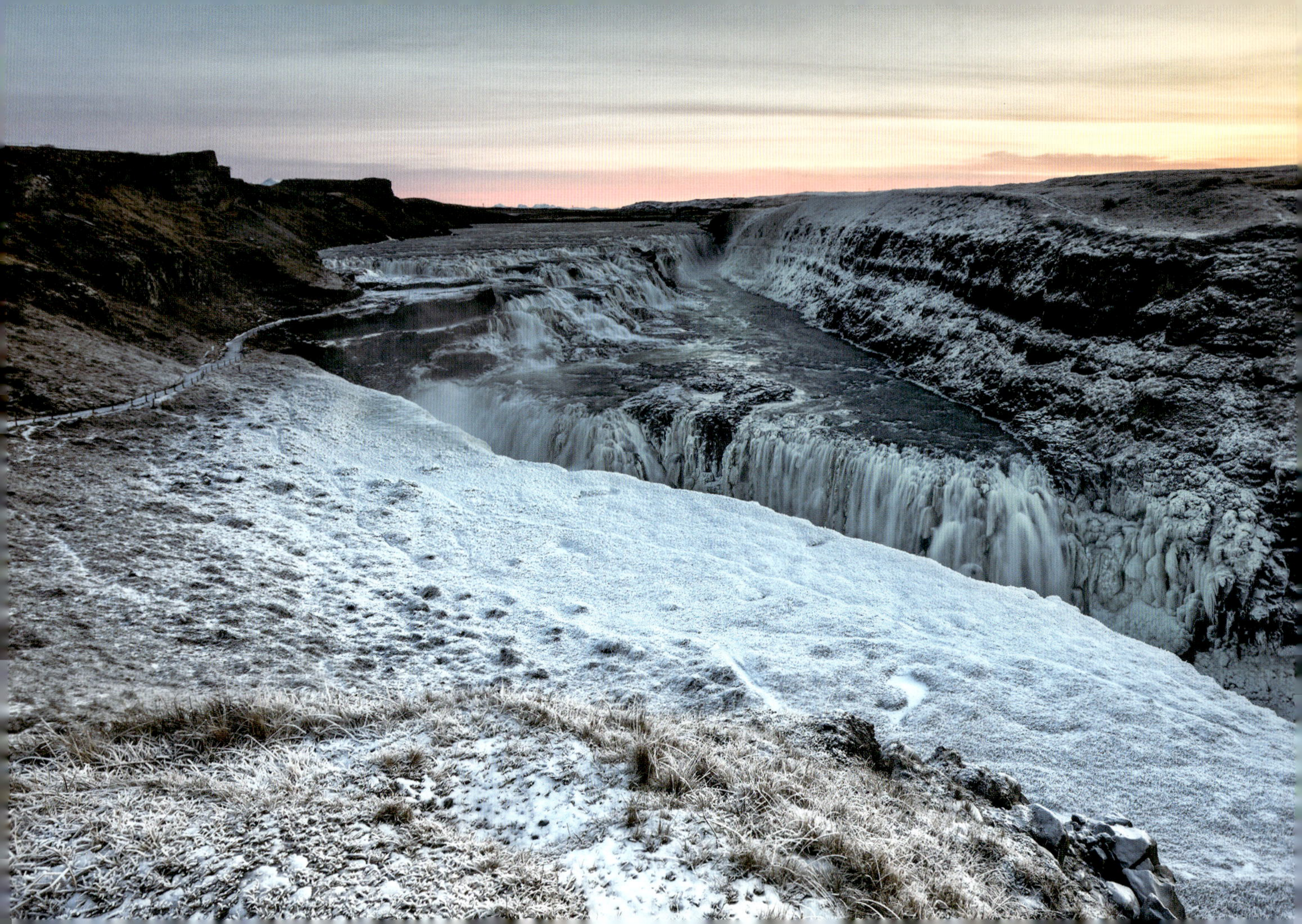

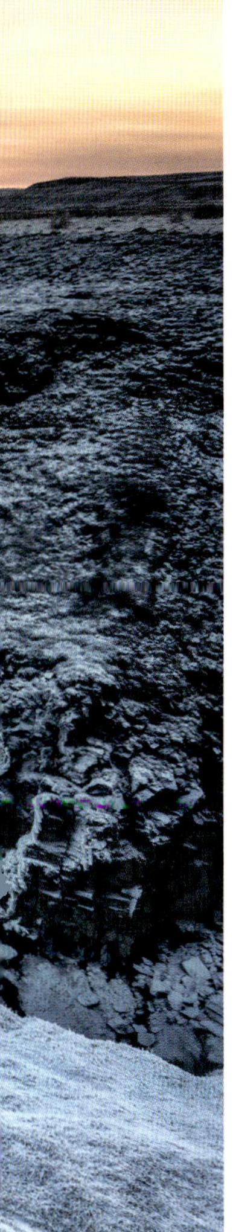

TOUR 4

THE EXTENDED GOLDEN CIRCLE AND THE HIDDEN WATERFALLS

The Icelanders call the area around three of the best-known attractions in the south the *Golden Circle*. The three most popular locations: Geysir, Gullfoss (a huge two-tier waterfall), and Þingvellir (the site of Iceland's ancient national parliament) make up a round-trip that you can book with a number of tour operators. The tour described here includes three additional wonderful waterfalls in the area around Selfoss.

TOUR 4 BASICS

Overall time required: 2–3 days

Travel time: About 1 hour to Selfoss from Reykjavík

Lodging: There are plenty of hotels and a campsite in Selfoss, as well as shops and gas stations. You can stay in Reykjavík, too, although this means more expensive lodging and adding an extra hour to your travel time.

TOP TIP
To avoid the crowds, try visiting these sites at unusual times of day. For example, if you visit Geysir at midnight, you will probably be able to marvel at the eruptions on your own.

WARNING!
The last two tours in this chapter—to the hidden waterfalls Háifoss and Þjófafoss—require a 4WD vehicle. They are both a long way from civilization and, even if you can get there in a regular car, you run the risk of damaging your vehicle or getting stuck along the way.

Among these, Brúarfoss—a secluded waterfall that flows into a unique blue gulley—is a major highlight. Few visitors find their way there and instead, they tend to get lost in the chaotic vacation home park where the path to the waterfall begins.

The sites listed here are some of the most popular in Iceland, so they are often swarming with visitors from Reykjavík during the day. I have counted as many as 20 buses parked simultaneously at Gullfoss.

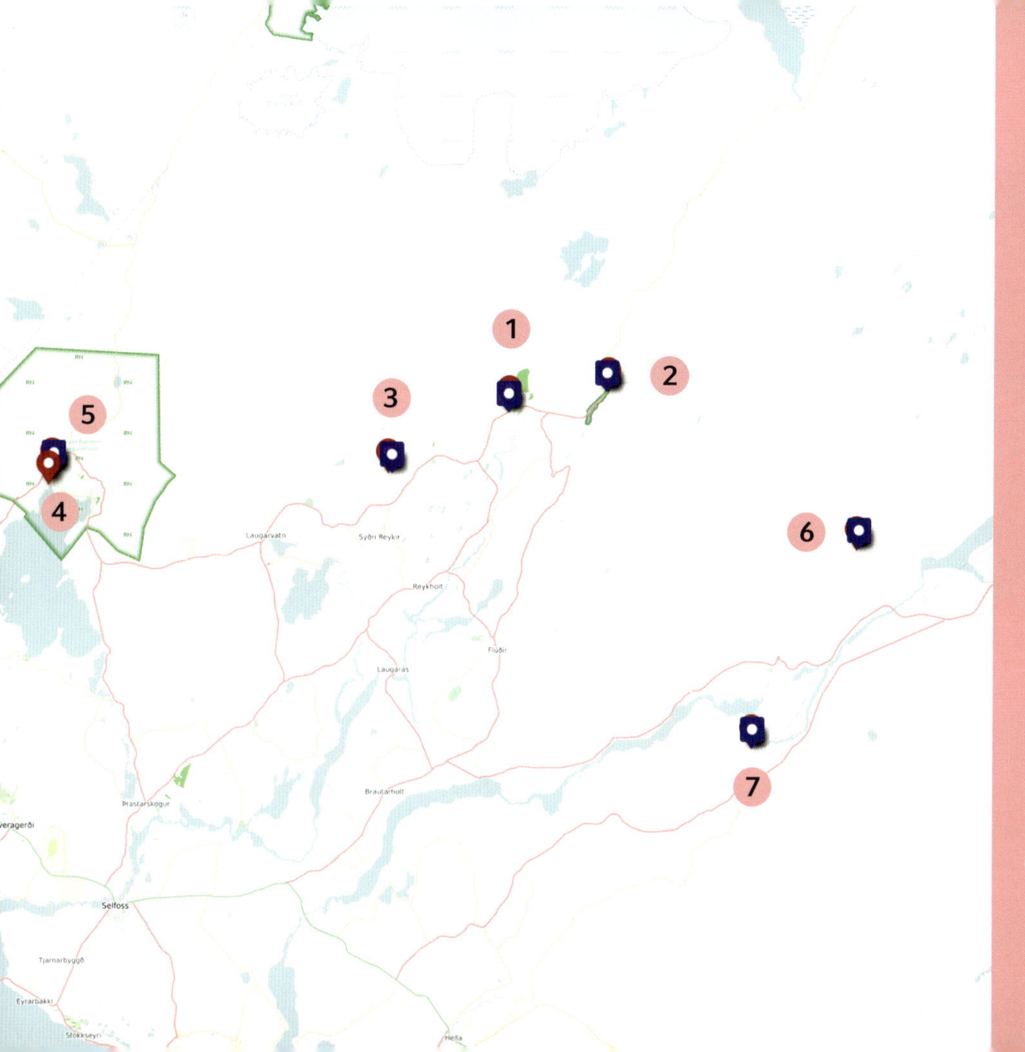

THE EXTENDED GOLDEN CIRCLE AND THE HIDDEN WATERFALLS

TOUR 4

1 GEYSIR AND STROKKUR

2 GULLFOSS

3 BRÚARFOSS

4 ÞINGVELLIR

5 ÖXARÁRFOSS

6 HÁIFOSS

7 ÞJÓFAFOSS

Parking Area

Photo Location

1 GEYSIR AND STROKKUR

Distance: About 50 minutes from Selfoss
Best time of day: Sunrise, sunset, or at night
Best time of year: Summer, fall, or winter
Equipment: No special requirements
Tour type: Self-drive
Parking area coordinates: 64.309415, –20.300758
Location coordinates: 64.312430, –20.300381

A geyser is a hot-water spring that sporadically erupts, sending hot water and steam up into the air. The most famous geyser in the world and the one all others are named after is at Haukadalur in Iceland—a highly active high-temperature geothermal area located close to Laugarvatn. The geyser has been inactive for a while now and, despite attempts by Icelanders to get it to erupt using soft soap, the Stóri Geysir (which means "Great Geyser") is still slumbering and erupts randomly and rarely.

By contrast, the smaller Strokkur ("Butter Barrel") geyser is the reason thousands of tourists make the pilgrimage to Haukadalur. Strokkur shoots a water fountain up to 80 feet into the air every 10 minutes or so. Although I have seen it numerous times, I am still amazed by this extraordinary natural force. The Icelanders have often discussed introducing paid entry or parking fees for the Geysir area, but so far, fees have not been implemented.

To get there, take Route 1 to the west out of Selfoss and turn right onto Route 35 just after the gas station at the end of town. Follow the road until you arrive at the parking area and visitor center at Geysir. The site includes a

Strokkur in golden winter light
(f/10 · 1/60 sec. · ISO 31 · 14mm · Filter: Soft GND16)

large, well-appointed gift shop and a café that is nice but quite expensive.

If you cross the road from the parking area, you end up directly in the geothermal area that Geysir and Strokkur are part of. There are signs of activity everywhere, with steam and bubbles emerging randomly from the Earth's crust. In recent years, the authorities have erected increasing numbers of fences and barriers to prevent people from injuring themselves. Plenty of signs warn of the extremely high temperatures that are present just below the surface.

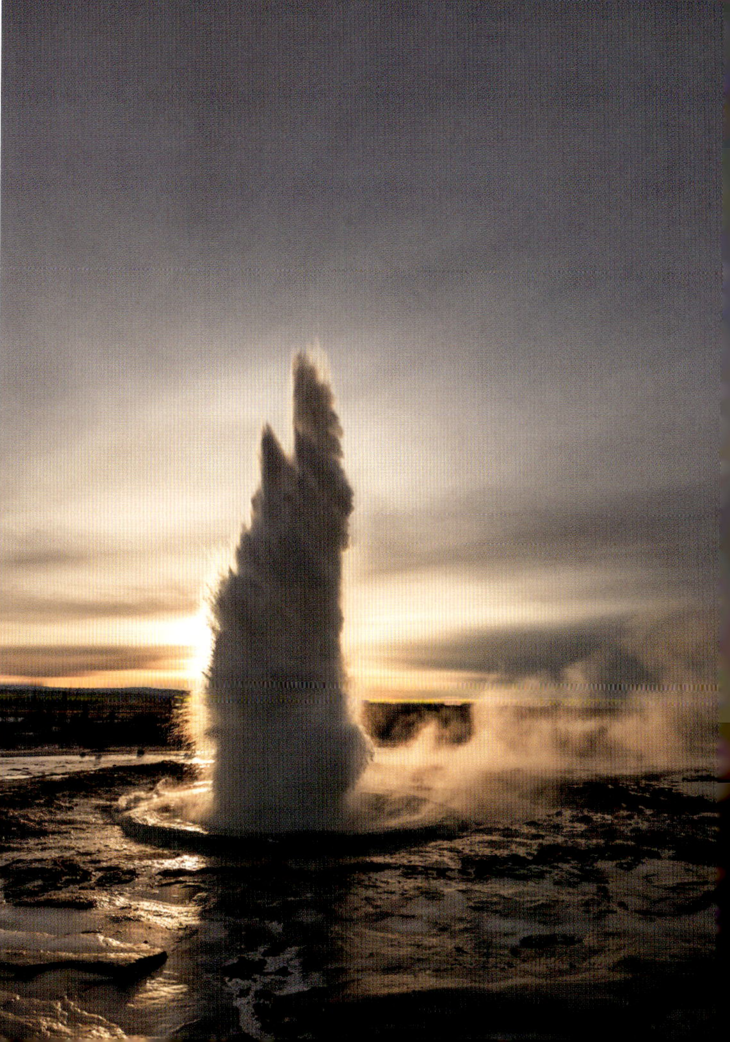

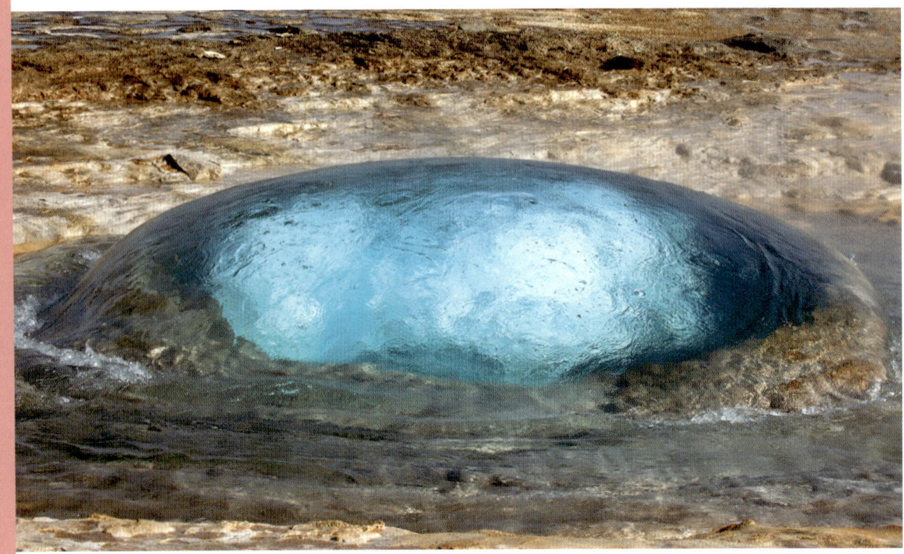

Just before it erupts, Strokkur's bubbling water glows bright blue (f/10 · 1/640 sec. · ISO 200 · 105mm)

Try just watching Strokkur for a while and make yourself familiar with its rhythm before you attempt to take any photos. Just before an eruption, the water actually starts to appear in increasingly large, pulsing gulps and, before the actual eruption occurs, a bubble forms just above the maw of the geyser and glows blue in the sunlight.

This bubbling is usually the precursor to an eruption, which hurls an enormous fountain of hot water and steam up into the air. Take note of the direction the wind is blowing and make sure you are standing upwind from the geyser if you don't want to give yourself and your camera a hot shower. Photos of the geyser also look better if you can find an angle that keeps the surrounding buildings out of the frame.

In general, I prefer not to include people in my landscape photos, but in this case, a couple of observers marveling at the spectacle of an erupting geyser can make an image all the more impressive. Whichever approach you take, visiting the site later in the day ensures that fewer people will be around and makes the experience even more dramatic.

I have captured some great images shooting into the sun on winter mornings with Strokkur in the foreground and the sun illuminating the wonderful landscape with golden, early-morning hues.

TOP TIP

About 15 minutes from Selfoss along Route 35 is a parking area with a sign pointing to Kerið. If you have time, take a quick detour to see this beautifully symmetrical 160-foot crater. The entry fee for the site is 350 Icelandic Krona (about $3.50) at the time of writing.

TOP TIP

There is a pleasant and surprisingly quiet campsite right near Strokkur. I have camped there a couple of times in summer and I thoroughly enjoyed wandering around the area at night.

Parking Area

Location

2 GULLFOSS

Distance: About 1 hour from Selfoss, or 10 minutes from Geysir
Best time of day: Sunrise, sunset, or at night
Best time of year: Summer, fall, or winter
Equipment: Rain jacket and a towel for your camera
Tour type: Self-drive
Parking area coordinates: 64.324981, –20.125385
Location coordinates: 64.326448, –20.123331

Ten minutes on from Geysir and Strokkur is Gullfoss ("Golden Waterfall"), one of Iceland's best-known waterfalls. The falls are formed by the Hvítá River, which plunges 100 feet over two levels set almost at right angles to one another. Below the falls, the water flows through a canyon that is up to 230 feet deep. Gullfoss is a monumental sight, and you can walk right up to the edge of the first level. Take care not to get too close to the edge. In 2017, a visitor fell into the falls for reasons that no one has been able to explain. His body was eventually found a month later.

Gullfoss is located about 10 minutes from Geysir/Strokkur on Route 35. There is a parking area above the falls with a newly built visitor center and café, and another, older parking area right next to the falls. To get there, just after you see the first blue sign for Gullfoss, turn right onto an unmarked road that follows the river until you reach the parking area. From the parking area, it is only a few yards on foot to the falls.

There are a thousand ways to photograph Gullfoss, but the views most people know are taken from the wooden rail that marks the

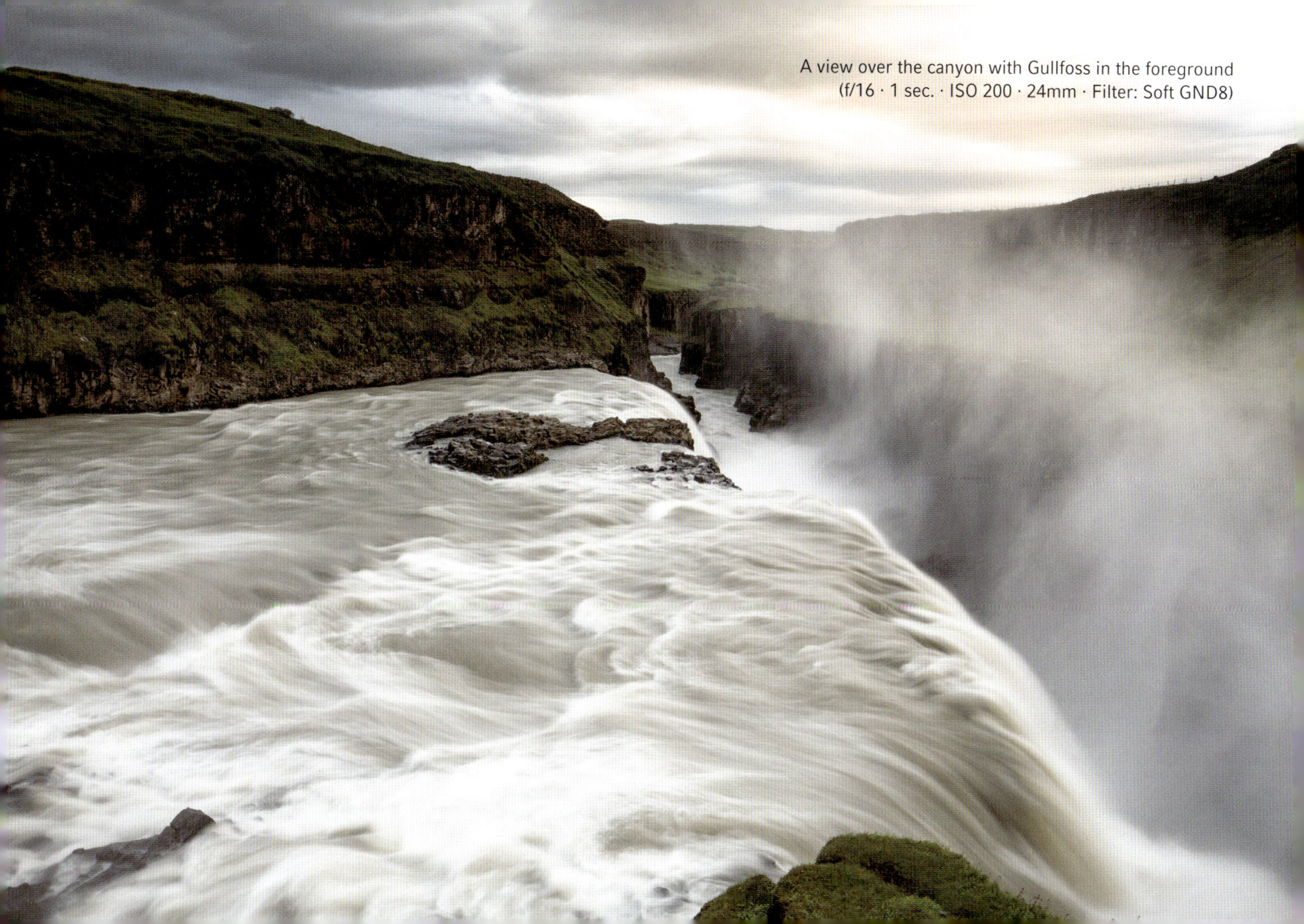
A view over the canyon with Gullfoss in the foreground
(f/16 · 1 sec. · ISO 200 · 24mm · Filter: Soft GND8)

TOP TIP
The wind gusts at Gullfoss can soak you and your gear with spray from the cascades. Try to get a feel for the rhythm of the wind and use the breaks between gusts to capture your photos.

path at the end of the parking area. Another great spot is on a small, natural stone platform near the edge of the falls, and just in front of that platform is a great view over the edge of the second level as the water plunges into the canyon below. The spray from the falls creates a mystical atmosphere and partially hides the wooden visitor platform. As at Geysir, if you want to enjoy the view without the usual crowds, it's worth visiting late in the evening.

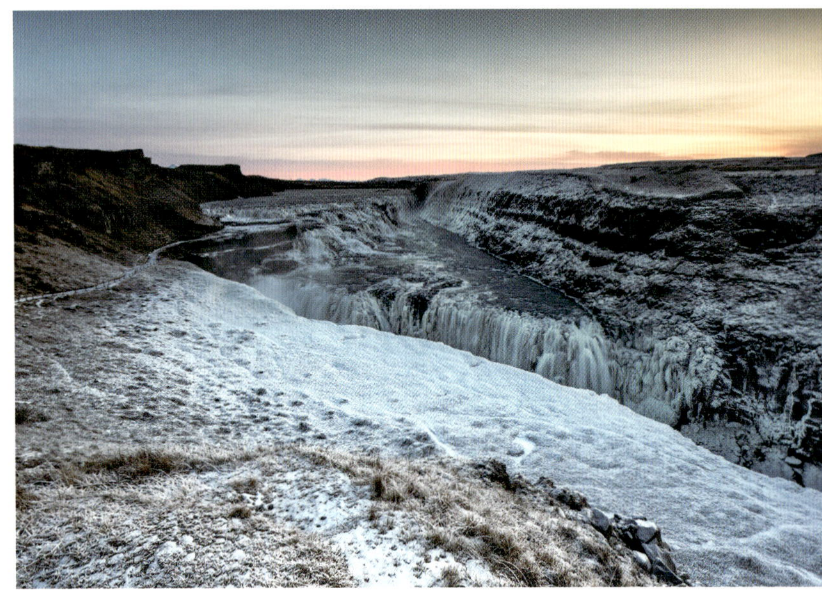

Sunrise on an icy winter morning bathes the landscape in wonderfully soft light
(f/8 · 1/5 sec. · ISO 100 · 19mm · Filter: Soft GND16)

Parking Area

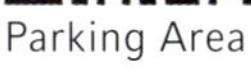

Photo Location

3 BRÚARFOSS

Distance: About 25 minutes from Gullfoss, or 15 minutes from Geysir
Best time of day: Sunset
Best time of year: Summer, fall, or winter
Equipment: Rubber boots or waders
Tour type: Self-drive
Parking area coordinates: 64.263611, –20.509444
Location coordinates: 64.264290, –20.515302

The next location on the traditional "Golden Circle" route is Þingvellir, but there is another treat you can visit on the way. Right next to the busy road to Þingvellir is a large area full of vacation homes, and hidden behind them is Brúarfoss, one of Iceland's most beautiful waterfalls. It is not so much its size, but rather its shape and the beautiful blue color of the water that flows into the ravine below that make it so attractive. There is a notch in the riverbed just before the falls, and the water flows in and around it in countless rivulets. This notch continues in the riverbed after the waterfall and forms a ravine with a strong current that fills the water with bubbles.

To reach Brúarfoss, take Route 35 from Geysir/Gullfoss toward Selfoss, and then take the turnoff onto Route 37 (Laugarvatnsvegur). You will soon see an area covered with small trees, which is where the vacation homes start. There are several badly signposted roads through the area and some roads are gated. To avoid confusion, navigate to the following coordinates—64.252000, –20.489539—and enter the village precisely there. At the second turnoff, follow the main road as it curves to

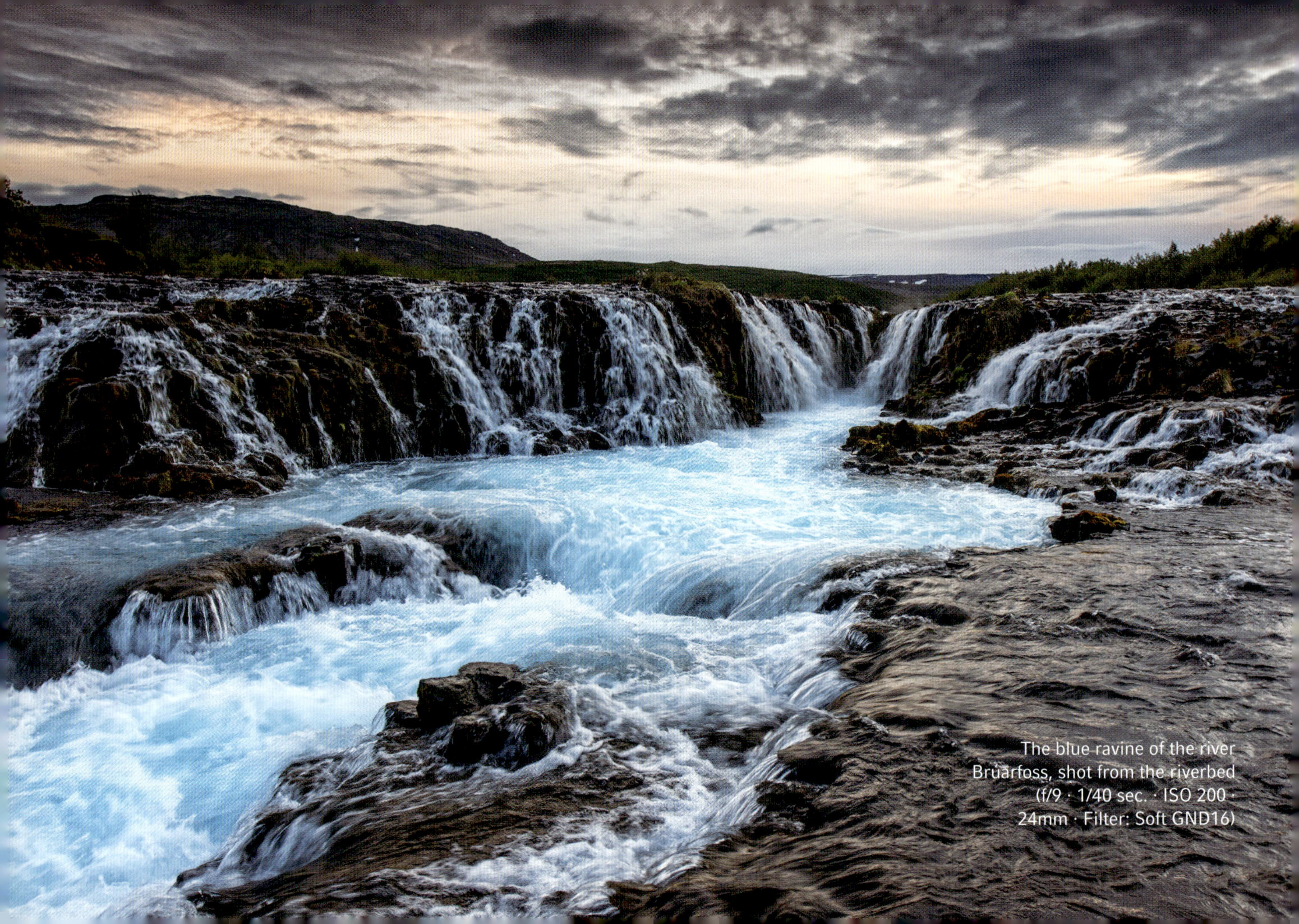

The blue ravine of the river Brúarfoss, shot from the riverbed (f/9 · 1/40 sec. · ISO 200 · 24mm · Filter: Soft GND16)

Vacation homes

the left. You will then see a long, straight road ahead, which you can follow to the parking area (see the coordinates listed above). This is not an official parking area, so make sure your vehicle isn't obstructing anyone. If you have found the right place, you should see a stream with a bridge over it. Cross the bridge onto a muddy path that takes a few steps uphill to a T-junction, where you turn right. The rest of the path is overgrown but, if you stick to it, it takes you directly to the waterfall. You will be able to hear the rushing water before you see it. If there has been a lot of rain, the path itself can be fully submerged. The first time I went there, I had to wade through about 10 inches of water. Since then, I always wear rubber boots when I am shooting at Brúarfoss.

There is a solid wooden bridge that crosses the river right next to the waterfall, and the best view of the falls is from about two-thirds of the way across. To get a view of the entire waterfall and the ravine without the rail on the bridge

WARNING!

Take great care here as the rocks on the riverbed are slippery, the current is strong, and the petrified lava has very sharp edges. One false move here could be fatal. Don't get too close to the deepest part of the ravine. A couple of yards in are enough to get a stunning, unhindered view of the waterfall in all its glory.

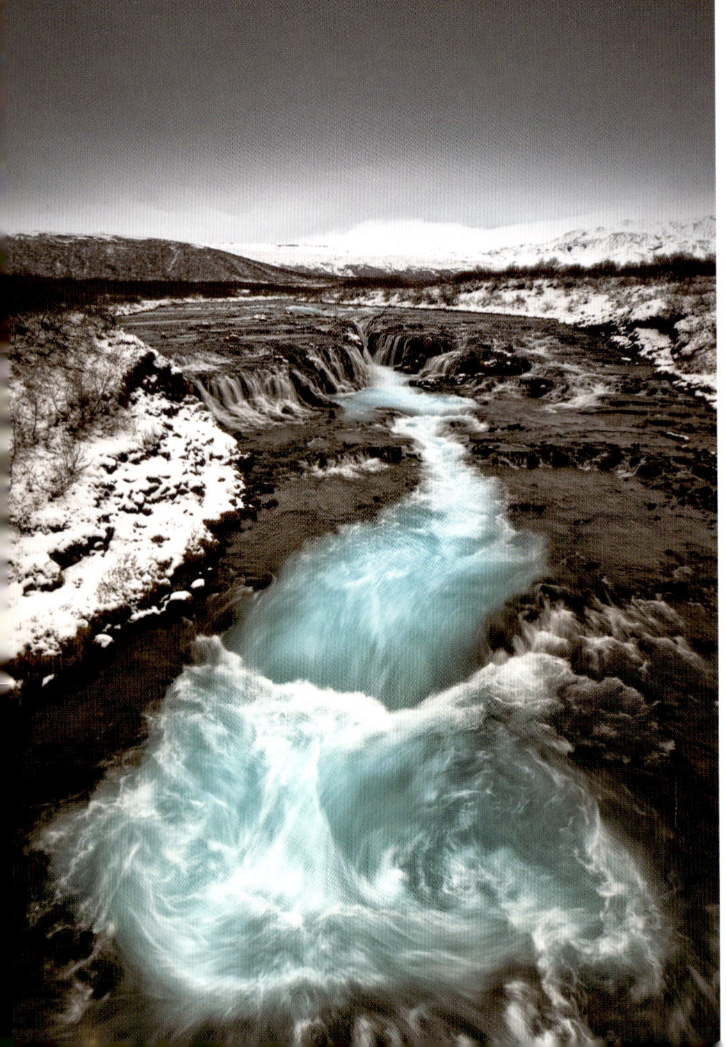

getting in the way, I straddle the rail with my tripod and rest its front leg on the beam jutting out beyond the rail.

There is another great view from the right-hand riverbank (looking at the waterfall from the bridge). Go back to your original starting point, where you will see a steep, narrow path that takes you down to the river. Take care here, as the path is usually very slippery. Walk a little way along the riverbank toward the falls and wade into the water toward the main channel.

The view from the bridge gives a great impression of the sublime beauty of the waterfall
(f/10 · 1/5 sec. · ISO 125 · 16mm · Filter: Soft GND16)

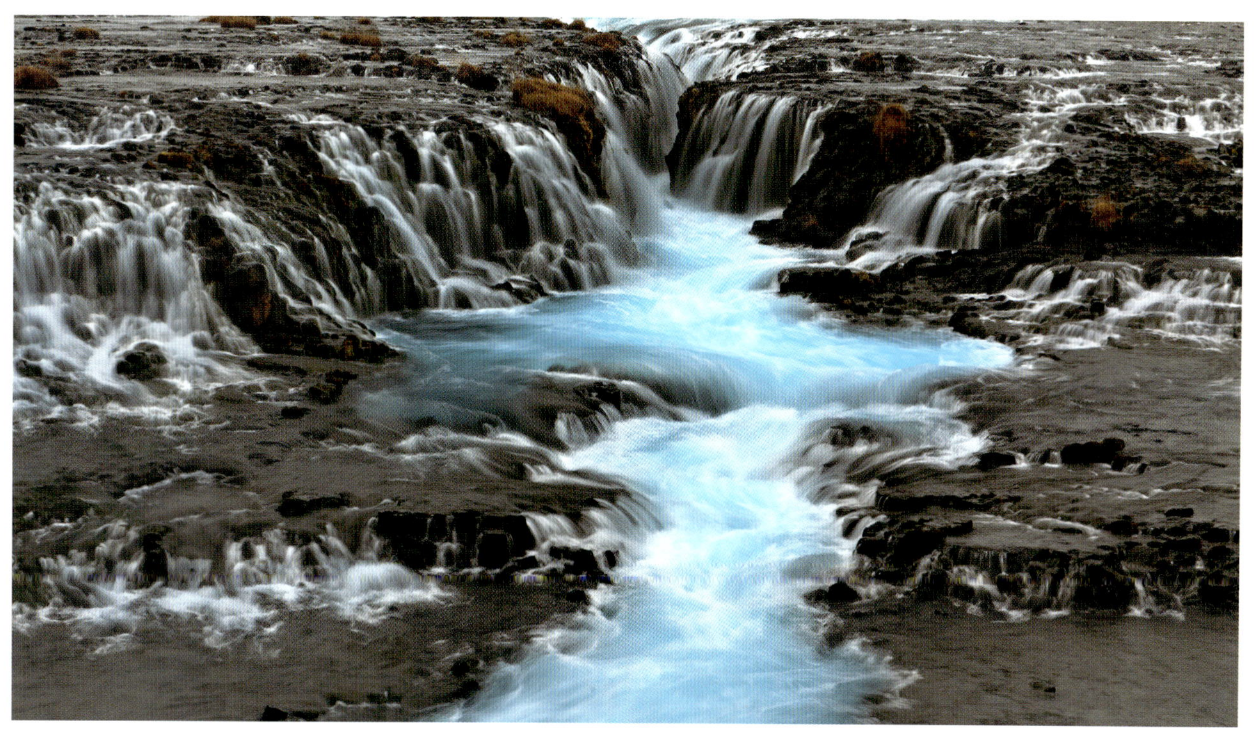

A cropped detail of a photo shot using a long lens shows the countless mini waterfalls that make up the main cascade (f/14 · 1/4 sec. · ISO 100 · 70mm)

4 ÞINGVELLIR

Distance: About 45 minutes from Selfoss or Brúarfoss
Best time of day: Sunset or nighttime
Best time of year: Summer, fall, or winter
Equipment: No special requirements
Tour type: Self-drive
Parking area coordinates: 64.264741, –21.114709
Location coordinates: 64.255908, –21.123565

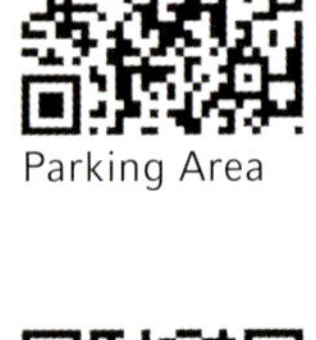

Parking Area

Photo Location

Þingvellir is located in southwest Iceland near Lake Þingvallavatn. It is a place of great historical significance, and is the site of the original Althingi, the national parliament of Iceland that was established there in 930 AD.

From the very beginnings of settlement in Iceland, the annual Althingi meeting took place on this site, where laws were made and judgments were handed down. The Althingi is one of the oldest parliaments in the world and was only abolished by the Danes in 1798. The modern Republic of Iceland was established there on June 17, 1944, and the 50th anniversary of the declaration was celebrated there as well.

The Icelandic history book Íslendingabók reports that the first settlers gave Grímur Geitskór the job of finding a suitable meeting place. After a long search, he chose Þingvellir because it was easy to reach from all the other settlements, and the river Öxará, which flows through the area, provided sufficient water and fish for all the participants.

In addition to its historical significance, Þingvellir is also an important geological

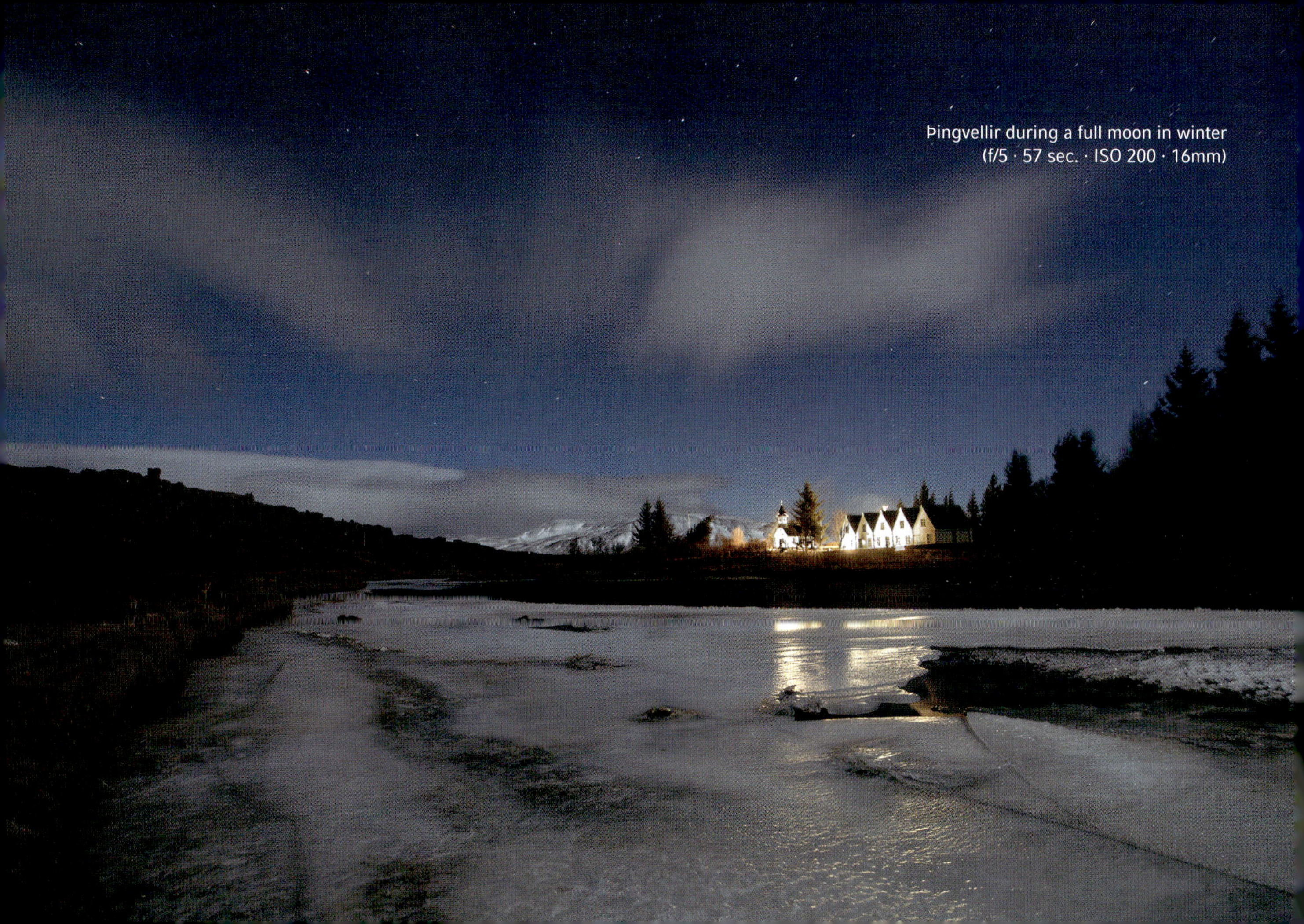

Þingvellir during a full moon in winter
(f/5 · 57 sec. · ISO 200 · 16mm)

site. It lies in a rift valley that marks the crest of the Mid-Atlantic Ridge and the boundary between the North American and Eurasian tectonic plates. If you take a walk along the Almannagjá (the "All Men Gorge," so-named because all participants at the Althingi could fit into the space between the rocks), the walls of the gorge are formed by the edges of the two tectonic plates. They are still moving and drift farther apart every year.

Along with Geysir and Gullfoss, Þingvellir forms the so-called Golden Circle, which is probably Iceland's most heavily marketed attraction, with crowds to match. There is a large, pay parking area above the site next the visitor center (in 2017, a day ticket cost 500 Icelandic Krone—about $4.75) and you will find another, smaller parking area at the opposite end of the Almannagjá. As of early 2017 the smaller lot was still free, and it makes a great jumping-off point for Þingvellir and Öxarárfoss (next section).

Take Route 37 from Brúarfoss and take the turnoff onto Route 365. Then take Route 36 to the right (northward) until you reach the tourist information point at Þingvellir. Route 36 carries on to the main parking area, so you need to turn left onto Route 361. Take a right at the next junction, drive past one parking area and stop at the next.

To reach our next spot, follow the marked walking path along the west side of the parking area to the left. You will pass a small pool and a rivulet that goes under the path. In the deep, dark past, this Drekkingarhylur ("Drowning Pool") is where women who were sentenced to death were executed by drowning. Men who were sentenced to death were either hanged or burned at the stake nearby.

You can continue on along the Almannagjá or take the alternative path to the church and the houses that surround it. If you take the latter route, there is small bridge to the south of the church, where you can capture some nice views of the houses with the Öxará River in the foreground.

There are informational signs along the Almannagjá that tell you more about the history of the site. If you follow the Almannagjá all the way to the end, you will end up at a wooden platform that gives you a view of the area from a perspective that is ideal for taking photos.

TOP TIP

The crowds of daytime visitors at Þingvellir are becoming larger all the time, so these days I only go there at less busy times. The true magic of the place becomes really palpable during a full moon in winter or in the half-light of an Icelandic summer night.

If you stroll along the Almannagjá at full moon in winter, you are sure to get a feel for how the sagas and myths of the past came to be. You are sure to spot trolls and other mythical creatures at every turn!

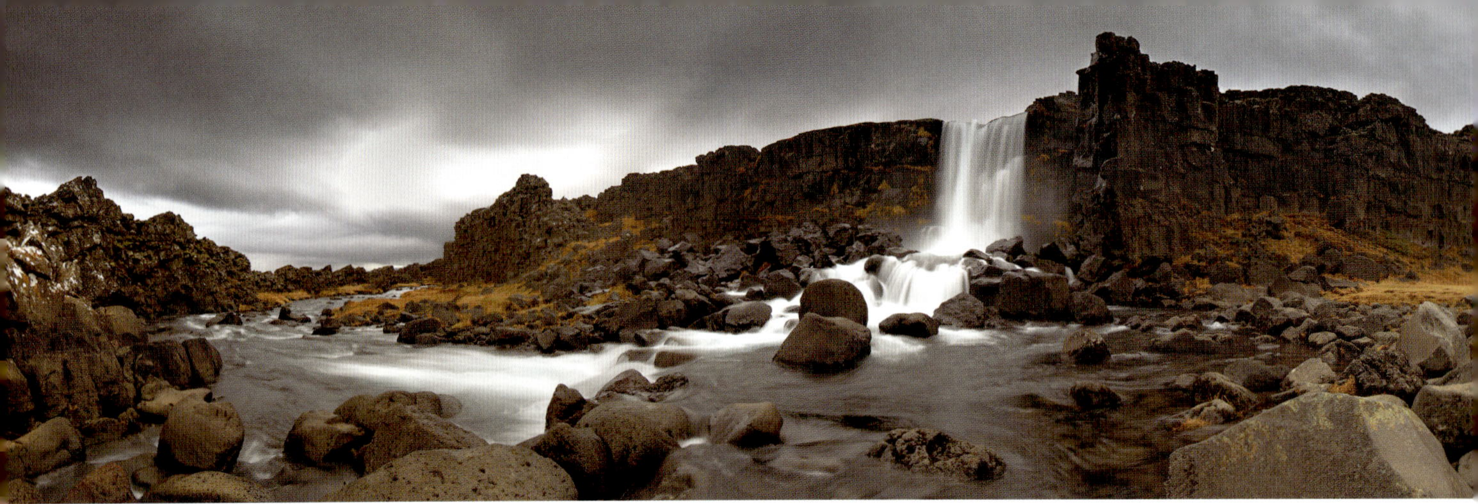

Parking Area

Photo Location

5 ÖXARÁRFOSS

Distance: About 45 minutes from Selfoss, or 45 minutes from Brúarfoss
Best time of day: Sunset or nighttime
Best time of year: Summer, fall, or winter
Equipment: No special requirements
Tour type: Self-drive
Parking area coordinates: 64.264741, –21.114709
Location coordinates: 64.255908, –21.123565

◀ Early winter mood lighting at Öxarárfoss (f/10 – 0.8 sec. · ISO 100 · 27mm · Filter: Soft GND16)

An icy winter night at the half-frozen Öxarárfoss (f/6.3 · 30 sec. · ISO 1600 · 16mm) ▶

This waterfall, which is probably man-made, is just a short walk from the parking area at Þingvellir. The Öxará River was diverted to Þingvellir to ensure there was enough water for everyone at the annual Althingi meetings.

The walking path is well surfaced and leads off to the right (in the opposite direction from the previous tour) and takes you down a small flight of steps into the gorge that leads to Öxarárfoss. If you follow the path to the left, you will hear the falls before you see them. When you get there, you will see a wooden platform that offers perfect views of the waterfall as it plunges over the canyon wall. In winter, the river is often reduced to a trickle.

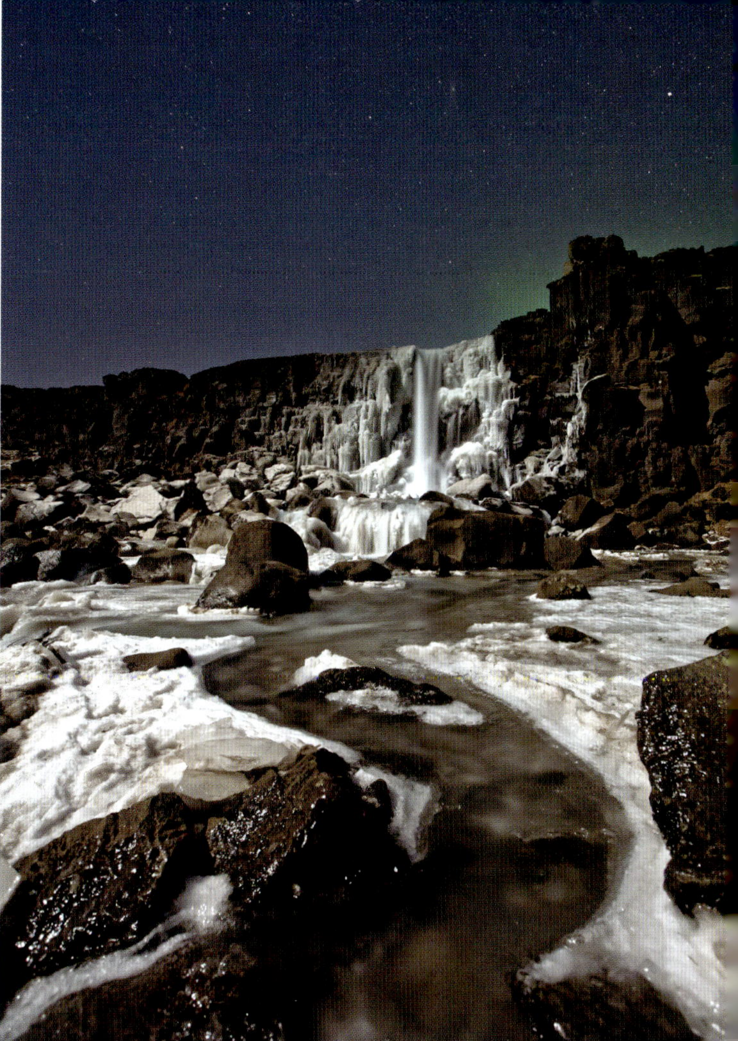

Parking Area

Photo Location

6 HÁIFOSS

Distance: About 90 minutes from Selfoss
Best time of day: Sunset
Best time of year: Summer or fall
Equipment: No special requirements
Vehicle: 4WD required
Tour type: Self-drive
Parking area coordinates: 64.206859, –19.678317
Location coordinates: 64.206753, –19.682075

At 400 feet, Háifoss is Iceland's third largest waterfall. Its sheer height, the deep canyon, and the secluded location make it a must-see. To get there, follow Route 1 eastward to the turnoff for Route 30 (Skeiða- og Hrunamannavegur), which you then follow to the north to the turnoff for Route 32 (Þjórsárdalsvegur). Take a right and drive for about 30 minutes to the turnoff to the left for Route 332 (northward). You will pass a café, and the farther you go, the worse the road gets. Even with a jeep, take care when negotiating rocks and potholes, as getting a flat out there in the wilderness is no fun at all. Once you reach the waterfall, you will find a parking area that is just as rocky and rutted as the road leading to it.

A broad path leads from the parking area to a platform with great views of Háifoss and the smaller neighboring waterfall Granni ("Neighbor").

You can capture an even better view if, instead of heading directly to the platform, you head off into the fields to the right. The ground is rocky but brings you directly to the edge of

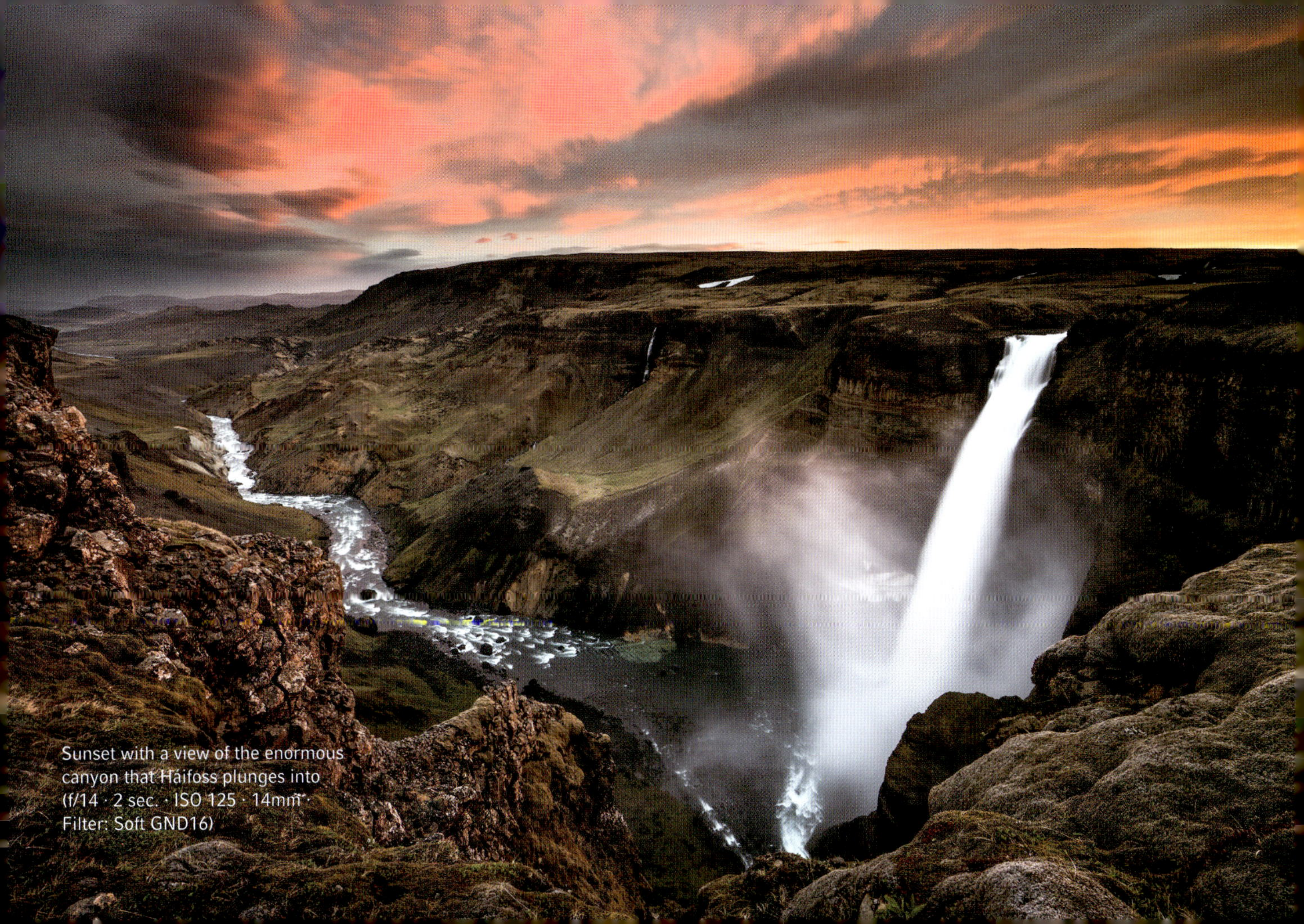

Sunset with a view of the enormous canyon that Háifoss plunges into (f/14 · 2 sec. · ISO 125 · 14mm · Filter: Soft GND16)

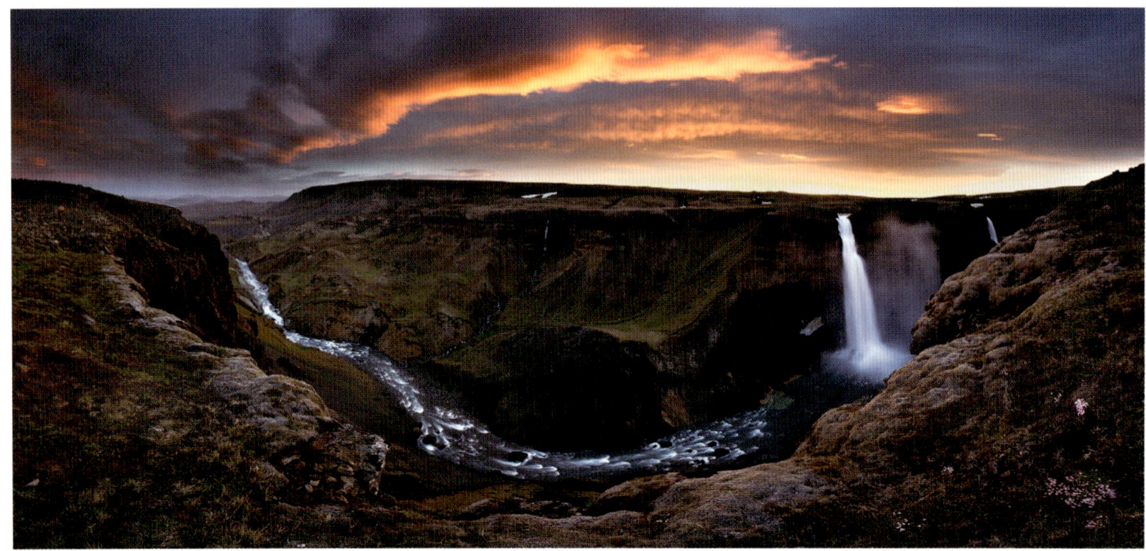

This panorama gives you an idea of the scale of the canyon and the two waterfalls that feed into it (f/14 · 1/6 sec. · ISO 125 · 14mm · Filter: Soft GND16)

the canyon, where you can see Háifoss and, to the left, the long canyon it flows into. There is a broad, moss-covered rock nearby that makes a great foreground detail for pictures of this spectacular scene.

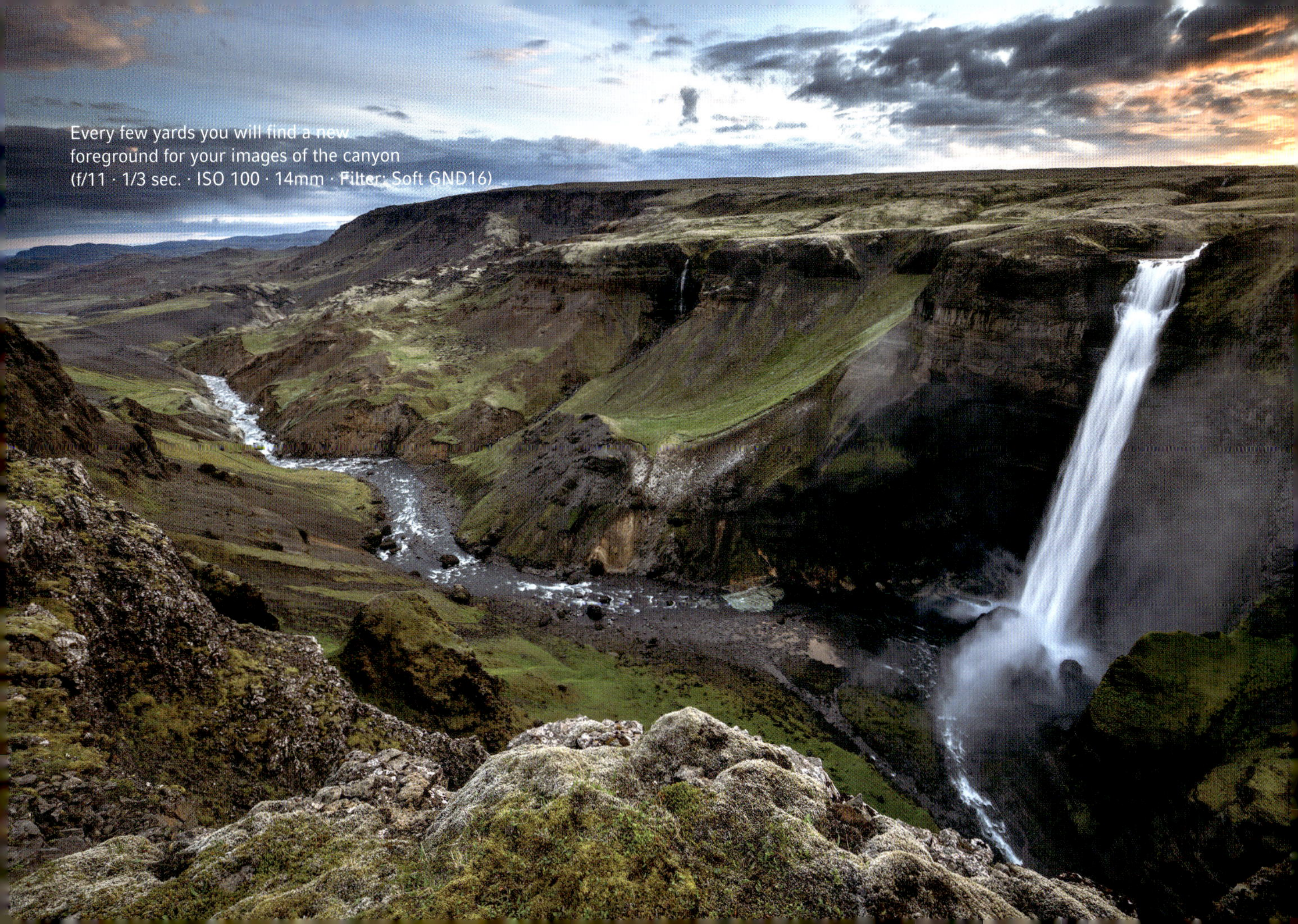

Every few yards you will find a new foreground for your images of the canyon (f/11 · 1/3 sec. · ISO 100 · 14mm · Filter: Soft GND16)

Parking Area

Photo Location

7 ÞJÓFAFOSS

Distance: About 50 minutes from Selfoss, or 45 minutes from Háifoss
Best time of day: Sunset
Best time of year: Summer, fall, or winter
Equipment: No special requirements
Vehicle: 4WD required
Tour type: Self-drive
Parking area coordinates: 64.056006, –19.867327
Location coordinates: 64.056725, –19.868485

Þjófafoss ("Thieves Waterfall") lies at the foot of Búrfell, a striking mountain that makes an ideal background for photos of the waterfall. The river Þjórsá forms a curve around the base of the mountain before plunging over a broad cliff into a semicircular pool.

To get there from Háifoss, drive back along Route 332 to Route 32. Turn left and continue on to the junction of Route 26 and F26. Turn right on F26 (which isn't completely paved), and after about 20 minutes you will see a turn-off to Þjófafoss on the right. Take this for about four kilometers until you see a small parking area, identified by a gate that someone put up in the middle of nowhere.

If you are coming from Selfoss, take Route 1 to the east to the turnoff for Route 26, where you turn left and follow the road for about 30 minutes to the turnoff toward Þjófafoss, and then proceed as described above.

Walk along the river toward the waterfall until you have a good view of the cascade and Búrfell. The jagged lava formations that sur-round the streambed make a great frame

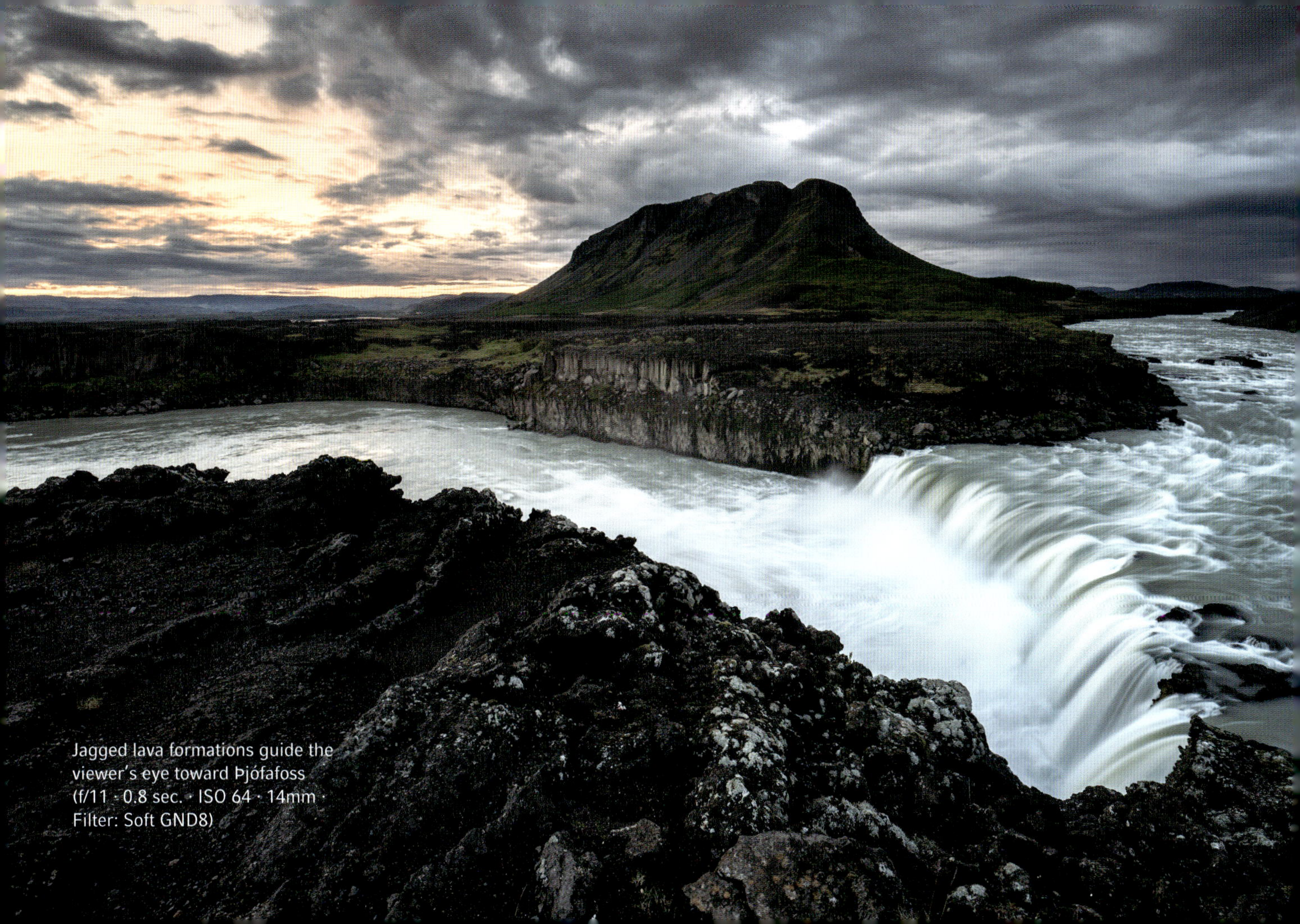

Jagged lava formations guide the viewer's eye toward Þjófafoss (f/11 · 0.8 sec. · ISO 64 · 14mm · Filter: Soft GND8)

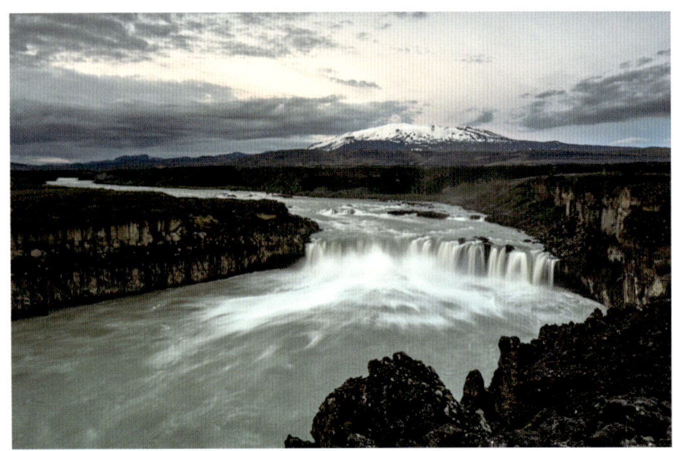

The view over the falls to the snow-capped volcano Hekla
(f/11 · 2.5 sec. · ISO 31 · 24mm · Filter: Soft GND8)

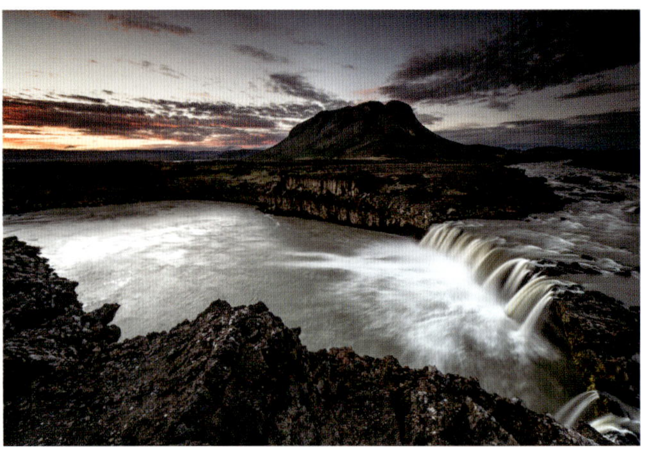

The last light of the fading day illuminates Mount Búrfell and gives Þjófafoss an eerie glow
(f/14 · 3 sec. · ISO 50 · 14mm · Filter: Soft GND8)

for your photos and add atmosphere to the scene.

This is also a great place to shoot panoramas. If you look to the right of the falls, on a clear day you will see a perfectly formed, snow-capped shield volcano called Hekla. This 4,900-foot volcano is one of Iceland's most active volcanoes and makes an exciting element in a panorama photo of the area.

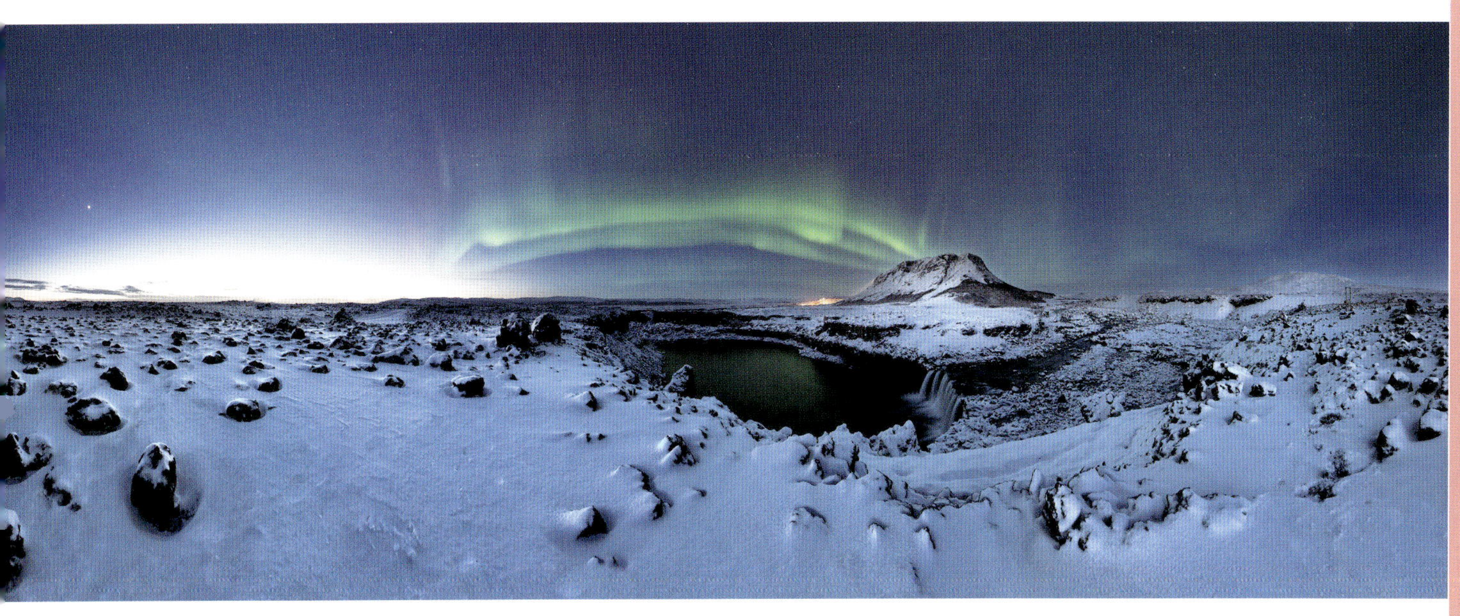

Northern Lights illuminate the sky while the sun sets, providing a unique panorama (f/2.8 · 10 sec. · ISO 1000 · 14mm)

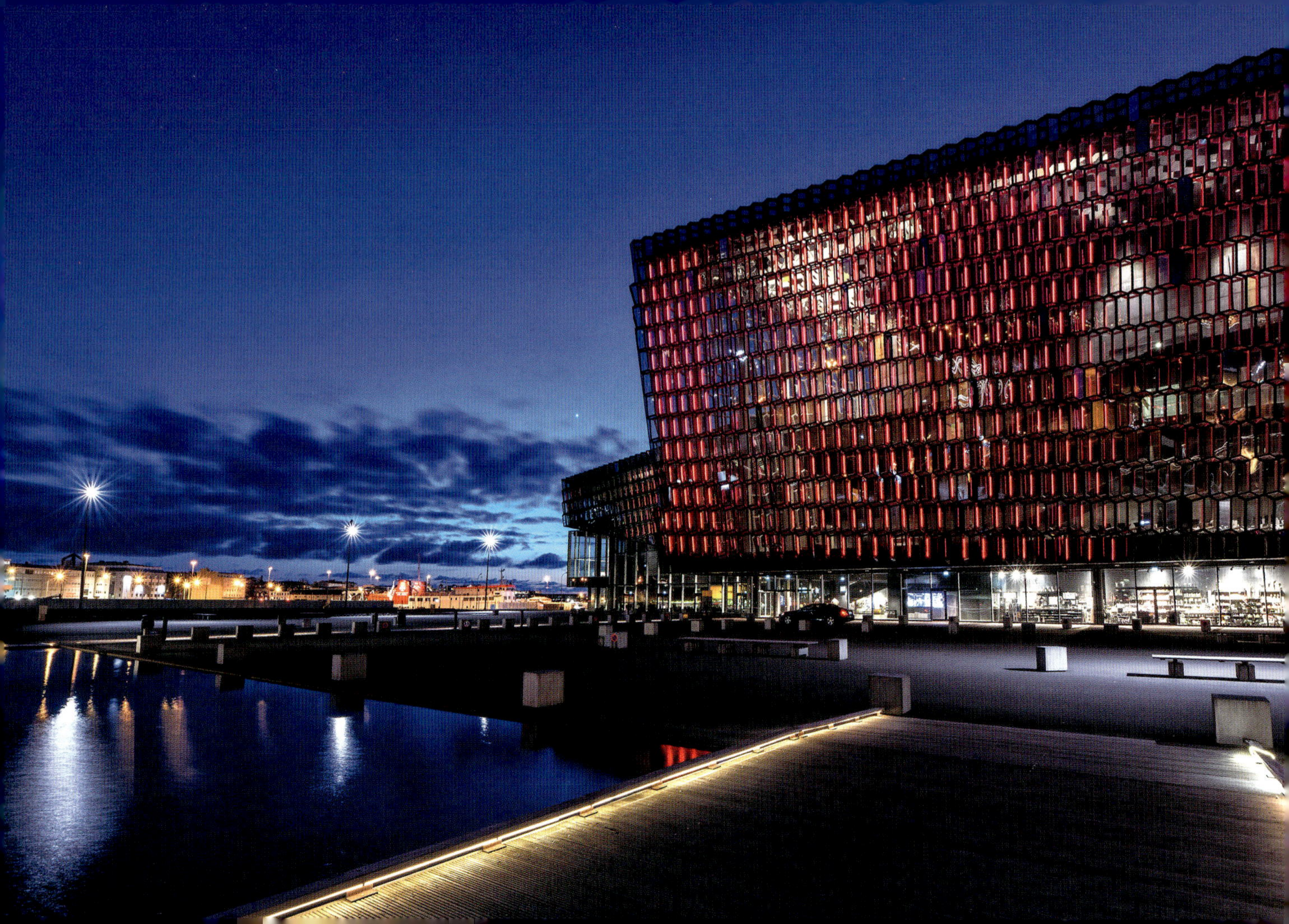

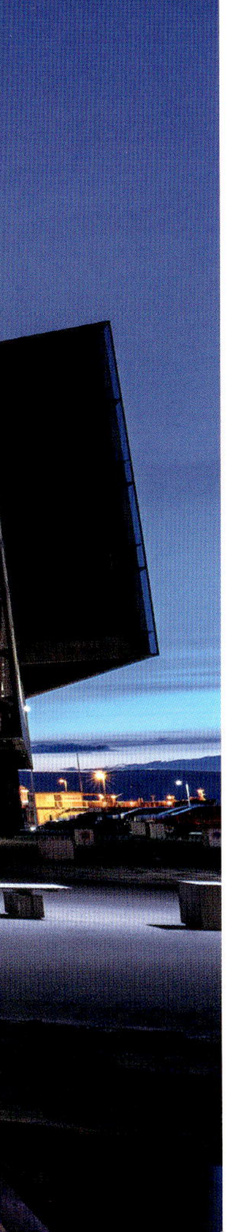

TOUR 5
REYKJAVÍK

Reykjavík is the capital of Iceland and is the starting and end point of all the tours described in this book. It is also a great place to visit in its own right. It has population of about 120,000, which is about a third of the entire population of the island. Reykjavík means "bay of smokes." According to the Landnámabók, it was founded by Ingólfur Arnarson, the first settler on the island. As well as a selection of great restaurants, shops, cafés, and bars, Reykjavík is also home to a number of museums and historically significant buildings. It is an ideal place for a stopover or for finishing up a trip.

Reykjavík is a young and lively city with public art everywhere, so there are plenty of photo

TOUR 5 BASICS
Overall time required: 1–3 days
Travel time: About 45 minutes from Keflavík Airport
Lodging: Reykjavík has a huge number of places to stay. I prefer privately rented apartments to hotels, as they offer more space and give you the opportunity to cook for yourself.

opportunities. There are unusually painted houses, art installations, and interesting architecture spread all around the city. One of the most interesting buildings is Hallgrímskirkja church. This church was completed in 1986, and more than 50 percent of the construction was financed through donations. The façade is reminiscent of the basalt stacks found all over Iceland, while the interior is a model of Scandinavian simplicity. I could easily write a whole book on Reykjavík, but I have selected my two favorite locations for inclusion here. You are sure to find many wonderful places when you visit the city.

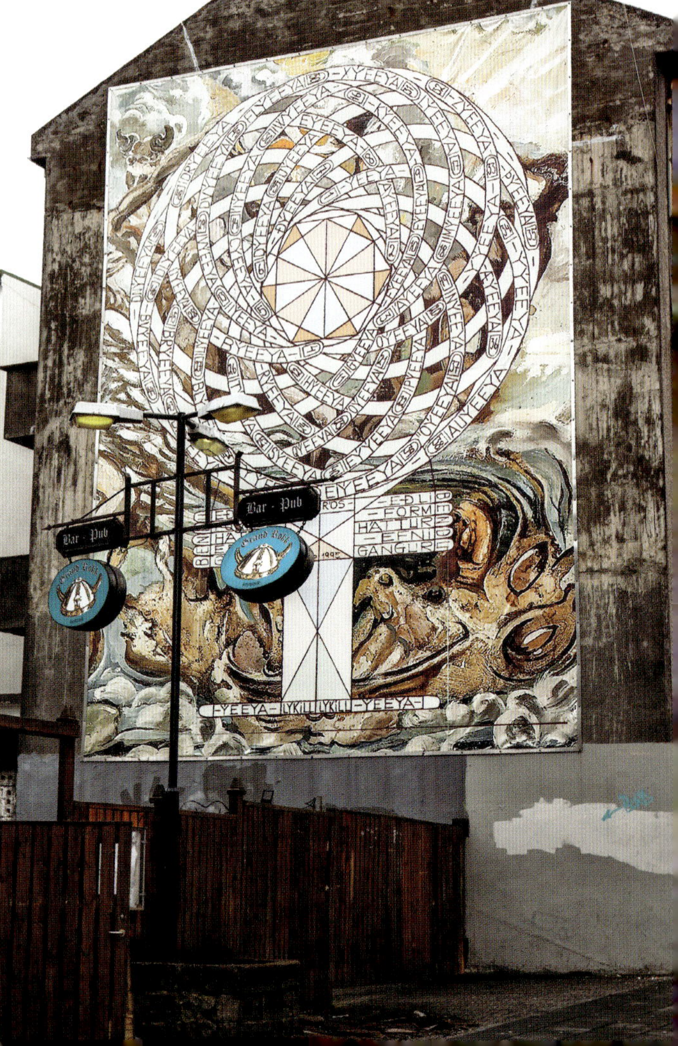

There is public art around nearly every corner in Reykjavík
(f/7.1 · 1/320 sec. · ISO 200 · 55mm)

TOP TIPS

In addition to plenty of photogenic attractions, Reykjavík has loads of great places to eat and world-famous nightlife. Here are some of the places I have enjoyed.

Food:

Messinn: This is definitely the best fish restaurant I know of. Reservations are essential (*www.messinn.com*).

Íslenski barinn: Great for local dishes or high-end burgers (*www.islenskibarinn.is/net/en*).

Bæjarins Beztu Pylsur: This local favorite is a hotdog stand in the center of town that is immensely popular. Ordering "Einar með öllu" (pronounced "eyner mjeth uttloo") gets you a hotdog with everything on it (*www.bbp.is/information-in-english*).

Cafés:

Stofan Kaffihús: Here you will find cozy atmosphere and great coffee. Some tables have charging outlets for phones and laptops. This is the place to go to meet Icelanders and, now and then, me (*www.facebook.com/stofan.cafe*).

Bars:

Iceland is home to countless microbreweries, each of which offers its own unique beers. Two of my favorites are:

MicroBar: Set in a snug basement close to Stofan Kaffihús (*www.facebook.com/MicroBarIceland*).

Skúli: Probably my absolute favorite bar, with good (background) music and great beer *(www.facebook.com/skulicraft).*

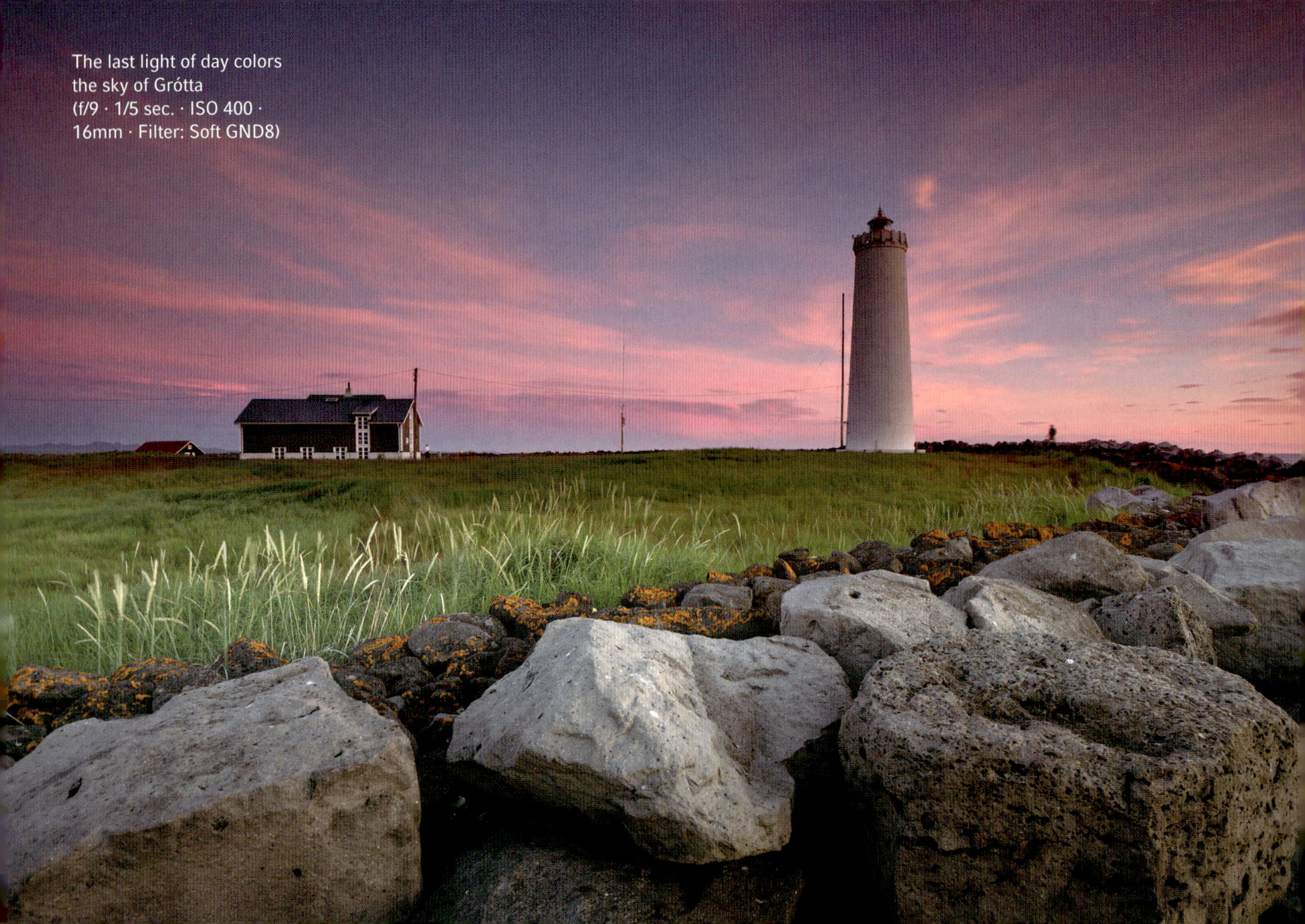

The last light of day colors the sky of Grótta (f/9 · 1/5 sec. · ISO 400 · 16mm · Filter: Soft GND8)

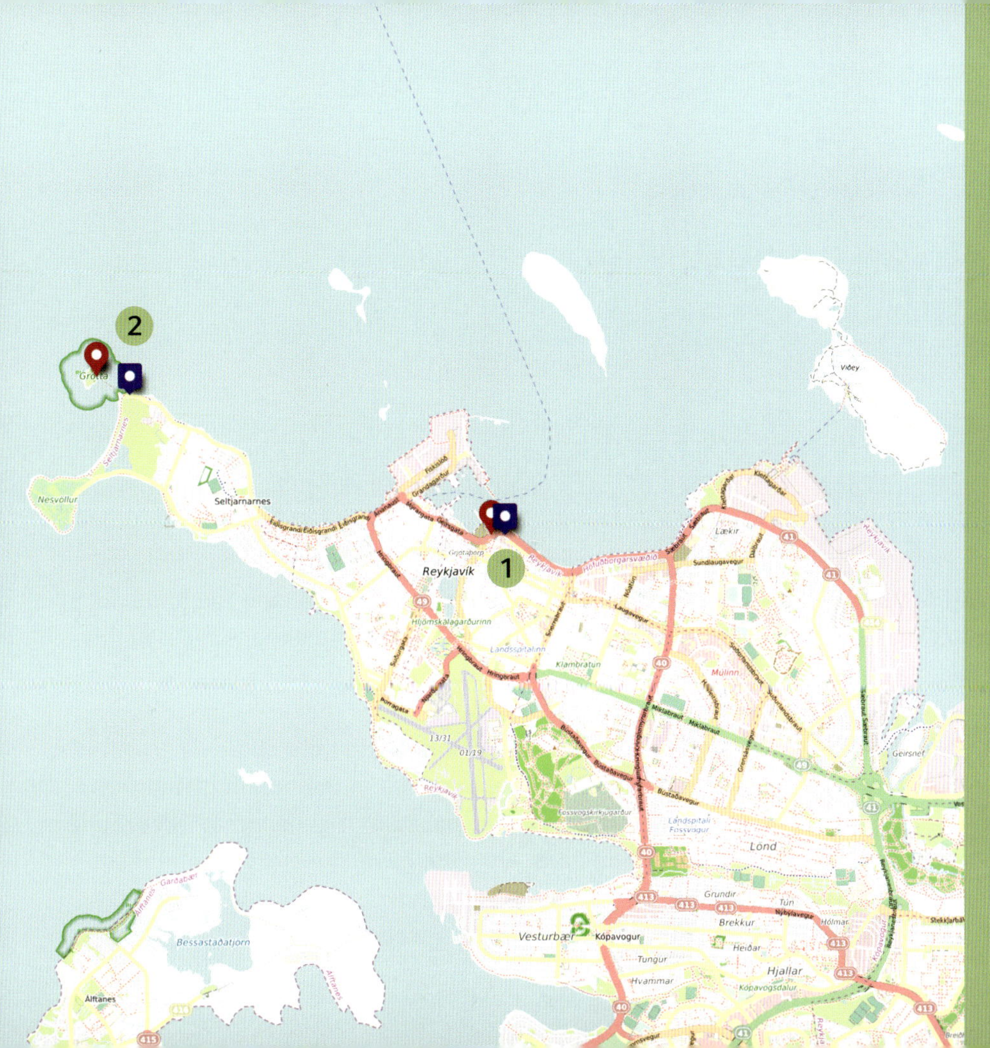

REYKJAVÍK

TOUR 5

1 HARPA

2 GRÓTTA

Parking Area

Photo Location

1 HARPA

Distance: On the waterfront in the center of the city
Best time of day: Sunset or nighttime
Best time of year: Summer, fall, or winter
Equipment: No special requirements
Tour type: Self-drive
Parking area coordinates: 64.149247, –21.929781
Location coordinates: 64.149416, –21.932887

Harpa is a concert hall and conference center. Despite the 2008 financial crisis—which halted construction on this center for a while—it was finally finished in 2011 thanks to the Icelanders voting to use public money to get their new landmark built, come what may. It is home to the Iceland Symphony Orchestra and the Icelandic National Opera. As well as the concert halls (which have moving walls for altering the acoustics), there is also a high-end flower shop and souvenir store where you can purchase stylish gifts to take home. The outer skin of the building has a honeycomb structure designed by Icelandic artist Ólafur Elíasson. The sheets of glass that make up the façade appear in different colors depending on the direction of the light illuminating them, and the building is artificially lit at night to make the most of this effect.

Night or evening is the best time to take photos of this amazing light show. There is a large pool in front of the building, and the boardwalks that span it make great foreground details. On calm days, the entire complex is reflected beautifully in the water. The best reflections can be seen from the left-hand side of

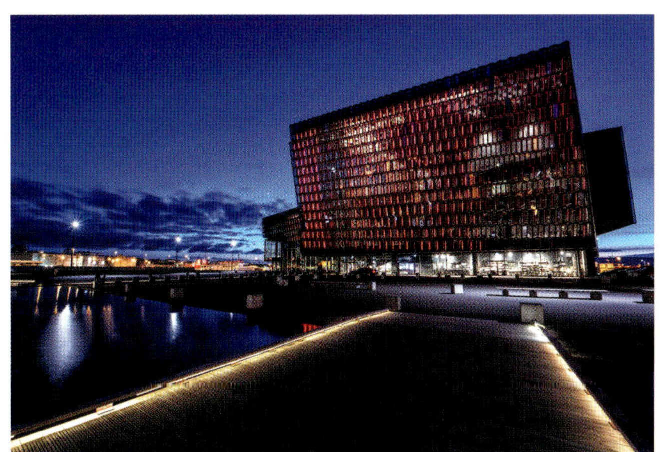

Harpa, beautifully lit during the blue hour
(f/14 · 15 sec. · ISO 250 · 14mm)

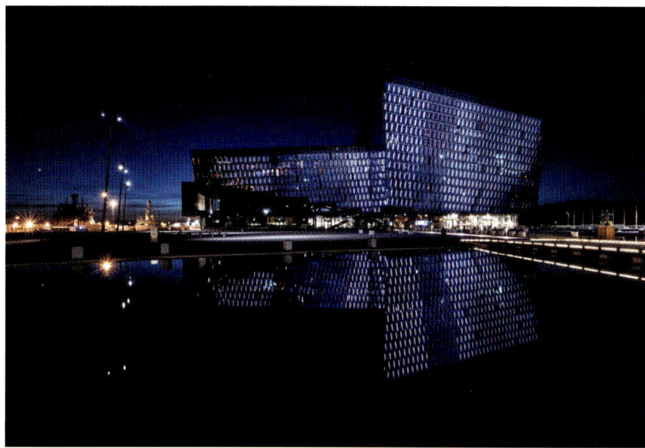

On a calm day, this unique building is beautifully reflected in its pool
(f/14 · 20 sec. · ISO 200 · 16mm)

the pool. It is worth spending some time taking multiple photos that capture the changing light in the façade.

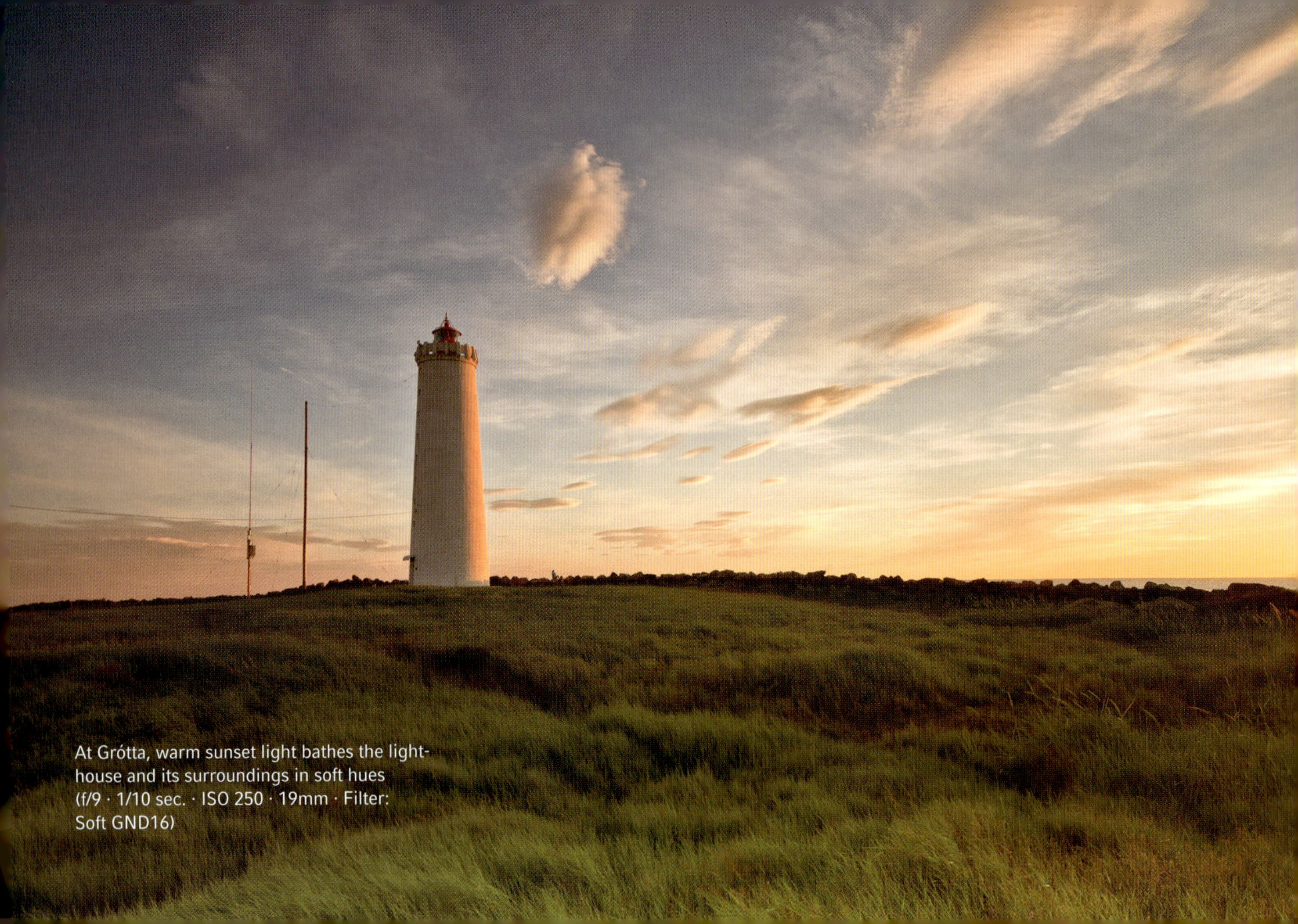

At Grótta, warm sunset light bathes the light-house and its surroundings in soft hues (f/9 · 1/10 sec. · ISO 250 · 19mm · Filter: Soft GND16)

2 GRÓTTA

Distance: 10 minutes from Harpa
Best time of day: Sunset
Best time of year: Summer, fall, or winter
Equipment: No special requirements
Tour type: Self-drive
Parking area coordinates: 64.162598, –22.013134
Location coordinates: 64.164433, –22.020745

Parking Area

Photo Location

One of Reykjavík's best-loved sights for tourists and locals alike is the lighthouse at the end of the Seltjarnarnes Peninsula. Countless couples go there to enjoy the sunset, and the best place to do this is at the sea-facing wall in the parking area. The lighthouse was built in 1947 on an island that was separated from the mainland during a storm. You can only get to the lighthouse at low tide by crossing a causeway called Gróttugrandi. To protect the seabirds that nest there, the island is closed to visitors between May 1st and July 1st.

If you visit the island, it's worth taking a walk around. If you climb the rocks that act as a breakwater, you can include some of them as an extra detail in your photos.

WARNING!
The best colors are to be found around sunset, but don't forget to keep an eye on the water level, as you can only get back to the mainland at low tide.

Photo Skills

USING GRAY AND GRADUATED GRAY FILTERS

Many of the images in this book were captured using gray and graduated gray filters.

GRADUATED GRAY FILTERS

If you have spent time shooting landscapes in tricky lighting conditions—such as sunrise or sunset—you will be familiar with the problem: either the sky is too bright and the landscape too dark, or vice versa. In other words, the overall contrast in the scene is too great for your camera's sensor to capture in a single image. You could capture a series of photos exposed individually for the various parts of the scene and then stitch them together using a computer—however, effectively stitching moving elements such as clouds and water is always tricky and often impossible.

I prefer to capture one-off images and perform as little image editing as possible, so I often use graduated gray filters (also known as "graduated neutral density," or GND filters) to help mitigate the challenge.

As the name suggests, a graduated filter allows incoming light to enter the lens with varying intensity. Usually, the filter effect is strongest at the top and becomes weaker toward the center of the filter. The lower half of the filter is clear and has no explicit effect.

Such filters are available either as circular, screw-in models or as rectangular glass or plastic sheets that you insert into a custom holder attached to the front of your lens. Such filters can then be rotated or moved up and down to fit the subject. With the holder-type filter, if the horizon isn't in the center of your frame, you can move the filter up or down, accordingly. Conventional screw-in filters are not as flexible.

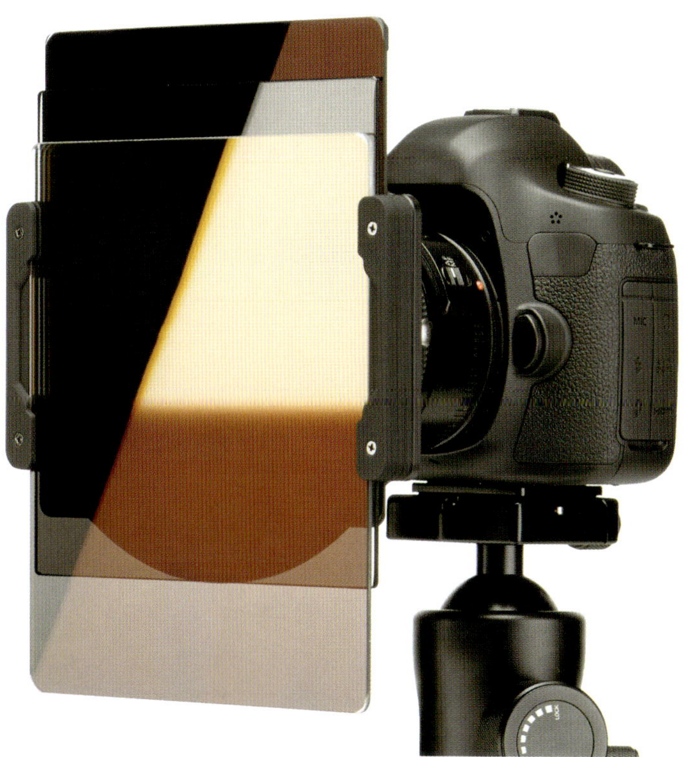

The Rollei filter system with three filters mounted simultaneously (Image courtesy of Rollei)

A 0.9/8 hard-gradient GND filter

A 1.2/16 soft-gradient GND filter

A 0.9/8 reverse-gradient GND filter

(Images courtesy of Rollei)

Graduated ND filters are available in various gradient types. The most common types are:

- Hard
- Soft
- Reverse

A hard gradient is where the darker portion of the filter ends suddenly with no drop-off in the intensity of the filter effect. With a hard gradient, details just above the center of the frame are still quite dark, so this type of filter is only suitable for subjects in which there is an obvious line (such as a horizon) separating two halves of an image. Use a hard gradient for daytime images of broad plains or the ocean, when you want to avoid overexposing the sky. A hard gradient is not suitable for capturing features such as mountains that rise above the horizon, as the filter will produce a visible line running through them.

A soft gradient gradually lightens toward the center, and the transition from filtered to unfiltered light is hardly visible. This type of filter is suitable for subjects with no clearly defined horizon. For example, in a mountain landscape, the peaks will appear slightly darker than they actually are, but the lack of a clear cutoff means the transition between the two halves of the filter won't be visible in the final image.

Reverse GND filters have a gradient that is lightest at the outer edge and darker toward the center. In other words, the filter effect becomes weaker toward the top of the frame. This type of filter is useful for shooting into the sun at sunrise or sunset at the ocean or in broad, open landscapes. Photographing the glacial lagoon at Jökulsárlón at sunrise is a good example of this type of situation. The filter effect is strongest just above the horizon where the sunlight is brightest.

GND filters are available in various strengths, with names that indicate the number of f-stops by which the filter darkens the subject.

Here are some examples:

- **ND 0.3** is equivalent to one f-stop darker
- **ND 0.6** is equivalent to two f-stops darker
- **ND 0.9** is equivalent to three f-stops darker
- **ND 1.2** is equivalent to four f-stops darker

The choice of available filters is huge, and individual filters are often quite expensive, so you need to consider carefully which filters you really need.

I used to carry a whole bunch of filters around, but after a while I realized I actually get on very well with a core set of filters, which cover all my basic photographic needs.

My basic GND filter set consists of:

- **Soft Gradient**
  GND 0.6/4 (two f-stops darker)
  GND 1.2/16 (four f-stops darker)
- **Hard Gradient**
  GND 0.9/8 (three f-stops darker)
- **Reverse Gradient**
  GND 0.9/8 (three f-stops darker)

I have tested many brands of filters and now use only filters made by Rollei, which are of extremely high optical quality with virtually no unwanted color effects and, unlike many others, they are made of hardened glass. They also have Rollei's patented Luminance Coating. The combination of hardened glass and the high-quality coating means the filters produce very few reflections and are easy to clean. Wiping away water drops doesn't create smears and doesn't scratch the glass. In contrast, plastic filters scratch easily and have to be replaced regularly. You can purchase Rollei filters and holders directly from the manufacturer at *www.rollei.com/products/photo-accessories/photo-filters.*

You can check out a complete list of my filters and the other gear I use at *www.martin-schulz.photography/en/equipment/*

GRADUATED NEUTRAL DENSITY (GND) FILTERS IN PRACTICE

As well as the filters themselves, you also need a filter holder and an adapter to attach the holder to your lens. If you use multiple filters simultaneously in a single holder, the strengths of the individual filters are added together.

With a filter mounted, aim your camera at a subject and move the filter up or down until you achieve the desired darkening effect in the sky. If you are working with hard-gradient or reverse-gradient filters, make sure the edge of the filter zone coincides with the horizon. This will ensure that the edge of the filter zone isn't

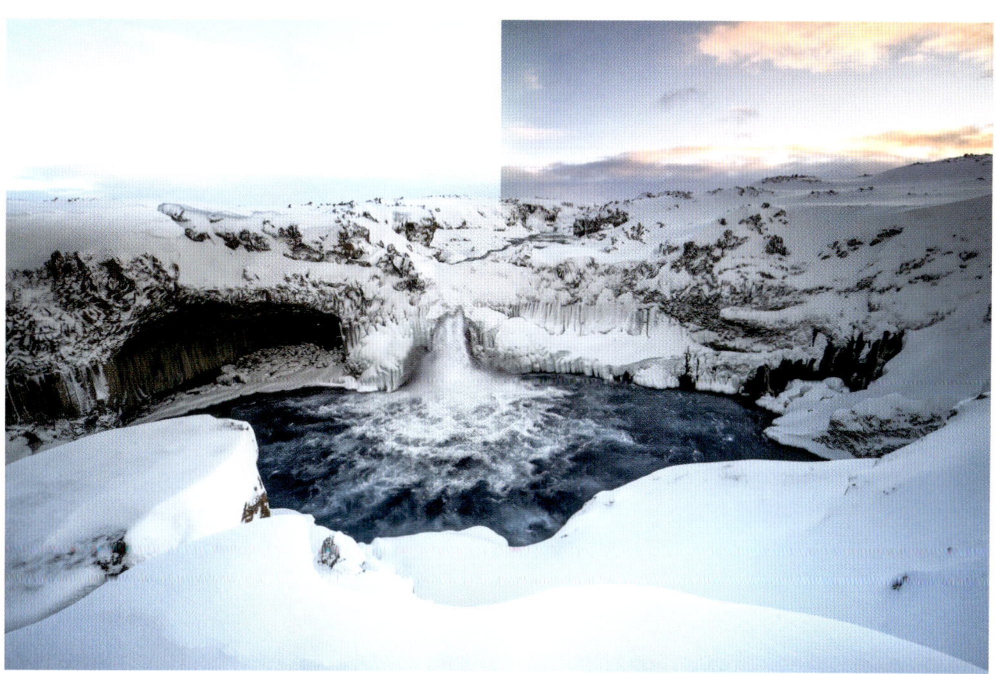

The left half of this image was captured without a filter and the right half with an ND 1.2 soft-gradient filter

visible in the final image. In extremely bright ambient light, you can use multiple filters in a single holder and you can shift them individually according to the needs of the shot. There are plenty of websites that offer calculators to help you work out which filter is theoretically the best for a range of situations.

The best way to calculate the contrast in your subject is to take a spot-meter reading for the brightest and darkest areas in the scene and note the exposure times the camera comes up with. In case you didn't already know, each step between the exposure times on your camera's dial is equivalent to halving or doubling the amount of light that reaches the sensor. In other words, 1/250 sec. allows only half as much light to reach the sensor as 1/125 sec., while 1/1000 sec. allows twice as much light through as 1/2000 sec. The same is also true for aperture values, where each click-stop either halves or doubles the amount of light that enters the camera.

You can use the exposure values you noted earlier to calculate the degree of contrast your filter has to compensate for. For example, the difference between values of 1/2000 sec. and 1/125 sec. is four f-stops (i.e., 1/125 sec. × 2 = 1/250 sec. × 2 = 1/500 sec. × 2 = 1/1000 sec. × 2 = 1/2000 sec.). An ND 1.2 filter is therefore (theoretically) the correct filter to use for this example. It would darken the brightest parts of the frame by a factor of 4, enabling you to use an exposure time of 1/125 sec. without overexposing the brighter parts of the frame.

However, theory and practice is not always the same thing. For example, at sunrise the light is quickly changing, so constantly recalculating the required values gives you no time to actually take photos. Instead, I simply select a filter according to the visual brightness of the sky relative to the foreground. In practice, this means I use one or other (or both) of the two soft-gradient filters in my kit.

GRAY FILTERS

Regular gray (or ND) filters work in a similar way to graduated ND filters but, instead of having a gradient, their entire surface is darkened. A regular ND filter darkens the entire frame evenly and—ideally—without falsifying the colors in the scene. But why do we need to darken the entire frame when photography is all about capturing as much light as possible?

Long exposures are an important part of the photography oeuvre, making nighttime photography possible and often giving daytime shots added vitality. In contrast, using regular metered exposure times to capture a scene usually freezes the action, making the patterns in the clouds or the individual drops of water in waves and waterfalls visible to the viewer.

If you want make your images more dynamic, you need to increase the exposure time. A photo of a waterfall captured using a long exposure time conveys the motion of the plunging water much better than a shot that freezes the action. The resulting blur also makes it possible for the viewer to sense the direction and power of the flow. The same is true for shots of waves hitting the shore, and the rolling movements form new and exciting patterns when captured in a long exposure. Clouds, too, appear much less static when captured this way. Long exposures are one of my personal favorite photo techniques.

Achieving long exposure times in daylight isn't just a case of closing the aperture all the way down and reducing the ISO setting as far as you can. Often, the only way to achieve the effect you are looking for is to use the artificial darkening provided by an ND filter.

Like GND filters, ND filters are available in screw-in and slot-in types. Again, slot-in filters offer greater flexibility, and are the only type you can effectively use with ultra-wide-angle lenses in which the front lens element protrudes beyond the end of the lens barrel. Some lenses also have built-in lens hoods that make

An ND 1000 gray filter
(Image courtesy of Rollei)

attaching screw-in filters impossible. Because the same filter holder can be adapted for use with different-sized lenses, a single rectangular slot-in filter can be used with virtually any lens.

I don't bother using low-strength ND filters, as the effects they produce can easily be simulated by altering the aperture and ISO settings.

The following ND filters are the ones I use most frequently:

- ND 64 (1.8), equivalent to six f-stops
- ND 1000 (3.0), equivalent to 10 f-stops

Slot-in ND filters can be used individually or in combination with other ND or GND filters. If you are using multiple filters, make sure the ND filter is positioned closest to the lens. Any light that gets in between the filter and the lens makes balanced exposures impossible, and some ND filters have a kind of built-in seal to prevent this happening. Strong ND filters sometimes have an adverse effect on autofocus systems. If your camera's autofocus system is affected, remove the filter to focus on your subject, then switch autofocus off before you reinsert the filter and release the shutter.

To calculate the exposure time required when using a filter, multiply the regular, metered exposure time with the filter factor. An ND 64 filter has a filter factor of 64 and an ND 1000 filter a filter factor of 1000. In other words, if you use an ND 1000 filter with a metered exposure time of 1/1000 sec., you need to set the exposure time to 1 second.

When working this way, it is essential to set your camera to manual (M) mode. This enables you to adjust ISO,

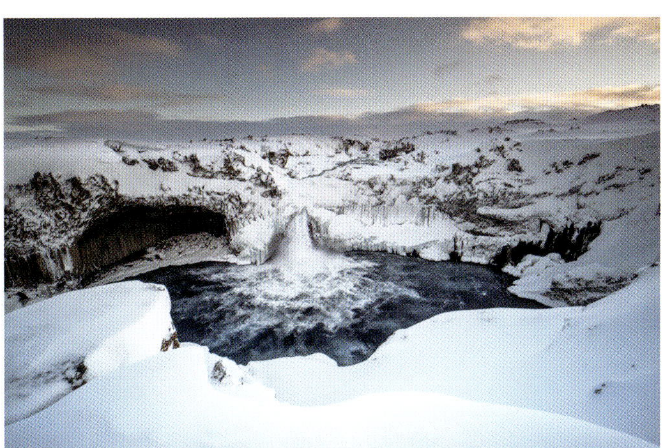

Shot using a GND 1.2 filter but no ND filter. The patterns in the water and the clouds are frozen.

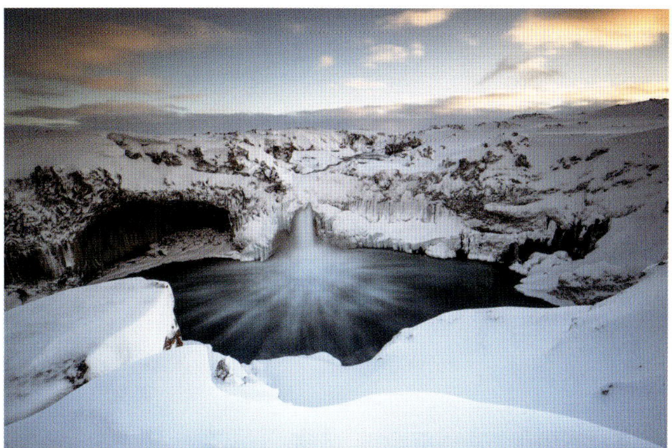

The same scene captured using GND 1.2 and ND 64 filters, which enabled a long exposure, giving the clouds and water a more dynamic look and feel.

aperture, and exposure time independently of one another according to the needs of each situation. The longest automatic exposure time supported by most cameras is 30 seconds, so you need to select Bulb (B) shutter mode if you want to set a longer exposure time than that. B mode enables you to manually select ISO and aperture values, while the shutter remains open for as long as you keep the shutter-button pressed. To keep your camera as still as possible, always use a remote shutter release or a dedicated app for this type of shot. Apps and some remote releases automatically display the remaining exposure time.

There are plenty of websites that offer tables of exposure values for filters of varying strengths. I prefer to use the Rolleimoments Photo App (available for iPhone and Android). The app is free and also offers weather forecasts and planning tools that include sunrise and sunset data for your chosen location.

In addition to a remote release, always use a tripod for long exposures. If you don't, camera shake is likely to creep in and blur your shots. Shots like this involve quite a lot of planning and are complex to shoot, but the results are definitely worth the effort.

PHOTOGRAPHING THE NORTHERN LIGHTS

If you are traveling in Iceland in fall or winter and appropriate weather coincides with sunspot activity, you may be lucky enough to witness the awe inspiring Northern Lights.

Northern Lights (scientific name: Aurora Borealis) occur when electrically charged protons and neutrons produced by eruptions on the surface of the sun hit the upper layers of the Earth's atmosphere and agitate air molecules that glow as a result.

Although I have been lucky enough to experience the Northern Lights on numerous occasions, I still experience a special tingle when the sky begins to shimmer and glow, and the lights begin their mesmerizing dance. The magic of the situation makes it easy to forget that I am actually there to take photos!

This section will help you become familiar with the Northern Lights. It explains how

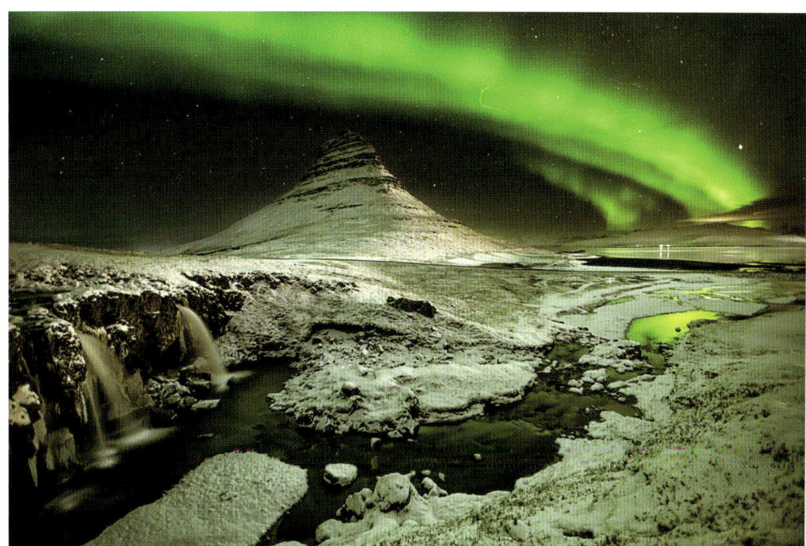

Kirkjufell
(f/2.8 · 30 sec. · ISO 1600 · 16mm)

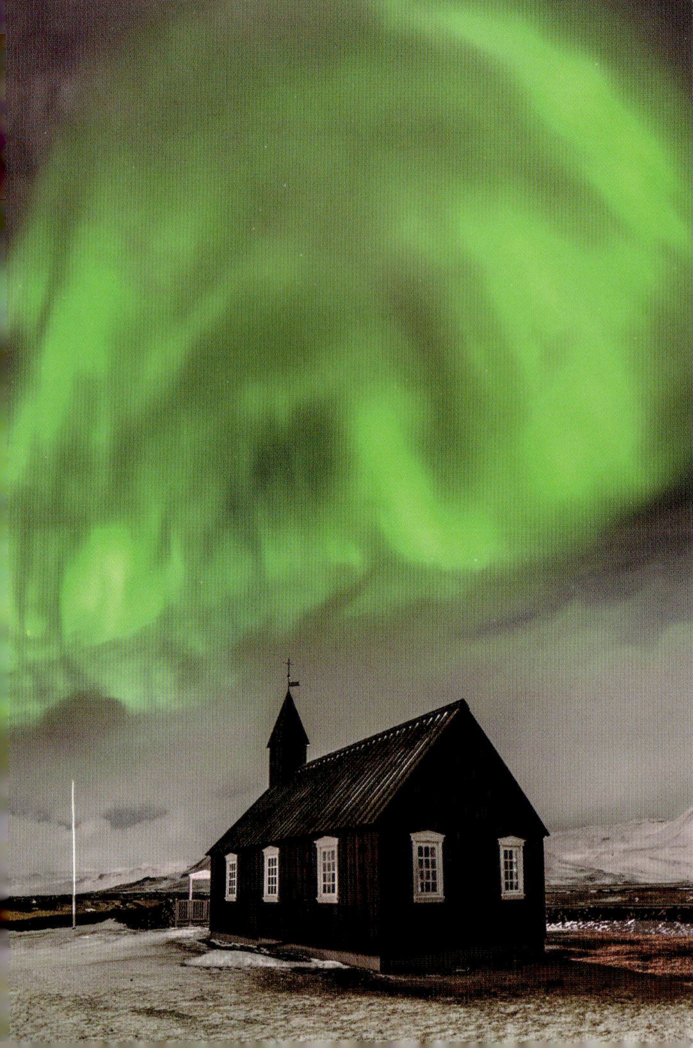

to prepare for a night sky full of shimmering green, and goes into detail on which gear and which settings to use to capture great images of this breathtaking natural phenomenon.

EQUIPMENT

The gear you use plays a significant role in the success of your photos.

Camera

The best type of camera to use is a digital single-lens reflex (DSLR) that captures low-noise images at high ISO settings. I use a Nikon D810 and a Canon EOS 5D Mark III. Both have proven excellent at capturing the Northern Lights, but other models from the major manufacturers should be just as good.

The black church at Búðir
(f/2.8 · 10 sec. · ISO 640 · 15mm)

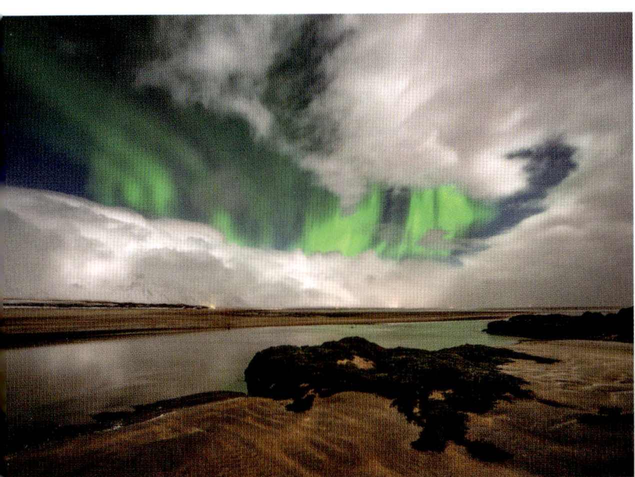

The red beaches at Búðir
(f/2.8 · 8 sec. · ISO 500 · 14mm)

Lens

Bright, wide-angle lenses are best for this kind of shot. Northern Lights often fill the whole sky, so you will need the widest angle of view you can get. The larger the maximum aperture in your lens, the lower you can set the ISO value and the less noise your images will contain. My favorite Nikon lens is my 14–24mm f/2.8.

Tripod

Photographing the Northern Lights almost always involves using long exposures, so a sturdy tripod is essential. You will also need a high-quality ball head that allows you to quickly and reliably adjust the camera position to match the ever-changing lights in the sky. I use a Feisol Tournament CT-3442 Rapid tripod (*www.feisol.eu/?lang=en*), which is a great value, is extremely light weight, and has proven to be reliable over the past few years.

Remote or Delayed Release

Even minimal camera shake can ruin your images, so it is essential to use some kind of remote release or your camera's built-in self-timer to release the shutter.

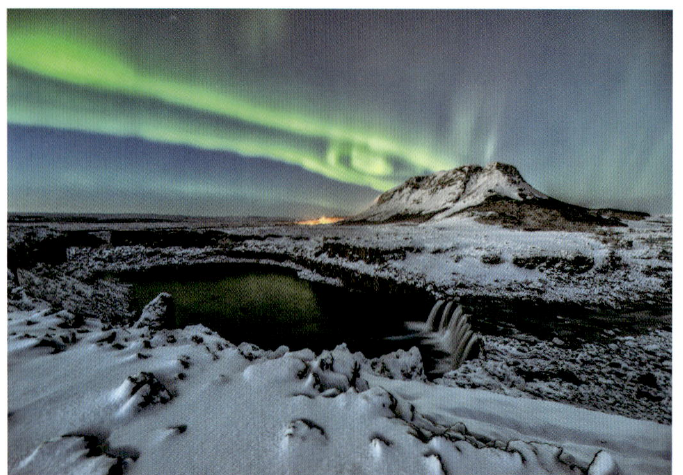

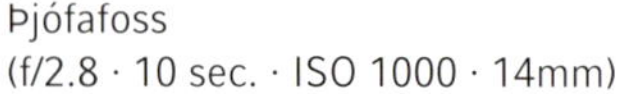

Þjófafoss
(f/2.8 · 10 sec. · ISO 1000 · 14mm)

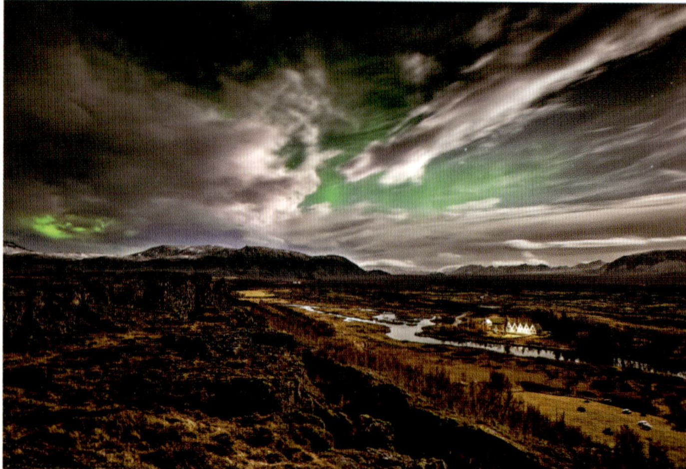

Þingvellir
(f/2.8 · 20 sec. · ISO 500 · 24mm)

Power and Storage

Always take plenty of spare batteries and memory cards along. Putting your batteries in your pants pocket keeps them warm and helps them retain a longer charge.

Let There Be Light!

Don't forget to pack a reliable pocket flashlight or headlamp. It is often difficult to find your way in rough terrain in the dark, and a flashlight will also shed light on your camera's controls when you are working at night. A flashlight with a red LED is less likely to disturb other photographers working in the vicinity.

Warmth from Within

The Northern Lights don't always appear on cue, so don't forget to take a supply of hot drinks along to make the waiting bearable.

Equipment Overview:

- Camera
- Bright lens
- Sturdy tripod
- Ball head
- Remote shutter release
- Plenty of spare batteries
- Plenty of memory cards
- Headlamp
- Hot tea or coffee

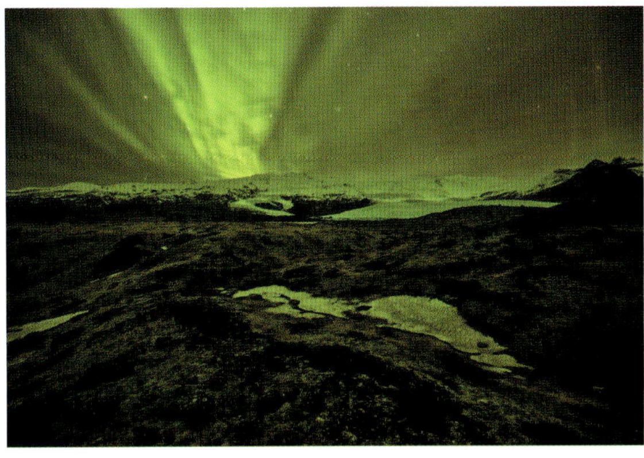

Fjallsárlón (f/2.8 · 15 sec. · ISO 1250 · 14mm)

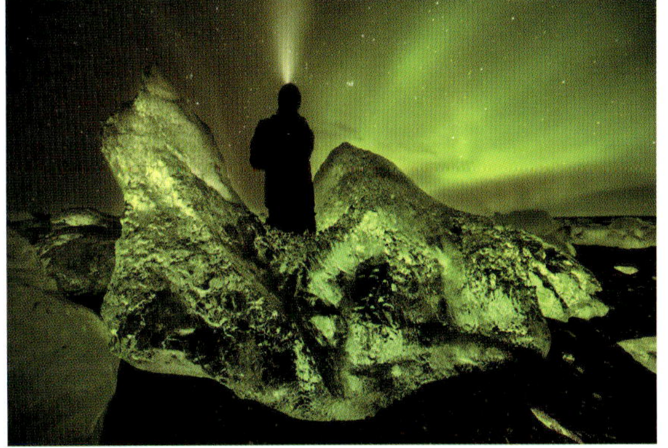

Breiðamerkursandur (f/2.8 · 15 sec. · ISO 1600 · 14mm)

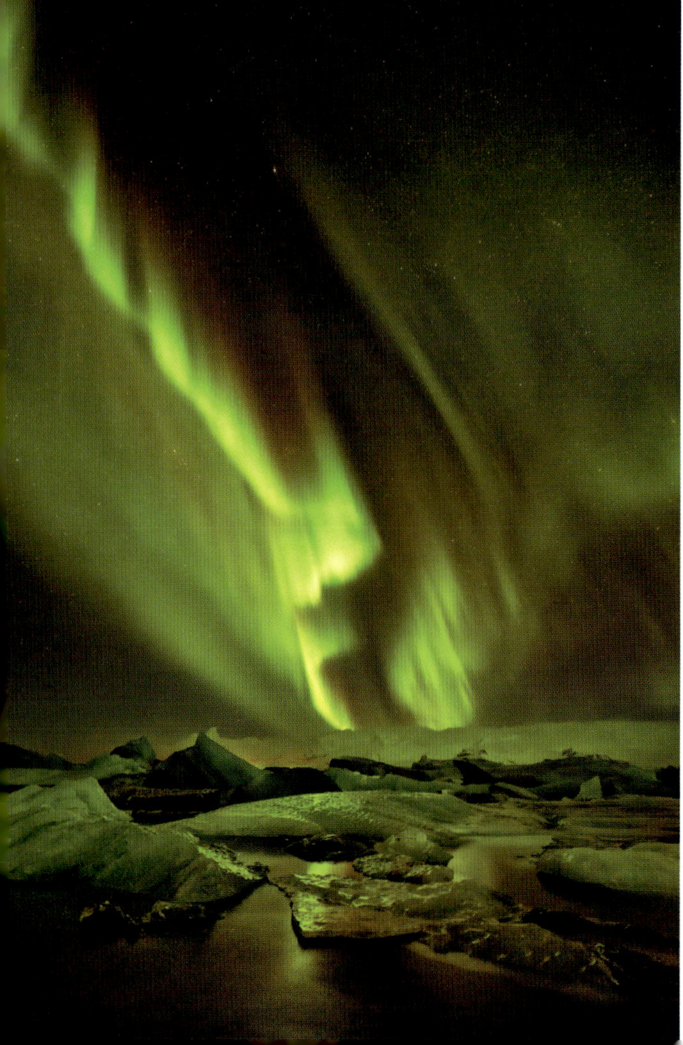

PREPARING FOR A SHOOT

Certain requirements have to be met if you want to successfully photograph the Northern Lights.

Because the summer nights in Iceland are never fully dark, the best time to travel is between the end of August and the end of March. I have had particularly memorable trips in September and February. The phases of the moon make a difference, too, and I always try to coordinate my travel with one or two full moons. Even though the Northern Lights themselves look best in the dark, a moonlit foreground often makes an image even more special.

There has to be plenty of sunspot activity for the Northern Lights to appear at all, and a clear sky is ideal.

The Icelandic Meteorological Office (*en.vedur.is*) offers weather and solar activity forecasts. Navigate

Jökulsárlón
(f/2.8 · 6 sec. · ISO 2500 · 16mm)

to *en.vedur.is/weather/forecasts/aurora* for Northern Lights forecasts. The forecasts are given on a scale from 0 to 9, and the larger the number, the more likely you are to see the aurora. But don't be put off by a 2 or a 3. I have captured great photos under such conditions.

The cloud cover forecast (*http://en.vedur.is/weather/forecasts/cloudcover*) has a slider that lets you view the conditions for the next few days. As with all forecasts, the results aren't guaranteed, but they can give you a fair idea of what to expect.

If you manage to combine darkness and a good forecast with a clear sky, you are well on the way to getting a great view of the Northern Lights. People often ask me which is the best time of day or night for capturing this type of shot. Over the years, I have found the effect to be pretty random. I have sometimes been lucky in the early evening, but have also had to wait until way after 3 a.m., and I have even had days when I didn't capture a single shot. Patience is the key ingredient for a successful shoot. Find a good location, get cozy in your car, and keep an eye open for signs of activity in the sky.

If you are staying in a hotel, ask the night desk to wake you if any activity shows up.

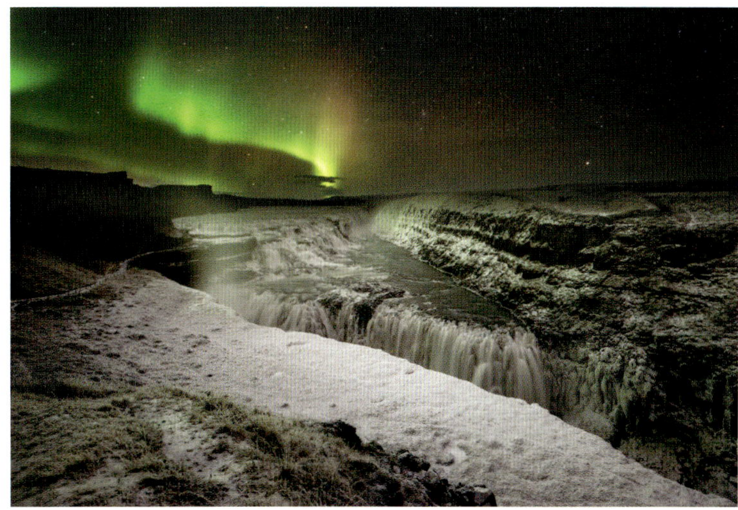

Gullfoss
(f/2.8 · 30 sec. · ISO 2000 · 20mm)

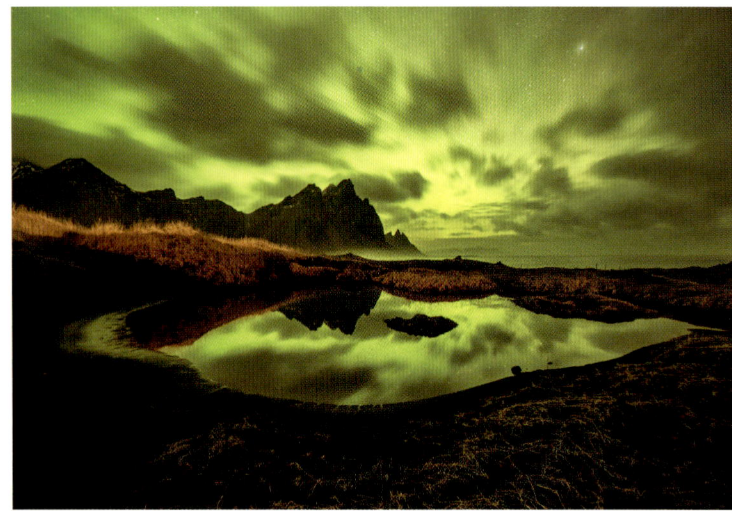

Vestrahorn
(f/2.8 · 30 sec. · ISO 2000 · 15mm)

CHOOSING A LOCATION

Northern Lights can appear anywhere in the sky, although weaker instances nearly always appear in the north. The lights usually start as a pale green arc that constantly alters its shape, size, and color. The original arc often splits into several smaller parts that move across the sky. When solar activity is particularly strong, you may witness the corona effect, which causes the lights to fan out from a central point as they head toward Earth.

With the exception of moonlight, the darker your surroundings the better. Try to find a location that is as far as possible from the light pollution caused by cities and other settlements.

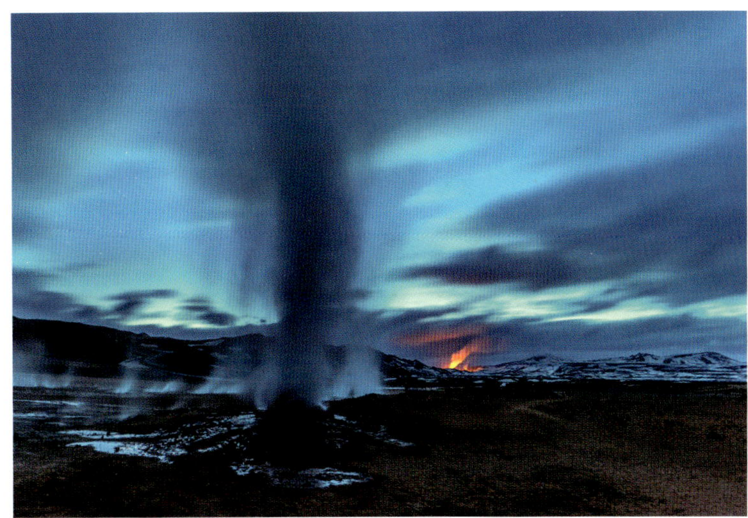

Hverir/Hveraröndd
(f/2.8 · 30 sec. · ISO 500 · 16mm)

Images of the lights alone are seldom successful, and photos often work better if they include suitable foreground details. Everyday subjects take on a whole new look and feel when you photograph them bathed in the ethereal light of the Aurora Borealis. The best locations are those where you point your camera north to capture the main subject, but you still need to be able to alter your viewpoint to follow the lights as they move and change.

CAMERA SETTINGS

Once you have acquired the right gear and found your way to a suitable location at an appropriate moment, you still need to set up your

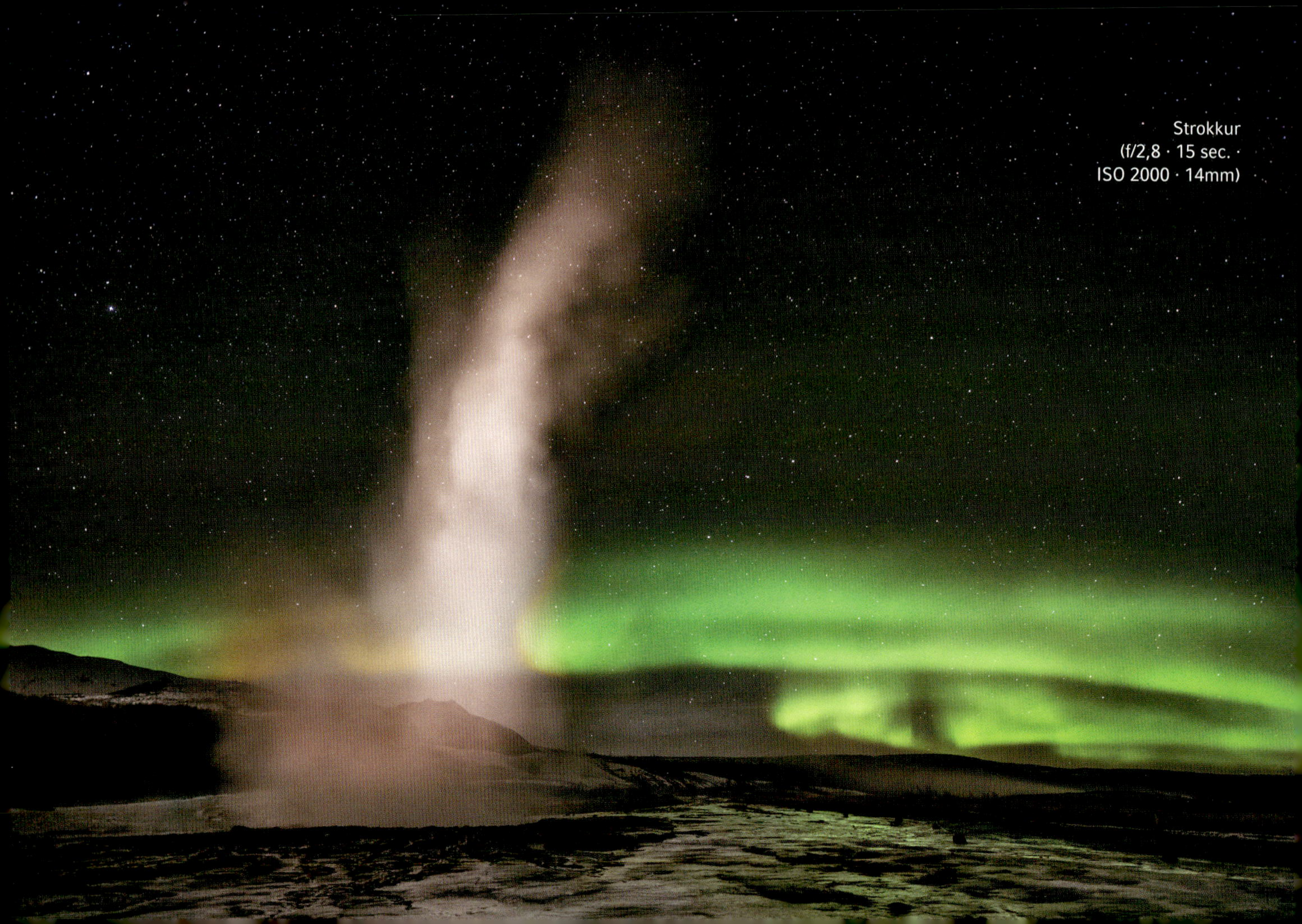

Strokkur
(f/2,8 · 15 sec. ·
ISO 2000 · 14mm)

camera properly to ensure excellent results. Unfortunately, there is no sure-fire method for capturing top-notch images.

The Northern Lights are never the same twice. They can be bright or faint, and the speed at which they move varies enormously. The settings required to capture the lights vary according to their strength and speed, and everyone develops their own strategies for dealing with these highly inconsistent conditions.

The following sections list some of the things you can do to make shooting easier from the outset.

ALWAYS SHOOT RAW

Shooting in RAW mode enables you to alter white balance, exposure correction, and a whole bunch of other settings as necessary after a shoot. The mercurial nature of the Northern Lights makes it virtually impossible to get a perfect setup while you shoot, and too much fiddling with the camera often means missed photo opportunities.

GET TO KNOW YOUR CAMERA AND SET FOCUS TO MANUAL AND INFINITY

You have to be able to operate your camera intuitively when you are shooting in the dark. If you have to use a flashlight every time you change your settings, you will waste valuable shooting time and you'll annoy the hell out of any other photographers working close by.

Because autofocus systems require light to function properly, they don't usually work in the dark. The solution here is to switch to manual focus. However, focusing manually in the dark is virtually impossible. To work around this, I simply focus my lens to infinity, and I have rarely had issues with out-of-focus objects in the foreground. If I do, I switch back to autofocus, use my flashlight to illuminate the object while focusing and switch autofocus off again once the lens has found the correct distance setting.

Note that the infinity sign on the focus ring of some lenses doesn't correspond precisely to the actual infinity setting in the lens. To make sure your lens really is set to infinity, use autofocus to focus on a distant object in daylight and use a piece of tape to mark the corresponding position of the focus ring. You can then manually set focus to precisely the right spot when you are shooting at night.

MANUAL EXPOSURE MODE

Automatic exposure modes are great under most circumstances, but photographing the Aurora Borealis most definitely requires manual exposure. Only manual mode allows you to make the constant tiny adjustments to ISO and exposure time that successful Aurora Borealis photography demands.

APERTURE, ISO, AND EXPOSURE TIME

Generally, the shorter the exposure time and the lower the ISO setting, the better your results will be. However, because these basic tenets are in direct contradiction of the fact that you will be shooting in the dark, you will have to make some compromises.

A short exposure time is essential if you want to successfully capture the patterns in fast-moving lights. A generally accepted rule of thumb says that you need to use an exposure time of 30 seconds or less if you want the stars to appear as well-defined points in your images. Any longer and the Earth's rotation will make them look like blurred tracks. The precise value will vary according to the focal length of your lens. Over the years, I have found 30 seconds to be a good base value. However, as previously mentioned, shorter exposure times are often preferable, and times of 8–10 seconds are ideal for fast-moving constellations.

To allow the maximum amount of light to reach the sensor, you need to use the largest-possible aperture (i.e., the smallest number). My lenses have a maximum aperture of f/2.8.

The third and final setting you have to consider is the ISO value. You probably use values of around 100 for regular daytime shoots, but you will have to increase this to anything between 800 and 3200 when shooting at night. The ISO setting will vary considerably, depending on the brightness of the night and the intensity of the Northern Lights.

SHOOTING CHECKLIST

- Switch autofocus off
- Use manual focus
- Set focus to infinity
- Switch to manual exposure mode
- Select the largest possible aperture
- Increase the ISO value to about 800
- Set an exposure time of about 10 seconds

I always make a test shot using these settings and adjust either the ISO value or the exposure time as necessary. If the patterns in the lights look good in an image that is otherwise underexposed, I leave the exposure time unchanged (or adjust it only slightly) and brighten the image by increasing the ISO value.

If you are lucky enough to be shooting during a long night of intense Northern Lights, you can experiment with your settings to see which combinations work best for you and your personal shooting style.

As you gain experience, you will learn to assess each situation individually and instinctively, and you will develop a feel for the settings you need without starting from scratch each time.

TOP TIP

Don't be misled by the appearance of your images on the camera monitor. The monitor always looks brighter in the dark, and images that look good at night often turn out to be massively underexposed when you view them on a computer in the cold light of day. I have often been suckered by this effect, and I have learned to check all my images using the histogram display. Roughly speaking, if all the peaks on the histogram curve are in the center, or are slightly to the left of center, the exposure is OK. However, if the curves are all bunched up at the left-hand edge, the shot is definitely underexposed.

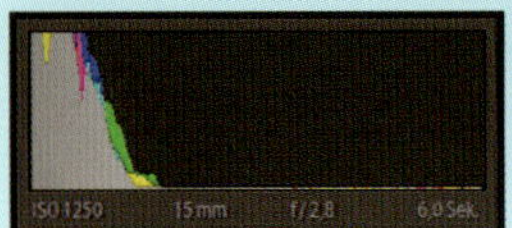

Underexposed

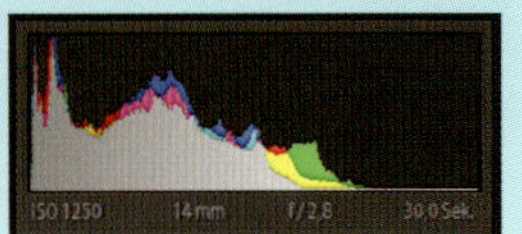

Correctly exposed

Recommended Websites

TOUR GUIDE OPERATORS

IceAk tours: www.iceak.is
Katlatrack Adventure Tours: www.katlatrack.is

ROAD CONDITIONS

Icelandic Road and Coastal Admin: www.road.is/travel-info/road-conditions-and-weather
Icelandic Search and Rescue: www.safetravel.is
Maps: http://en.ja.is/kort/?type=map

NEWS AND CURRENT AFFAIRS

Iceland Review: www.icelandreview.com
Visit Reykjavík: www.visitreykjavik.is

WEATHER

Icelandic Meteorological Office: en.vedur.is/weather/forecasts/areas

NORTHERN LIGHTS FORECASTS

Icelandic Meteorological Office: en.vedur.is/weather/forecasts/aurora

MISCELLANEOUS

Bæjarins Beztu Pylsur (hotdogs): www.bbp.is/information-in-english
Blómasetrið – Kaffi Kyrrð (café): www.blomasetrid.is
f-stop (backpacks): www.fstopgear.com
Feisol (tripods): www.feisol.eu/?lang=en
Fjöruhúsið café: www.facebook.com/FjoruhusidHellnum

Íslenski barinn (burgers): www.islenskibarinn.is/net/en
Krafla Power Station: www.landsvirkjun.com/company/powerstations/kraflapowerstation
Messinn (restaurant): www.messinn.com
MicroBar: www.facebook.com/MicroBarIceland
Mývatn Nature Baths: www.myvatnnaturebaths.is
Rollei (filters): www.rollei.com/products/photo-accessories/photo-filters/
Skúli (craft beer): www.facebook.com/skulicraft
Stofan Kaffihús (café): www.facebook.com/stofan.cafe

Index

T

Ð

Þ